The Barker-

An American Crime Family

W. D. Smith

Forward by Tony E. Stewart

ACKNOWLEDGMENTS

I wish to thank all those who have inspired and encouraged me over the past several years to not only improve on my artwork, but who have also encouraged me to write. Many have helped point me in the right direction, with research material, recommended books, and thousands of bits and pieces I never would have found on my own without their help and advice of these, and so many other people:

Tony E. Stewart, Linda Mattix, Louis LaCava, "Wilbur Underhill" (Facebook persona), Autumn LeMasters, Ted and Marsha Prince, Muddboss C. Flynn, Ron Rosner, Mr. Denny Zitek of Cheyenne, Wyoming, Chris and Amanda Williams of Kansas City, MO., Janelle Woodbury, Laramie County, Wyoming Historical Society, Wichita Public Library, Wichita, Kansas, Freda Ann Dillard of Dallas TX, Pam Paden Tippet, Toney Aid of West Plains, MO., West Plains Public Library, MO., Mike Jeffries of the Sapulpa Historical Society / Museum, Sapulpa, OK, Brandy Dicks at Red Door Art Gallery, Wahpeton ND, Minnesota Historical Society, Redwood Falls, MN Historical Society, Cloud County, Kansas Historical Society, David Zimdars of the Beloit Wisconsin Historical Society, George Albright III, Pat Hughes, Julie Thompson, and many, many others too numerous to list here. Without your help and continued encouragement, this project would not have been possible! I think you all from the bottom of my heart!

CONTENTS

Forward by Tony E. Stewart

Fire away and fall back into W.D. Smith's extraordinary new book, *"The Barker-Karpis Gang, An American Crime Family. A History of the Last Great Outlaw Gang."* Finally, the compelling true story told for the first time in this rip-roaring bulletproof account. Smith tells it the way it happened...blasted from the business end of a Thompson sub-machine gun to the FBI's greatest historical gun battle and the aftermath of events that follows.

This is genuinely the best book ever written on the Barker-Karpis gang and outlaw associates such as Dillinger, Baby Face Nelson, Pretty Boy Floyd, Harvey Bailey and many others. With over 300 pages of newly updated researched facts and over 200 photographs *(many never-before published)*, including drawings and illustrations, this book comes highly recommended to the highest caliber. W.D. Smith brilliantly worked outside the box to bring fourth the greatest story ever told on crime, corruption and the greatest criminals of all time.

Hands down...this book is a must to read!

Sincerely,

Tony E. Stewart

Author of *"Dillinger, the Hidden Truth"*

CHAPTER 1:
BARKER FAMILY HISTORY

Arizona Donnie "Kate" Barker (1873 – 1935)

From the mid-1920's to 1936, the Barker-Karpis gang was one of the most ruthless band of robbers and murderers to terrorize the Midwestern U.S. They managed to fly under the radar of law enforcement for several years before they were finally recognized as one of the worst gangs the Division of Investigation, as the FBI was then known, would ever face. As law enforcement began to place all the pieces of the puzzle together, they would find that the Barker network included other individuals who also worked closely with the Dillinger gang, Charles Arthur "Pretty boy" Floyd, George "baby-face" Nelson, Harvey Bailey, and others. They eluded scrutiny for so long mainly due to the way they operated in virtual anonymity, and their use of fast cars to hit quickly and get away quicker.

Those were the days before police radios and the lack of any sort of real communication between police departments. So the police had no way to tie many of these crimes together as being committed by the same gangs. In addition, they had corrupt friends in various police departments throughout the country who were willing to cover for them for a cut of their loot. The Barker gang itself grew out of the old Central Park gag in Tulsa, and by the end of their run, it consisted of over 25 members, with the core of the group being Fred and Arthur "Doc" Barker, and Alvin Karpis.

Lloyd William Barker, the second oldest, doesn't seem to have been as involved in his brother's activities. He served honorably in the Army during the First World War. However, in 1921, he was convicted of robbing the mail in Baxter Springs, Kansas and sentenced to 25 years in the Federal prison at Leavenworth, Kansas. He wasn't released until 1938. This probably saved his life. They were joined in 1931 by Alvin Karpis.

Their mother, Arrie "Ma" Barker who liked to be called "Kate", just tagged along with them. She took no part in their actual crimes, but she would lose her life as well, only to be vilified wrongfully in history by J. Edgar Hoover as the "mastermind" of the gang. Hoover invented the whole story, fearful of the outcry against his department if the public found out his men had killed an old woman. In researching the history of the Barker boys' ancestry, there is nothing that has been found that would explain just why these men turned out to be such violent, ruthless individuals. Their ancestors were, from all appearances, solid, hard-working, law-abiding, God-fearing pioneers from Kentucky, North Carolina and Virginia.

The only explanation for their actions lies in the behavior of their overbearing, domineering, hot-tempered mother who refused to discipline them. It was Arrie Barker herself who planted the seeds that grew into the Trees of Destruction. Not only for them, but ultimately for herself as well.

These families settled in the rough and largely untamed foothills of the Ozark Mountains, in the Southwestern region of Missouri. Life was hard, and it produced a rough class of people. Daniel Boone had come to Missouri with his family in 1799 to escape the western expansion of civilization. His youngest son, Nathan Boone, found a grove of Ash and Walnut trees in an area a short distance Southwest of Springfield. Here, he built his home and raised fourteen children. He named the town that grew up around his home "Ash Grove". By the time he died in the late 1850's, Boone owned over a thousand acres of land and a great many slaves.

During the Civil War, Missouri was technically neutral, and an attempt to secede the state from the Union failed. However, this didn't spare the state from the ravages of war. The first major battle West of the Mississippi River took place on August 10, 1861, twelve miles southwest of Springfield along Wilson's Creek. Confederate forces under the command of Major General Sterling Price and Brigadier General Benjamin McCulloch met an attack by a Federal force commanded by Brigadier General Nathaniel Lyon. After Lyon was killed, he was replaced by Major Samuel D. Sturgis. The Confederates routed Colonel Franz Sigel's Federal column as it approached Skegg's Branch, but Sturgis knew his men were running out of ammunition and ordered them to withdraw to Springfield. It was a victory for the Confederates but it came at a heavy cost. They lost over 1,000 men killed and wounded, while the Federals lost over 1,235. Southwestern Missouri would remain largely in Confederate hands until the end of the war. [1]

There was a great deal of bitterness between factions in Kansas and Missouri even before the war began. A virtual border war had erupted in 1854 between the anti-slavery "Free-Staters" in Kansas who wanted Kansas Territory to be a free state, and the pro-slavery "Border Ruffians". Violence escalated, and on May 21, 1856, a mob from Missouri rode into Lawrence,

Kansas. They ransacked the town, burned two newspaper offices, and the Free State Hotel. Into this fray entered a fanatical abolitionist from Ohio named John Brown. [2]

On May 24, 1856, Brown and his followers raided a pro-slavery town on Pottawatomie Creek, and took several men away whom they hacked to death with swords. The murderers escaped and made their way to Harper's Ferry, Virginia, where they planned to mount a full-scale slave insurrection. They seized the Federal Arsenal there, but after a short skirmish, they were soundly defeated and placed under arrest. Brown was hanged for Treason in 1859. [3]

Both sides engaged in guerilla warfare, with the pro-Union guerillas being referred to as "Jayhawkers", but one of the worst of the pro-Confederate partisan ranger forces was led by William Clarke Quantrill. On August 21, 1863, Quantrill took a large force of over 400 men into Lawrence, Kansas, where they burned the town and murdered 183 men and young boys. Union forces took swift revenge by driving residents out of four Missouri border counties and burning everything they had. They drove Quantill's men out of Missouri, where they spit up into smaller bands to harass Union forces. Quantrill would eventually go east where he was killed during a raid into Kentucky. Several of these raiders would become well-known in history. [4]

William T. "Bloody Bill" Anderson was probably the most sadistic of them all. In September 1864, he led a raid on Centralia, Missouri where he and his men seized a train and murdered over 124 Union soldiers. The Centralia massacre soon led to Anderson being pursued by a Federal force led by Lieutenant Colonel Samuel P. Cox, who caught up with Anderson on October 26, 1864 and killed him. [5]

Other former members of Quantrill's raiders included Cole Younger and his brothers, and Jesse and Frank James. These men fought on after the war ended, going on the become rather proficient at robbing banks and trains from 1866 into the early 1880's. Many people saw these bandits as "Robin Hood" like folk-heroes instead of villains, who robbed from the insolent Yankee occupiers and gave to the poor. They mourned deeply when Jesse was shot in the back and killed on April 3, 1882. It is against this backdrop that our story begin. [6]

The earliest known Barker ancestors were Elias Barker (1743 – 1805) and his wife Rachel Isabelle Stewart (1745 – 1802), from Berkeley County, Virginia (it became part of the new state of West Virginia in 1863). They settled in Madison County, Kentucky by 1790 with their children, Joseph (born 1765), Elias Sr., (born 1768), William (born 1772), James (born 1776), and Stephen (born 1779). [7]

Their son, James Barker was born December 27, 1777 in Virginia. James married Margaret Temperance Noland in Madison County, Kentucky August 24, 1796. James and Margaret had a large family, with several of their children born in that part of Madison County, that later became the new county of Estill. They eventually settled in Lafayette County, Missouri, where James died November 1854. Margaret died in 1850. [8]

Elias Barker, the eldest son of James and Margaret Barker, was born about 1803 (some sources cite 1799) in Estill County, Kentucky. Estill County records show two marriages for an Elias Barker. The first is to Rachel Barker July 23, 1816 and the other to Betsy Warner on December 13, 1821. Whether this man who married Rachel and Betsy, was James's son isn't certain. We do know Elias was in Missouri by 1830. On July 20, 1829, Elias married Sarah Evangeline Dennis in Cooper County, Missouri, and they had a large family. He married again to Elizabeth (Doty) Dennis in LaClede County on July 16, 1868. Elias died August 1, 1874 in LaClede County, Missouri, after falling off a horse. His children by Sarah Dennis were: [9]

1. John Washington BARKER – born September 8, 1837 Lafayette County, Missouri. He married Elvira Adeline MCDOWELL February 7, 1856 in Stone County, Missouri.

2. James BARKER – He was born about 1841 Lafayette Co. Missouri. He married Julia Elizabeth YOUNGBLOOD on July 7, 1865.

3. Matilda BARKER – She was born about 1842 in Lafayette County, Missouri. She married Ezra SANDERS August 10, 1869

4. Sarah BARKER – She was born about 1844 in Lafayette Co. Missouri. She married James A. DAVIS, January 29, 1888.

5. Jacob (Jake) BARKER – He was born about 1846 in Lafayette Co. Missouri, and married Mary Jane LORANCE (or LAWRENCE) on December 21, 1865.

6. Nancy E. BARKER – She was born about 1849 Lafayette Co. Missouri and married George W. EDWARDS on July 24, 1887.

7. Aurena BARKER – She was born about 1851 in Laclede Co. Missouri. She married John SHAFFER on February 22, 1869.

8. Amanda BARKER – She was born 1853 in Laclede Co. Missouri, and married Richard BOTKINS on January 25, 1874.

9. William Riley BARKER – He was born 1858 Laclede Co. Missouri, and married Martha A. VERMILLION on April 19, 1877.

JOHN WASHINGTON BARKER was born September 8, 1837

and died October 8, 1913 (per death certificate) in Stone County, Missouri. He married Elvira Adeline McDowell, the daughter of Wiley and Margaret (Williams) McDowell, in Stone County on February 7, 1856. Elvira was born October 12, 1838 in Simpson County, Kentucky, and her family was in Taney County, Missouri by 1850, and Stone County, Missouri by 1854, when Wiley married a second time to Nancy Dennis. John and Elvira were the paternal grandparents of the Barker brothers. [10]

By 1860, John and Elvira was living in LaClede County with their first child, (George) Elias, who was listed on the census as being one year old. By 1870, they had returned to Stone County, and resided in Washington Township. Their household now included Elias, age 11, William age 6, and Adeline, age four months. Living near John was his brother James, and wife Julia. The names of their children were Martha A., age 4, and Nancy E., age 10 months.

In 1880, John and Elvira were living in Flat Creek Township of Stone County, Missouri with children (George) Elias, age 21, William W., age 17, Munice, age 12, John, age 9, Mary A., age 6. Charles, age 4, and Thomas, age 1. [11]

It was the eldest son, George Elias Barker, who was the father of Herman, Lloyd, Arthur, and Fred Barker. George was born October 8, 1859 in Lebanon, LaClede County, Missouri. By all accounts, he grew up without much of a formal education and was a quiet, soft spoken man. He worked the best he could to provide for his family. In the 1890's, George was living in Aurora, in Lawrence County, Missouri, and it was here he met and fell in love with a feisty, dark-haired girl named Arizona Donnie Clark. They were married in Lawrence County on September 14, 1892. The license reads as follows:

"Marriage License – State of Missouri – County of Lawrence.

This license authorizes any Judge, Justice of the Peace, Licensed or Ordained Preacher of the Gospel or any other person authorized under the laws of this state to solemnize marriage between GEORGE E. BARKER of Aurora, County of Lawrence and State of Missouri, who is over the age of twenty-one years and ARRIE CLARKof Mt. Vernon, County of Lawrence and State of Missouri, who is over the age of eighteen years.

Witness my hand as Recorder, with the seal of office hereto affixed, at my office in Mt. Vernon the 14th day of Sept. 1892. W. C. Trimble, Recorder State of Missouri, County of Lawrence.

This is to certify that the undersigned Minister of the Gospel did, at Aurora in the said county, on the 14th day of September A.D. 1892, unite in marriage the above named persons. W. B. Cochran, Minister of the Gospel. Filed for record Sept. 16th, 1892. W. C. Trimble, Recorder."

Arizona Donnie Clark was born October 17, 1873 in Ash Grove, Greene County, Missouri to John Clark and Emmaline Eliza (Parker) Clark, who were married in Greene County on December 8, 1864. John Clark was born about 1833, probably to Robert and Delia Clark, in Brown County, Illinois. Emmaline was born November 28, 1847, in Arkansas according to census data. The Clarks were a God-fearing, hard-working family, and their farm was located close to present-day 14599 West Farm Road 52, just a short distance southwest of her grandparents' farm. This was, in all likelihood, where Arrie and her siblings were born. Emmaline's maternal grandparents, the Sewell's, descended from pioneers from Sampson County, North Carolina.

Not much is known about Arrie's paternal lineage beyond her father, John Clark. No definite information has been found regarding his family. However, a John and Sarah Clark appear in the 1850 census of Brown County, Illinois, in the household of

Robert and Delia Clark. The ages of the John and Sarah in that census very closely coincide with the ages of both John Clark and the Sarah (Clark) Tyler, who were living with the John Turner family near Ash Grove in 1860. Sarah had married Caleb Tyler in Greene County on August 3, 1856. In 1859, John Clark had purchased two tracts from the government. The first consisted of 39.4 acres which he purchased on June 1st. On November 1st, he purchased an additional tract of 80 acres. According to the 1860 census, his property was valued at around $800. In 1870, John and Emmaline were living in Boone Township, Greene County, Missouri with their children Lecta A., born about 1866, and Jesse, born 1870 (age given was five months). [12]

John died about 1878 when Arrie was only five years old, and Emmaline remarried July 8, 1879 to Reuben Roy Reynolds. In 1880, they were living in Boone Township with Lecta A., Jesse, Arizona, and Eva Ann Clark. In 1900, Reuben and Ann were living in Lawrence County, Missouri, in Vineyard Township with four additional children: Baretta M, Lulu Ophia, a son Chesley Winfield and Mary Goldie Reynolds. By 1914, Reuben and Emmaline moved to Tulsa and remained there for many years before moving to the West Coast. Emmaline died in Cowlitz County, Washington on January 24, 1942. Reuben died January 26, 1943. They are buried at Whittle and Hubbard Cemetery, near Castle Rock. [13]

Jesse Clark was born January 26, 1870. He was 5 ½ months old at the time the 1870 census was taken on June 28th. He married Flora Florence Hunt in 1906, and they lived in Lawrence County, Missouri until after 1920. They then moved to Carthage, in Jasper County, Missouri. Flora was born in Jasper Township, Ozark County, Missouri on December 13, 1878, to Jeremiah V. and Martha Ann (Craigo) Hunt. They had five children: Myrtle M., (1907 – 1909), Earl J. (1911 – ?), Hattie Faye (Clark) Hamilton (1913- ?), wife of Paul Eugene Hamilton (1913 – 1995), Eva M.

(Clark) Lauat (1915 - ?), and Marlin Laverne Clark (1920 – 1998). They remained in Carthage until their deaths. Jesse died June 15, 1956, and Flora died May 16, 1960. They were buried at Sycamore Cemetery near Miller, Missouri. [14]

Eva Mae Clark was born in November 1877. She married Elmer Riley Hays. They most likely moved to Tulsa at the same time her mother and step-father moved there. She and Elmer had five children; Paul Aussie, Norma, John Hugh, Herbert Frederick, and Loretta Mae Hays. Eva died in Tulsa March 21, 1947. Sometime about March 1954, Elmer suddenly vanished without a trace. His children believed some former co-workers robbed and murdered him. [15]

Arrie's half-siblings and their descendants have proven more difficult to trace. Her sister Baretta M. Reynolds was born in 1880, but is said to have died about 1904. Lulu Ophia Reynolds was born 1883, and in June 1901, she married George Beecher Perryman Jr., a Creek Indian, by whom she had two children: Theodore Perryman (1902 – 1903) and Okena Perryman (1904 – 1959). Ophia died about 1910, and George remarried. But in 1937, he got drunk, fell down a flight of steps, and died instantly from a broken neck.[16]

Chesley Winfield Reynolds was born February 5, 1885 in Lawrence County, Missouri. He, like his father, served on the Tulsa Police Department. He married a girl named Cora about 1904, and he later moved to Cowlitz County, Washington, near his parents' home with his second wife, Stella. He died there February 9, 1955. He and Stella are also buried at Whittle and Hubbard Cemetery, in Castle Rock.[17]

Mary Goldie Clark was born September 1, 1888 in Miller, Lawrence County, Missouri. She married Melvin M. Vosburg of Iowa about 1910. They had three sons: Melvin Charles, born about 1911, Harold L., born about 1914, and Delbert James Vosburg, born about 1917. By 1930, they had moved to California, and resided at 3357 Magnolia Avenue in Long Beach,

Los Angeles County. Sometime after 1940, Goldie remarried to a man named Hanners, but she still resided at the same address as previously, and this was her home at the time of her death on May 11, 1972. She was survived by her son Delbert, three children, and five great-grandchildren. [18]

Ma Barker's half-siblings, about 1895.
L to R: Lulu Ophia, Chesley Winfield, and
Mary Goldie Reynolds.

Emmaline Eliza Parker's family left an easier paper trail to follow. Her parents were John A. Parker and Anna Jane Sewell, who were married about 1846 in McNairy County, Tennessee. Not much is known about John Parker's parents. He was born February 26, 1820, possibly in Georgia. The only Parker living in close proximity to the Sewell's in McNairy County was Edmund D. Parker, who was living next door to Anna's uncle, Frederick

Sewell, in McNairy County in 1850. Edmund is believed to have come from Georgia into Lincoln County, Tennessee by 1830 along with a Thomas Parker. They are on census records in Lincoln County, Tennessee in 1830 and 1840. Edmund was born in 1794 and died in McNairy County in 1859. He is buried there at Mount Zion Cemetery. Edmund was the only Parker living within proximity to the Sewell's old enough to have been the father of John A. Parker. No information has been found regarding Edmund's wife, though there is another Parker buried there who seems much too young to have been his wife, and was most likely a daughter. [19]

Anna's parents were German (or Jarman) Sewell and Grace Bennett. German's parents were Samuel Sewell and Mary Jarman (pronounced "German"), of Duplin and Sampson Counties of North Carolina. By 1830, German and several of his brothers, including Elias, William, and Frederick, left North Carolina and moved to McNairy County, Tennessee. About 1845, some of the Sewell brothers packed up and moved west into Missouri. German and his elder brother William settled first in Barry County, Missouri before 1850. But by 1860, they had moved to Greene County. No record of either German's nor Grace's deaths have been found, but they may be buried in Williamson Cemetery. [20]

Her uncle William Sewell was born June 16, 1775 Duplin County, North Carolina, and died March 24, 1849 in Greene County, Missouri. His wife was Catherine Butler, whom he married about 1795 -1800. Catherine was born about 1776. Both had died before the 1850 census, as they aren't enumerated. Her grave isn't marked. They are buried at Hammontree Cemetery, in Cass Township, three miles southeast of Walnut Grove near the intersection of Farm Road 65 and Farm Road 28. The cemetery is approximately 200 feet north of the intersection and 80 feet west of the road in an open pasture.

John A. Parker and Anna Jane Sewell married about 1843 in McNairy County, Tennessee, and headed west with the Sewell's after their eldest son, William, was born in Tennessee in 1844. The next child, Emmaline Eliza Parker, was born November 28, 1847 in Arkansas, according to the 1850 Barry County, Missouri, census for District 5. Barry County's southern boundary adjoins Arkansas, so this is very likely. The next two children, Nancy and Mary, were born in Missouri about 1848 and 1849. [21]

By 1860, they had settled in the northwestern part of Greene County, near Willard, with additional children; David, born 1851, a daughter, Palestine, born 1852, Lewis, born 1853, Elzara P., born 1854, Margaret, born 1858, and John O, born 1859 – listed as being 9 months old. By 1870, two more sons, James and Jacob, were added. John isn't enumerated on the census, and may have died young. John and Anna Jane settled on a 100-acre tract of land just a short distance southwest of Walnut Grove, bounded on the north side by a branch of Clear Creek and along Farm Road 38 and Farm Road 33. [22]

Greene County deed records show that J. A. Parker bought land from Henry McKinley on May 21, 1866, which was recorded August 29, 1866 in Book O, page 455. He bought another tract of land from W. and R. Frazier on November 15, 1870. This tract was recorded January 1, 1871 in Book X, page 329.

The following map shows the location of John A. Parker's farm southwest of Walnut Grove, and the possible location of Arrie (Clark) Barker's birthplace, just north of Ash Grove, in Greene County, Missouri. Anna Parker died February 18, 1910. John died a few months later, on October 7, 1910. They are interred at Williamson Cemetery, within a mile or so northeast of their farm, on Farm Road 33.

People who knew Arizona Clark described her as a tough, ill-tempered girl who also loved to sing in church, her parents being devout Presbyterians. However, she yearned for a life of excitement, which was fueled no doubt by the frequent visits of the notorious Jesse James gang through Ash Grove. Jesse and Frank James were considered folk heroes by many of the locals, and Arrie is said to have been devastated when Jesse was shot in the back and killed while he was straightening a picture on the wall. His killer, Robert "Bob" Ford, would be reviled in history *as "the dirty little coward who shot Mr. Howard, and laid poor Jesse in his grave."*

Jesse and Frank James in the 1870's

The old adage, "opposites attract", seems to have been the case with George and Arizona Donnie Clark. Whereas he was quiet and soft spoken, she was outspoken, headstrong, and often ill-tempered. Arrie, (she often used the nickname "Kate"), ruled the roost, and it proved to be a recipe for disaster.

When George and Arrie Barker married they were living near Aurora, Missouri, where they bought a lot in town on September 5, 1898.[23] George worked as a sharecropper and at any other sort of work he could find, but about 1899, he sold the lot he had purchased, and sometime between 1900 and 1903, moved the family to Webb City, Jasper County, Missouri. The rumors that he was a "worthless drunk" are certainly not evident in existing records for this family. He consistently worked and never left while the boys were at home. The Cartersville/Joplin/Webb City directories show him as a consistent worker. He was listed in the 1903 Webb City Directory as living at 205 North Pennsylvania Avenue, as an Ore Buyer. In 1905, George is listed in Webb City at 222 West 2nd Street, as an Ore Buyer for Prime Western Smelter Company. Another 1905 entry for George E. Barker lists him as a miner

working for the Queen Jack Mine, and residing on Smelter Hill.
24

George Elias and Arrie Barker
about 1900

George and Arrie Barker had four sons, all born in Aurora, in Lawrence County, Missouri. Their first son, Herman, was born October 30, 1893. Lloyd William, called "Red", was born next, on March 14, 1897. Arthur Raymond (per his World War One draft record), called "Doc", was born January 4, 1899, and Frederick George "Freddie", was born December 12, 1901. The Barker boys attended the Webb Grade School, and like most boys their age, they were prone to get into mischief. Herman gained quite a reputation as a prankster, even riding his horse through the front doors of saloons in imitation of his idol, Jesse James. But soon, the Barker boys' "mischief" led to petty theft, burglary, and more serious offenses. There is no doubt that Arrie's stories about the James Gang had a great deal to do with their behavior.

ORIGIN & MIGRATION OF GEORGE ELIAS & ARIZONA (CLARK) BARKER FAMILY IN MISSOURI 1859 - 1930

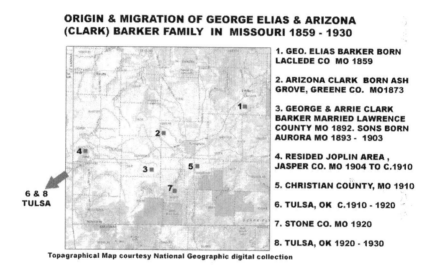

1. GEO. ELIAS BARKER BORN LACLEDE CO MO 1859

2. ARIZONA CLARK BORN ASH GROVE, GREENE CO. MO1873

3. GEORGE & ARRIE CLARK BARKER MARRIED LAWRENCE COUNTY MO 1892. SONS BORN AURORA MO 1893 - 1903

4. RESIDED JOPLIN AREA , JASPER CO. MO 1904 TO C.1910

5. CHRISTIAN COUNTY, MO 1910

6. TULSA, OK C.1910 - 1920

7. STONE CO. MO 1920

8. TULSA, OK 1920 - 1930

Topographical Map courtesy National Geographic digital collection

In 1910, Herman had his first run-in with the authorities when he was arrested for petty theft. He was released to his mother. On March 5, 1915, he was arrested once again, this time for highway robbery, but after Arrie threw a tantrum, he was again released into her custody. It was during this time that the police in Webb City also arrested Doc on several juvenile offenses. Each time, Arrie would throw a tantrum in front of the Judge. When that didn't work, she would begin sobbing and pleading for mercy. This generally worked, and the boys would be released to her. Because she refused to discipline them, they continued to get into more and more trouble with the law, and became incorrigible little hoodlums.

Arrie continually fumed about how her sons were being "mistreated" by everyone, and "persecuted" by the police; evidently oblivious to the fact that it was her permissiveness that laid at the door of all their run-ins with the Law. *She* was the reason they turned out bad.

One day, Arrie allegedly told her neighbors *"They're marked. The police here won't ever stop picking on my boys."* she grew so furious that she demanded that George move them to Tulsa, Oklahoma, where her family had also moved. She overruled every objection he had until he finally threw up his hands and gave in. He knew it was of no use to argue with her. Ironically, her step-father, Reuben Roy Reynolds, was a cop in Tulsa. He first appears in the Tulsa City Directory as a police officer in 1914, was Deputy Sheriff in 1921, and by 1931 was working as a security guard. His family lived there until moving West after 1940. [25]

George and Arrie Barker first appear in the Tulsa City Directory in 1914, and their address was given as 704 Park Avenue (Park later became S. Trenton). George was working as a laborer. In 1916, he was working for the Crystal Springs Water Company located at 114 E. 12th Street. In 1917, their address was listed as 702 Park Avenue, and George was still working at Crystal Springs. It was while they lived here that Arthur got into trouble for stealing a government vehicle in 1918. George and Arrie were still there in 1919, but Park Avenue had been renamed Trenton Avenue, so the 1919 Tulsa City Directory stated their address as 702 S. Trenton, with George still working for Crystal Springs as a Sterilizer.

They packed up and moved back to Stone County, Missouri by the end of 1919, and without the boys. Herman was in prison in Minnesota, and Doc was in jail in Tulsa, but Lloyd's and Fred's whereabouts in 1920 are a mystery. It's possible George might have been laid off temporarily from Crystal Springs. Whatever the reason, they were listed on the 1920 census for Stone County, Missouri, in Lincoln Township. [26]

BARKER HOME at 702 S Trenton Ave., Tulsa OK

Residence of George E. and Arrie Barker and their boys Herman, Lloyd, Arthur "Doc" and Fred, from about 1913 to 1920. A two-story addition built onto the rear of the house was added much later. It was for sale in June 2016 for $129,500.

PHOTOS BY AUTUMN LeMASTERS June 25, 2016

According to the census, George owned his residence, and was working as a farmer. By 1922, George and Arrie were listed in the Tulsa City Directory where George was again working as a bottler for Crystal Springs Water Company, and living in West Tulsa. Fred Barker was also listed as living in West Tulsa, and working for the Acme Water Company.

Their residence changed by the time the next Tulsa City Directory was printed. In 1923, George and Arrie lived at 403 North Cincinnati Avenue. George was no longer working for Crystal Springs, but was now employed as a Watchman. In 1924, their address is given as 401 North Cincinnati Avenue, and George was working as a janitor at the National Bank of

Commerce Building. In 1926, they were still living at the same address, and George was working as a Stationary Engineer. In 1927, their address was the same, and George was still a Stationary Engineer. 1928 is the last year George and Arrie were listed together in Tulsa. They were still living at 401 North Cincinnati Avenue, and George was working as a clerk.

Christmas time photo of Arrie Barker
Date unknown

In every City Directory where George Barker is listed, he is shown as being gainfully employed. The evidence is completely inconsistent with the off-repeated notion that he was a "worthless drunk." The fact is, he was a steady worker. Also, there is no evidence that George himself was ever arrested.

Herman kept ties to Webb City, since he was still getting into trouble there after 1915. Lloyd, seeing the handwriting on the wall, enlisted in the Army in Tulsa on August 17, 1918, just short of three months before the Armistice ending the First World War. He served as a Cook with the 162nd Depot Brigade, 87th Division, and was honorably discharged with the rank of Sergeant in February 1919. But, alas, Lloyd also fell back into old habits after coming home. In 1921, he was arrested in Tulsa for vagrancy, then later that year, he was involved in robbing a mail courier at Baxter Springs, Kansas. He was sentenced to 25 years in prison, and entered Leavenworth on January 16, 1922. He remained there until 1938, and after being released he went straight. When the U.S. entered World War Two, he reenlisted in the Army and served as a Cook at Fort Custer, in Augusta, Kalamazoo County, Michigan. After the war, he was again honorably discharged, moved to Denver Colorado, married, had a daughter, got a job as an assistant manager, and in 1949 his wife blew his head off with a shotgun as he came home from work. She was sent to an insane asylum for life.

George and Arrie's home at 702 Park Avenue (now 702 S. Trenton) was just a few blocks east of 6th and Peoria Streets, where both Central Park, and the Washington-Forsyth Elementary School were also located. It was here that a group of juvenile delinquents organized into a what became known alternatively as "the Central Park Gang" and "the East Side Gang". These young hoodlums committed burglaries and petty crimes throughout the area. One of them, Eva Jacobs, who was known in the local papers as "the bandit queen", forced a family out of their car at gunpoint and robbed them. She was only 17 when she and most of her gang were finally arrested in 1922. [25]

Members of the notorious Central Park Gang included Herman, Lloyd, Arthur and Fred Barker, Kenneth and Edgar Burnside, Merritt "Doc" Darnell, Lawrence "Larry" DeVol, Will Green, Harry Campbell, Elmer Hull, Jimmy "Blackie" Sexton, Frank Hadley, Edward Lansing, Gregory O'Connell, Roy Nance, George "Burhead" Keady, Mack Gray, Howard Musgrave, Volney Davis, Ray Terrill, Jimmy Lawson, Phoenix Donald, a.k.a. "William Weaver, Roland "Shorty" Williams and several others.

On July 4, 1918, Arthur "Doc" Barker was arrested for having stolen a government car on June 26 in Tulsa. He somehow managed to escape and fled to Joplin, where he stayed until he was recaptured there in 1920 and returned to Tulsa. But he again managed to escape. Then in January 1921, using the alias "Claude Dale", he was arrested for the attempted burglary of the bank in Muskogee, Oklahoma.

Doc was released a short time later, and was soon implicated in more serious trouble. Tulsa's new Catholic hospital, St. John's, was under construction and on the night of August 26, 1921, three men broke into the building to rob the office safe. They were interrupted by the night watchman, Thomas J. Sherrill, whom they killed while fleeing the scene. Soon thereafter, Volney Davis and Doc were arrested and charged for Sherrill's murder. They were convicted, and sentenced to life in prison at McAlester.

On January 9, 1922, members of the Central Park Gang were involved in a shootout with police officers, shortly after a burglary in Okmulgee, Oklahoma. Officers Captain Homer R. Spaulding, L. M. Lairmore, and M. E. Spence encountered a stalled car in the road in front of the Wooster Oil Company at Second Street and Choctaw Avenue, and stopped to give assistance. He then noticed burglary tools and explosives in the vehicle. One of the occupants, Jimmy Sexton, pulled out a pistol and opened fire on the policemen. The other officers returned fire, killing Sexton. Captain Spaulding, though initially thought to be lightly injured, had actually been mortally wounded. The bullet had hit his Femoral Artery, and he died on January 19th. Three other gang members, one later identified as Volney Davis, escaped. Two others, Ed Lansing and Frank Hadley, were captured and told Police they had been on their way to rob a bank in Muskogee when they had car trouble. Lansing was initially sentenced to death that September, but his sentence was commuted to life on December 23, 1922. Hadley, was sentenced to life on October 7, 1922.

CHAPTER 2:

HERMAN BARKER

Herman Barker, George's and Arrie's first born son, was born October 30, 1893 in Aurora, Lawrence County, Missouri. The family couldn't be found on the 1900 Lawrence County census, but there is little doubt they were there, as stated earlier, all four of their boys were born in Aurora. Sometime before 1900, George moved them to Webb City, in Jasper County, where he worked in the lead and zinc mines and various other jobs. The miners worked long, grueling hours, which left George little time to deal with the unruliness of his sons. Every attempt he made to discipline them turned into angry arguments between him and Arrie. After a while, he just finally gave up. When confronted about their wrongdoings, he said, *"You'll have to deal with Ma. She handles the boys."*

Herman's first brush with the Law came in 1910, when he was arrested for burglary. By 1914, George and Arrie had moved to Tulsa, when Herman was listed as a cook in the Tulsa City Directory, and boarding at 704 Park (704 S. Trenton). [1] On March 5, 1915, Herman was arrested in Joplin for "highway robbery"[2]. Arrie threw a tantrum and got him released. He returned to Tulsa and was living with them at 704 S. Trenton, and again listed in the City Directory as a cook. In 1916, he was again picked up in Joplin on a number of burglary charges, and in August was sentenced to 40 years in the Missouri State Penitentiary. However, he managed to escape, and fled to Montana.

In October 1916, under the alias "Bert Lavender", he was arrested in Billings, Montana for burglary and grand larceny and sentenced to six to twelve years in the Montana State Penitentiary at Deer Lodge, in Powell County.[3] When the United States entered the Great War, as World War One was then called, Herman still clung to his alias of "Bert Lavender" when he filled out his draft registration.

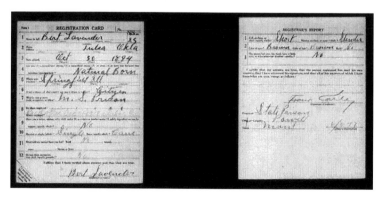

Even though he was later identified as Herman Barker, an escapee from Missouri, he was made to serve his sentence in

Montana under his alias until he was released in 1921. After getting out of prison, Herman violated his parole and fled to Minnesota, where he was arrested for burglary under the alias "Clarence Sharp", and sentenced to prison there. He was released from the Minnesota State Penitentiary in 1925 and returned to Tulsa to form a new gang. This new outfit included Ray Terrill, Elmer Inman, Alvin Sherwood, Joe Howard, Bill Munger, Ralph Scott, A. A. "Danny" Daniels, Charles Henry Stalcup, (who used the alias "Pale Anderson") and several others.

On June 7, 1926, Herman and Elmer Inman were captured in Fort Smith, Arkansas, driving a 1926 Paige Cabriolet stolen in Fairfax, Oklahoma from J. H. Ward. They were subsequently extradited to Oklahoma to answer charges there for robbery. But they didn't stay in jail very long before being released on bond, thanks in large part to their crooked pal, Ottawa County Judge Quillikee Phillip McGhee. [4]

McGhee was a native of Delaware District, Oklahoma Territory, and a Cherokee Indian. He was born November 22, 1886 to Thomas Jefferson McGhee and Martha Jane Hanna. He married Ellen Letitia Hanna February 1, 1904 in Jasper County, Missouri, then returned to Delaware County, where he was admitted to the Bar in 1914. In 1920, he was elected Judge in Ottawa County, by a huge margin. His popularity was no doubt influenced by the notoriety of his father, who had served during the Civil War as a 1st Lieutenant in Company E, First Cherokee Mounted Volunteers CSA, under Brigadier General Stand Watie. General Watie's Cherokee Regiment was the very last Confederate army in the field to surrender – a full four months after the Civil War "officially" ended with the surrender of General Robert E. Lee, overall Commander of all Confederate forces, at Appomattox Courthouse, Virginia on April 9, 1865. [5]

Judge McGhee was corrupt, and worked with an equally corrupt Deputy Sheriff, Frank Warner. Together, they secured

Herman Barker's release from Fort Scott authorities to prevent him from being prosecuted in Osage county for the same car theft. They also got Elmer Inman released.

McGhee, attorney Frank Burns, and the Justice of the Peace in Ketchum, Jeff D. Sexton, used a bogus warrant for an alleged burglary in Ketchum to gain custody of the two. Bond was made on June 22nd, and they were returned to Craig County, Oklahoma and released shortly thereafter. The same stunt had been used by McGhee ten days previously in Memphis, Tennessee, where Barker had been arrested for a jewelry store robbery in McAlester. McGhee used the warrant to prevent Pittsburg County authorities from extraditing him there to face charges. He would later be disbarred and indicted for aiding and harboring a felon.[6]

The Judge and his cronies operated an almost fool-proof scheme. Whenever one of their criminal friends got into trouble in another county or state, regardless of the charge, the arresting authorities would receive a notification that the suspect was wanted on serious charges back in Ottawa County, and that they were offering a substantial reward. The Ottawa Sheriff's department would go pick up the suspect using the bogus warrant, bring him back to Miami, then release him after he paid a fee of $1,200 or more. The "reward" cited would be paid to the arresting authority, and the difference would be split between McGhee, Warner and their cronies. This backfired on them late in 1927, when arrest warrants were issued against McGhee, Warner, and several others. McGhee and two other attorneys were disbarred, and then tried on the charges and found guilty. McGhee was sentenced to seven years in prison at McAlester.

Herman Barker. About 1915

On February 25, 1936, a report was filed with the FBI stating that on July 4, 1926, shortly after being sprung by McGhee, Fred and Herman Barker were in Independence Kansas casing a bank to rob. About one mile West of Tyro, on Highway 166 in Montgomery County, they approached a car being driven by Charles Faurot. With Faurot was his fiancée, Myrtle Rogers.

When Mr. Faurot and Ms. Rogers got close to the Barkers' car, Herman stopped them and without provocation killed Mr. Faurot. Subsequently, A Washington County, Oklahoma man, Everett Bible was arrested, wrongfully accused of the murder, convicted, and sentenced to the Kansas State Penitentiary. The informant stated that shortly after the murder, Herman and Fred Barker came to her home. She stated that she observed their peculiar actions and from their comments made while reading a newspaper concerning the murder, was confident that they were the individuals who had killed Mr. Faurot. The informant also stated that Herman Barker had told the entire story to Elmer Inman. She further stated that it was her desire to see Mr. Bible exonerated for a crime he didn't commit. [7]

It was 1926 that Herman began using the alias "J. H. Hamilton", and it was under this name that he allegedly married Mary Carol Antone. Carol's father, Cornelius Darius "Tony" Antone, was a full-blood Oneida Indian from New York State who had come to Indian Territory (as Oklahoma was then known) about 1884 to move logs to the railroad terminal at Red Fork – which was about fifteen miles southwest of Tulsa. While there, he met a woman named Lydia Van Loon. They were married June 9, 1886. [8]

Antone Stockade. Cornelius Darius Antone and wife Lydia (Van Loon) Antone, with their children, early 1900's (Courtesy Mike Jeffries, Sapulpa Historical Society/Museum, OK)

Their home became known as the 'Antone Stockade", and it holds a prominent place in the history of Creek County. Lydia was actually the first white woman in the area. She and Cornelius had six children but three died young.

1. Elizabeth "Lizzie" Antone was born February 14, 1888. She and her first husband, Michael Francis Slayman, married October 3, 1906 in Muskogee. They had four

children before Michael's death in 1919: [9]
a. Mary Slayman - Born in 1908
b. Francis Slayman - Born in 1910
c. Dorothy Slayman - Born in 1913
d. Myrtle Slayman - Born in 1919.
Lizzie remarried in Tulsa, Tulsa County, Oklahoma on February 11, 1922 to Lawrence James Richards. [10]
2. Mary Carol Antone - Born April 16, 1890. Died December 1962, Oklahoma City, Oklahoma.
3. Myrtle Antone - Born November 2, 1892 and died about 1905.
4. Jesstina Antone - Born August 23, 1895 and died February 9, 1896.
5. Thomas Cornelius Antone - Born December 25, 1896. Died Aug. 15, 1966 in Oklahoma City, Oklahoma. He served in the U. S. Marine Corps during the First World War.
6. Charlies Darius Antone was born 1898, and died before 1900.

Sometime before 1900, Lizzie, Mary Carol, and Myrtle were enrolled in the Chilocco Indian Agricultural School in Kay County, Oklahoma. Carol hated it, and ran away and returned home after a short time. However, her mother convinced her to return until she finished her education. Afterwards, she returned to Sapulpa, and married Earl E. Ladd on July 11, 1914, but they were divorced a short time later. [11]

Carol stated that she and Herman were married in Crowder, Pittsburgh County, Oklahoma by the Justice of the Peace there about November 1924. However, Herman was still in prison in Minnesota, and wasn't released until 1925. No marriage record for them has ever been found. It is possible that the Justice of the Peace failed to turn the record in to the county, but in all probability, her relationship with Herman would be closer to "paramour" or his "common law" wife. Also, since Herman wasn't using his real name, but the alias, "J. H. Hamilton", there is some question as to whether or not their marriage, if it actually took place, would have been legal anyway. In the latter part of 1930 she married Seth Camberlin Tankersley, but he left her, never to be heard from again. [12]

"J. H. and Mrs. Carol Hamilton", ran their gang's operations out of McGhee's Radium Springs Health Resort, which was located about a mile South of Salina, in Mayes County, Oklahoma. This resort lay along the Kansas, Oklahoma and Gulf Railroad where the old State Road made a sharp turn left, before turning right again to cross Saline River. It was said to be heavily armed and equipped with a powerful spotlight to warn gang members if the police were nearby. Years later, it was owned and operated as the "Radium Springs Sanitarium" by Dr. James Allen Nolen. In 1951, Nolen was the subject of an FDA investigation for misbranding drugs and fined $2,000. It was flooded when Hudson Lake was created, and it lay just below the shoreline of Salina State Park. The old railroad bed, as well as the old state road bed can still be seen leading into the water.[13]

Settlement of Oklahoma Territory began in earnest after the discovery of oil in the 1890's. Oil wells were drilled everywhere. Some wells didn't hit anything but Sulfur Water, but even then, enterprising land owners found a way to make money by advertising it as "Radium Water". They made outlandish claims that it could cure many, if not most, illnesses. People from all over the country flocked to these resorts, with the most well-known facilities being centered in and around Claremore. McGhee got in on the action also, and used his facility as the headquarters for his criminal friends' operations. [14]

On December 20, 1926, Herman, Ray Terrill, and others, broke into the State Bank of Buffalo, in Wilson County, Kansas where they stole $6,000 in cash and American Express Travelers Checks worth another $2,000. Almost three weeks later, on

January 16th, the safe from the bank in Rogersville, Missouri is stolen. The next day Terrill, Herman and their gang broke into the bank in Jasper, Missouri. They had stolen a truck and backed it up to the bank. The trick was to winch the safe into the back of the truck, take it back to their hideout at Radium Springs, empty it, then dump it over the side of the Lindsay Mayes bridge into the Grand River below.

Old Highway 20 bridge over the Grand River between Salina and Pryor. It was built in 1922.

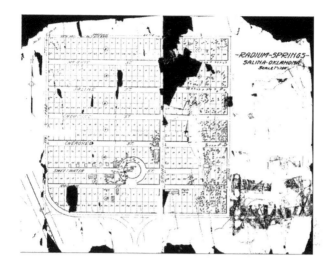

Radium Springs Resort, Salina, OK. Plat Map 157-A

They had done this several times, but on this particular night, the gang was spotted by a local businessman who alerted authorities. In addition to the truck, they had two other vehicles. One car sped towards Kansas, while Barker and Terrill took off in another car to their hideout at 602 East Main Street, in nearby Cartersville, Missouri. The Police had been informed that the house in Cartersville was being used by a gang of criminals, and they had it under surveillance. Upon seeing Barker and Terrill, they quickly surrounded it and ordered the occupants out. A gunfight ensued, during which Herman was hit in the left leg with buckshot, and both he and Terrill were captured. Nearly two dozen shotgun pellets were removed from Herman's leg, leaving only one lodged behind his kneecap that couldn't be removed. He walked with a pronounced limp for the rest of his life.

On January 19, Terrill was returned to McAlester to finish his sentence, but he jumped out of the car and escaped. As for Herman, because there wasn't enough evidence to tie him to the bank burglary, he was turned over to the authorities in Washington County, Arkansas to face charges for a bank robbery there. However, he and another prisoner escaped from the jail in Fayetteville after Herman sawed through the bars in the window.

On or about May 17, 1927, Carol talked Herman into taking a long trip out to the West Coast to get some rest and to give him time for his leg to heal. After a few weeks, they began their return trip back to Tulsa. Their funds began to run low by the time they reached Cheyenne Wyoming, so on August 1st Herman decided, against Carol's advice, to cash some of the American Express Travelers Checks that had been stolen from the bank in Buffalo, Kansas seven months earlier. They stopped at the American National Bank at 16th Street and Capital Avenue in Cheyenne to cash the checks. [15]

Using the alias "R. D. Snodgrass, Herman cashed three of the traveler's checks for $30.00. A sharp-eyed clerk noticed something didn't seem right and asked Herman to come back inside. He ignored the clerk, got into his car, and sped off. The clerk immediately notified the authorities. Sheriff George J. Carroll in Pine Bluffs, about 40 miles East, was also notified and given a description of the car, the driver, and his female companion. [16]

Deputy Sheriff Arthur Emil Osborn was busy doing some carpentry work at the Laramie County Fairgrounds when the clerk at the Standard Hotel notified him that the Sheriff needed to speak with him. He rushed to the hotel to take the call. Sheriff Carroll explained the situation, gave him a description of the car and its occupants, and told him to try to apprehend the bandit.

After hanging up the phone, he turned to the hotel manager, Fred Anderson, and said *"I feel like this is going to be my lucky day. I haven't caught a car in a long time, and I believe I'm going to catch this one!"* He drove West on the Lincoln highway watching for the two-tone blue Chrysler Coach, loaded down on the driver's side running board with camping equipment, with a large blue trunk on the rear as described by the bank clerk in Cheyenne. He spotted it about a mile and a half west of town, and quickly turned his car across the road, forcing Herman to slam on his brakes and come to a screeching halt. [17]

Osborn got out of his car and walked up to the running board of Barker's Chrysler. He smiled and said, *"I believe you folks are some people I want!"* Carol responded, *"I'm sure you're mistaken. You can't want us. We haven't done anything wrong!"* Yes, I'm certain I want you!" Osborn answered.

At that moment, Herman pulled out a .32 caliber Colt automatic pistol and pointed it at Osborn, and shouted *"Put your hands up and get in!"*. Startled, Carol jumped out of the car. She then heard two gunshots. Herman had shot Osborn as he reached to grab the gun. Seeing Osborn lying in the road, she began to cry and scream hysterically.

Herman yelled, *"Get back in the car NOW!"* As she got in, Herman gunned the engine, swerved around Osborne's car, and continued East through Pine Bluffs. A few miles out of town, he turned right onto the old Cemetery Road, which is today State Road 164, and runs due south parallel with the Nebraska state line. The barren, rocky terrain, as well as the weather, would prove to be serious hindrances in tracking down the killer. Carol would later describe how Herman drove across Cemetery Hill in the "fog and the rain" and down across the state line into Weld County, Colorado close to the Pawnee Buttes. [18]

Cemetery Road becomes Weld County Road 105 at the state line. From there, it is believed Herman then turned West down Weld County Road 136, then South again on County Road 89 into Grover. From there, they traveled down Southeast along the road running parallel with the railroad. A few miles further, they pulled off the road to allow a farmer to pass by with his tractor, then drove on.

Fearing they might be spotted they hurriedly unstrapped the large blue trunk off the rear luggage rack. Hoping to change the car's appearance enough to thwart being recognized by the police, they threw the contents into the car and left the trunk behind. [19]

It was found several days later. From there, they traveled across the grasslands, then turned South again. Carol stated later that their car got stuck in the mud four miles North of Raymer. This would have been at the south fork of Pawnee Creek, which is almost exactly four miles North of Raymer (also called "New Raymer"). They managed to get the car out of the mud, continued on through Raymer, and then headed east out of Colorado. By August 5, they were back in Tulsa.

Deputy Osborn was discovered by some men from nearby Scotts Bluff, lying face down in a ditch. They turned him over and saw that he was unconscious but still alive, but just barely. The men carefully picked him up, and laid him into a vehicle and rushed him to the office of Dr. M. L. Morris in Pine Bluffs, where he died about fifteen minutes later. Upon examining Osborn's body, Morris found that the first bullet had entered his left arm just above the elbow, traveled down into his torso above the left kidney, ripped through his intestines in six places, then lodged in his right pelvic region. The second bullet had been fired as he fell, striking him in the back of his left shoulder. Osborn's pistol, a .32-20 Colt Army Special revolver, was found still holstered. He never drew his weapon.[20]

Arthur Emil Osborn was 45 years of age, leaving behind his parents, William and Sarah Osborn of Edison, Nebraska, his wife Beulah, and young children Mary Faye, Arthur Ray, and Wayne Neville. Their eldest daughter, Maxine, had died in 1916. He was born January 27, 1882 in Edison, Nebraska and had settled in Pine Bluffs in 1900, working as a carpenter and building contractor. He married Beulah Bird in Cheyenne County, Nebraska in 1912. Osborn had served a term as Mayor of Pine

Bluffs, and was a member of Gates City Lodge No. 32, A.F. and A.M. of Pine Bluffs, and of Wyoming Consistory No. 1. He had been appointed Deputy Sheriff on January 1, 1926, succeeding C. R. Buschow.

As the search for Osborn's killer widened, the trunk they had tossed aside was found near an abandoned school at Sligo, about 13 miles Southeast of Grover, and about 27 miles Southeast of Pine Bluffs. However, they overlooked several items which proved valuable to the police. Articles of clothing, shoes, and other things with the name "Mrs. J. H. Hamilton" written on them were found inside. [21]

By this time, authorities began to believe that another bandit, Elmer Inman, was the gunman and word was sent out throughout most of the country and also to Canadian authorities. Laramie County Sheriff George J. Carroll issued thousands of circulars describing the killer and his female companion, and offered rewards of over $1,200 for leads that might result in the capture of the culprits who had killed his deputy. [22]

Herman and Carol made it back to Tulsa in their muddy car on August 5th and rented a room under the aliases "Mr. and Mrs. Smallwick at a boarding house owned by Mrs. W. B. McConnicko. While here, they traded the Chrysler for a Ford Coupe, in which they made their way to Batesville, Arkansas where Carol claimed she owned a farm. However, evidence suggests they were still in Tulsa during the second week of August.

.

Deputy Sheriff Arthur E. Osborn

HERMAN BARKER'S ESCAPE ROUTE

AUGUST 1, 1927
HERMAN BARKER KILLS DEPUTY SHERIFF ARTHUR E OSBORN NEAR PINE BLUFFS, WYOMING. ESCAPES SOUTH INTO WELD COUNTY, COLORADO ACROSS THE PAWNEE BUTTES GRASSLAND.

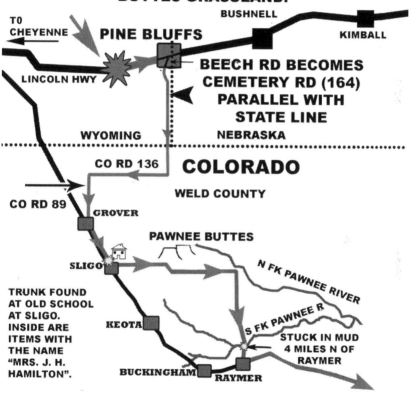

On the night of August 9th, four men in a truck and another vehicle attempted to rob the People's Bank of Southwest City, in McDonald County, Missouri. Shortly after midnight, they were interrupted by Night Marshall William Henry Hatfield. One of the alleged robbers knocked him unconscious, then shoved the barrel of a shotgun in his mouth and pulled the trigger, blowing his brains out. The truck's occupants heard the shot and exited the scene. A local doctor, Edward Croxdale, was later arrested for Hatfield's murder and sentenced to life in the Missouri State Penitentiary, but he was paroled by 1940. Local authorities dismissed robbery as a motive for Hatfield's murder, since Croxdale was a known bootlegger, and Hatfield, a retired Methodist minister, was a vocal advocate of Prohibition. Croxdale may have unknowingly interfered with the robbery attempt at the bank. The truck was found burned a few days later in Vinita, Oklahoma. [23]

Meanwhile, in Seneca, Missouri; just a short distance north of Southwest City, Kenneth Prader discovered that his new grey Chevrolet four-door sedan had been stolen during the night. The following week, Herman Barker drove up in the car, and informed Carol that he was leaving to meet some friends to "do a job" and that he would be back soon. [24]

The job was to rob the Crystal Ice Company, in Newton Kansas. Herman's gang knew the company handled large sums of money. Newton is located in Harvey County, about 28 miles due North of Wichita. The Ice Plant was located along the railroad at 416 Oak Street. Barker, and his two companions, Porter Clay Meek and Charles Henry Stalcup, had met at Coffeyville, Kansas to plan the robbery. They had scouted out this job while staying in the whorehouse located right behind the Ice Plant. This was a perfect location. The whorehouse was a two-story brick building that allowed the gang to have a bird's eye view of the plant and the small payroll office out front where the safe was located. From their perch, they noted the routines of everyone coming in and out.

Porter Clay Meek was the eldest of the three. He was born October 23, 1881 in Crawford County, Arkansas to George W.

and Mary Elizabeth (Brandenburg) Meek. By 1900, they had settled in Tecumseh City, Pottawatomie County, Oklahoma Territory. Porter's brother, Milton H. Meek, had been shot and killed in March 1911 by Pottawatomie County Deputy Sheriff J. B. Tilghman, for being drunk and disorderly, and resisting arrest. By 1917, Porter was in the Oklahoma State Prison. [25] His father George died in Mayes County, Oklahoma in 1911, and his mother died in 1912. He was paroled by 1919, when he and W. F. Fuller robbed a gambling hall over the Grand Theater in Tulsa. They were arrested, but the prosecuting witness failed to appear in court. Meek then left for Dallas Texas. On September 20, 1920, he, Pres Fanning and Earl Rife, robbed a card game at the Waldorf Hotel. Meek was sentenced to 25 years for this crime, but was again paroled after serving only a short time.

Charles Henry Stalcup was born January 9, 1892 in Howe, Leflore County, Oklahoma Territory. His parents were John Wesley and Ida Alice Stalcup, who had divorced shortly before 1910. John was a prominent attorney in Picher, where he and his second wife Rosa had settled. Charles, however, despite his father's reputation, was well-known to authorities in Miami as a rough character who had been in and out of prison in both Oklahoma and Kansas.

In 1927, Charles and his wife Wilma were living at 15 D Street, SW. He and another ex-con, A. A. "Danny" Daniels ran the Osage Pool Hall at 28th South Main Street. The pool hall was a front for local hoodlums, including the Barker brothers, to plan their robberies. Ralph Scott, Alton Purdy, Gene Johnson, James Parduo, and others hit small businesses, banks, jewelry stores, and other targets of opportunity far and wide. About April of 1927, the city of Miami revoked their license after it was learned Daniels and Stalcup had criminal records. Stalcup had been arrested in February by Muskogee officers in connection to a jewelry store robbery in Lawton the previous August. He was taken to Lawton and Muskogee but released for lack of evidence. He was arrested again on April 4th by request of Missouri officials in connection with the robbery of the Bank of Billings, Montana, but charges were dropped on May 14 after a preliminary hearing.

Soon, it was time for them to make their move at the Ice Plant. They were in Prader's stolen Chevy Sedan, and In the late hours of August 28, They quietly made their way on foot and approached the payroll office. It was a brick building roughly 12 feet square on the end of the plant opposite the whorehouse. They caught the security guard completely by surprise, quickly tied him up, and locked him in a freezer. They then cracked the safe. It contained about $200 in silver and other change. They bagged up the dough and left. [26]

The entire job took mere minutes. The trio got into their car, drove down North Pine Street then left on East 4th, and headed quickly South down North Main Street towards Wichita. They gloated in how smoothly they had pulled off the heist, but unbeknownst to them, this would be their last hurrah. Destiny lay just a few short miles down the road.

It was an uneventful night in Wichita for motorcycle patrolmen Joseph Earl Marshall and his partner Frank Bush, riding in the side car. The night was clear and the air was warm and dry as they drove along the quiet streets. Reports of the robbery had already reached Wichita and the two policemen were watching for suspicious automobiles on the streets. Just after 1:00 a.m., they saw a car speeding past, headed south on North Lawrence.

Officer Marshall quickly took off in pursuit. They pulled the car over at the intersection of North Lawrence and 11th Avenue. Marshall and Bush dismounted from their bike and cautiously approach the vehicle.

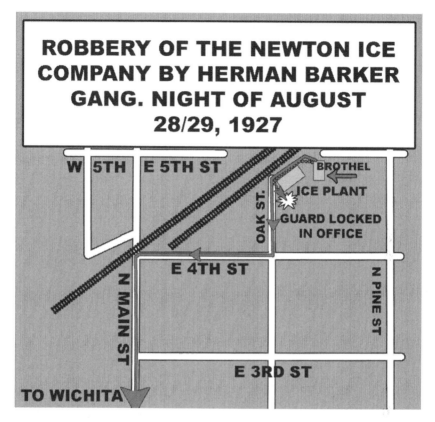

ROBBERY OF THE NEWTON ICE COMPANY BY HERMAN BARKER GANG. NIGHT OF AUGUST 28/29, 1927

"Where's the fire, Mister?"

Marshall asks and he approached the driver's side door. Bush moved right to approach towards the passenger side. Something isn't right. They unsnap their holsters. Marshall noticed the driver looking down as if fumbling about trying to find his driver's license.

As Marshall walked up to the car to question him, Herman suddenly grabbed him around the neck in a head lock and pulled him through the window. He placed his .32 Colt automatic against the officer's head and pumped three bullets into him. The first bullet entered Marshall's right eye and exited from the left side of his head. The second bullet struck him in the mouth, and the third slug ripped into his left arm as he fell to the ground.

Seeing his partner shot, Bush curses and returns fire as Barker starts the car and drives off. He emptied his weapon at the car, and sees Barker slump behind the wheel. As Bush quickly reloads, Meek jumped from the passenger's side with his gun firing wildly. Bush returned fire, striking Meek in the leg, but Meek quickly jumped to his feet and vanished into the night. His luck would run out later the following day. Barker was hit in the lower chest, and ripped through his lungs. Charlie Stalcup, sitting in the back seat, was also hit twice through his legs.[28]

Herman Barker being stopped by officers Marshall and Bush (Illustration by the author)

Officer Marshall was quickly rushed to St. Francis hospital in a Lahey and Martin ambulance. Detective James L. Fugit and Earl

T. Martin, of Lahey and Martin Mortuary, rushed to Marshall's home to inform his wife of the shooting, then took her to the hospital to be with him. He died at 3:27 a.m.

Frank Bush (left) and Joseph E. Marshall on motorcycle
(Wichita Eagle. August 30, 1927)

Barker hit the gas pedal and sped wildly turning left down 11th Avenue. He careening erratically back and forth as other patrolmen join the chase. As Barker reached St. Francis Avenue, he turned right, nearly losing control. His vision soon began to fade, and his breathing becomes more laborious as blood pooled into his lungs. Accounts vary as to what happened next. One witness at an all-night burger joint reported seeing the bandit's car heading East on Pine on the wrong side of the road. The newspaper stated he was headed South on St. Francis. One thing is for sure. His wild ride came to an abrupt end at the intersection of St. Francis and East Pine.[29]

Customers at the burger joint heard the tires from Barker's car squalling as he tried to stay on the road, but it was to no avail. He veered off the road as he swerved out of the path of an oncoming car, and slammed into a tree at the southwest corner of the intersection. Hearing the crash, they rush out to investigate, It wasn't long until they heard sirens as the other officers in the chase arrived on the scene. Dazed, Herman opened the car door and fell flat on his face. Somehow, he managed to get to his feet one last time. He could barely breath as the blood pooled up into his throat from the tunnel Bush's bullet bored through his chest. Everything quickly began fading to black. He staggered a short distance away from the car across to the southeast corner of the intersection. He knew this was the end of the line as he placed the Colt against his right temple. *"Forgive me, Ma!"* he groaned as he pulled the trigger. Herman Barker, George's and Arrie's first born son, was dead. 30

Herman Barker lies dead, Wichita, Kansas. August 29, 1927.

UNDERTAKERS

Funeral Parlors

Ambulance

Hall Undertaking Co.
SERVICE

32 S. Main

Phone 800

MIAMI CITY DIRECTORY (1927)

Hall Undertaking in Miami, Ottawa Co., OK who handled Herman Barker's funeral (Miami, OK City Directory 1927)

Herman's body was taken to Gill Mortuary at 423-425 North Emporia Avenue, where it was discovered that Officer Bush's bullet had inflicted a mortal wound, entering below the left armpit, ripping through the chest cavity, and exiting the right side. Herman's intense pain plus the knowledge that even had he survived his wounds, he would most likely be executed for the murders of Osborn and Marshall, drove him to take his own life. [31] Stalcup was found lying in the back seat, was arrested, and taken to the hospital to treat his injuries.

Lawrence Hall, who ran Hall Funeral Parlor at 32 South Main Street, in Miami, Oklahoma with his wife, Margie, was sent to pick up Herman's body and return him to Oklahoma for burial. However, Assistant Wichita Police Chief Roy Criswell refused to release the body until City Physician, Dr. J. E. Wolfe completed his inquest. Once that was competed, his remains were released to Hall on August 30. [32]

Herman's funeral was held on September 1st by Rev. A. P. Cameron at 2:00 p.m., at Williams-Timberhill Cemetery near Welch, in Craig County. His friend Q. P. McGhee had purchased the burial plot for him and his family. Williams-Timberhill was often referred to in the newspapers as an "outlaw cemetery", and rumors circulated for years that Barker was secretly buried in the middle of the night. This, of course, was pure myth.[33]

Gill Mortuary, Wichita Kansas, November 1927.
Photographer unknown

THE END OF HERMAN BARKER
Wichita Kansas, August 29, 1927

BARKER, MEEK & STALCUP PULLED OVER AT LAWRENCE AND E 11TH. MARSHALL KILLED

DYING, BARKER KILLS SELF AT ST FRANCIS & E PINE ST. CHARLES STALCUP CAPTURED

The following day, Wichita police were swarming the streets in search of Porter Clay Meek. He was soon spotted a few blocks north of where he bailed out of Barker's car, in a neighborhood near the railroad roundhouse. He was tired, hungry and thirsty, and as he walked down the street, he saw Charles Mullenix sitting on the front porch of his home. He asked for a drink of water then went on his way. Mullenix noticed a pistol sticking out of Meek's belt, waited for him to leave, then called the police. [34]

Funeral of Joseph E. Marshall, September 1, 1927, Wichita, Kansas. (Photographer unknown) Courtesy Downing & Lahey West Mortuary, Wichita, Kansas

A short while later, Meek entered a store to buy a beer and a pack of cigarettes. The store clerk also saw the pistol and she, too, notified the police after he left. As the manhunt continued, a fourteen year old named Harold Burkholder told police that he saw a man who looked like the one they were looking for. Detective Merle Colver had Burkholder get in his car and show him where he had seen him. He led them to a vacant house, and called out, *"Come out and put your hands up!"* Instead, Meek came out shooting and yelled, *"Like Hell I will!"* Burkholder was shot in the leg as Colver returned fire. He hit Meek in the side and through the heart, killing him instantly. His body was taken to the Lahey and Martin Funeral Parlor, at 922 East Douglas Avenue. Harold Burkholder was honored for his heroism and given a medal. Officer Marshall's funeral was held there at 4 p.m. on September 1. Ironically, Meek's remains were laid out in the parlor directly across the hall. Marshall was buried at Wichita Park Cemetery. Meek's body was returned to his family in Oklahoma. [35]

As Stalcup laid in his hospital bed, he confessed to the Ice Plant robbery in Newton. When the police searched Barker's car, they find two bags, containing silver coins, and loose change. When Wichita authorities ran the car's tags, they learned that it had been stolen in Seneca. The owner, Ken. Prader, was notified, and he arrived a few days later to retrieve it. Since Stalcup was the only one of the three to survive, he was charged with First Degree murder in the death of officer Joseph E. Marshall. On November 4, 1927 he was found guilty, and sentenced to life in the Kansas State Penitentiary. In 1961, he applied for Executive Clemency from the Governor of Kansas. It was denied, but he reapplied in 1962. He was eventually released and moved to Little Rock, Pulaski County, Arkansas. He died there at the age of 93 on December 1, 1985.[36]

Sheer Hell on Earth ensued in the Barker home in the wake of Herman's death as Arrie became completely unhinged. Lloyd, Doc, and Fred were in prison, and now her first born was dead. Her grief turned to anger, and that anger turned to hatred. A substantial amount of that hatred was directed at Herman's "hussy" wife, Carol, whom she believed was responsible for his death. Arrie refused to believe that Herman had taken his own life, believing he had been murdered by the police.

As for Carol, she knew not to show her face at Herman's funeral. Instead, she claimed she hid herself behind some nearby shrubs and watched as he was laid to rest. Not only was she hiding from Ma, but also from the authorities in Wyoming as well. They were hot on her trail, and she knew it would only be a matter of time before they caught up to her. Frightened and desperate, and not knowing quite what to do or where to turn, she made preparations to end her own life. Her plan was to go to Williams-Timberhill Cemetery, lay on Herman's grave, and blow her brains out.

She had already made several nocturnal visits to Herman's grave, and it wasn't long before someone spotted her. The authorities got wind of Carol's visits, so they took up positions near the cemetery and watched. As it turned out, she never returned, but soon they were told she had been hiding at a local attorney's home. In all likelihood, the attorney was none other than Q. P. McGhee.

Photo by Autumn LeMasters, June 25, 2016

About mid-September, Carol left Oklahoma to stay with her sister Lizzie's relatives a short distance West of Neosho, in Newton County, Missouri. It was there on the morning of September 16, that she was arrested at a house near New Salem Church by a group of officers, which included Newton

County Sheriff Beach W. Bridges, Deputy Foster McConnell. Sheriff George J. Carroll of Wyoming, Ottawa County, Oklahoma, Deputy Joe Anderson of Cardin, a Post Office inspector of Tulsa, and another officer from Picher, Oklahoma. Carol, using the alias "Mrs. Ruth Parker", put up no resistance, and was returned that afternoon to Wyoming to face charges in connection with the murder of Deputy Sheriff Arthur Osborn.

Carol subsequently pleaded guilty as an accessory to Osborn's murder. She fully expected to get the death penalty, and even told the court to "end me" for her role in the crime. She indicated that she would rather be executed than spend the rest of her life behind bars. Instead, she was sentenced to only two years, but since Wyoming had no prison facilities for women, she was incarcerated at the Colorado Women's Prison in Pueblo. She arrived there on September 29, 1927 as Inmate Number 14172. Two years later, she was paroled into the custody of Herman's pal, Q. P. McGhee, on October 2, 1929. After returning to Oklahoma, McGhee got her a job at the Carleton Hotel in Sapulpa, where she moonlighted as a prostitute.

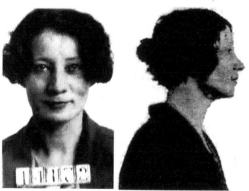

Carol "Hamilton" (Barker)

Carol would still be associated with the Barker gang for several more years, often buying groceries for Arrie after George left, and while Herman's brothers were still locked up. She eventually became the girlfriend of Fred Barker's best friend, Alvin Karpis.

After Herman's death, Arrie's world came crashing down. It was just her and George at home struggling to get by on what little he was able to earn at his age, and he was almost 70 years old. By this time, his health prevented him from holding better paying positions. However, in her daydream world, she yearned for her sons to become what George could not – wealthy – so that she could live in luxury, with money, nice clothes, jewelry, and a nice place to live. But that wasn't reality, and it was always someone else's fault that her boys turned out bad. Never did she stop to think that it was her own doing; that she, herself, was to blame by not disciplining them when they were young. The proverbial chickens had come home to roost, and now it was just her and George. She turned into even more of a cantankerous old Hellcat than before.

Whether out of boredom, frustration or both, Sometime in 1928, Arrie and some of her lady friends from the neighborhood began hitting the speakeasies and seeing other men on the sly behind their husbands' backs. It wasn't long before George found out, and all Hell broke loose. He had tried his best to work and provide for his family, and now she had crossed the line. He was devastated. This betrayal ripped his heart out, and he just couldn't take it any longer.

He had worked his fingers to the bone to support her and the boys. He had wanted to discipline them, only to have her fight him tooth and nail, and undo everything he had tried to do. He stood by and watched helplessly while they turned into petty hoodlums and killers. Herman was dead, and now he had caught Arrie cheating on him. Other men would have either shot her, themselves, or both. As far as he was concerned, on top of the sheer Hell of seeing his oldest child die, this latest outrage was unforgiveable. She had finally pushed quiet, easy-going George Elias Barker over the edge. He exploded with rage, packed what little possessions he had, and moved back home to Joplin. This was the last straw. From all accounts, he never had another thing to do with her for the rest of her life.

George and Arrie Barker
about 1927

CHAPTER 3:

THE RISE OF THE BARKER-KARPIS GANG

FRED BARKER   **ALVIN KARPIS**

With George leaving, life soon began to take a nose-dive for Arrie. Lloyd was in the Federal penitentiary in Leavenworth, Kansas. Arthur had been sentenced to life for the murder of a night watchman, and was in the Oklahoma State Prison in McAlester, and Fred was in the Kansas State Penitentiary serving a five-year sentence for burglary. By the Fred got out of prison in 1931, Arrie was still living at 401 N. Cincinnati at the corner of East Archer Avenue, about a block north of the Frisco Railroad. The house had become little more than a run-down tar paper shack.

And just when she thought things couldn't get any worse, the New York Stock Market crashed on October 29, 1929, plunging the entire country into the Great Depression. It was worst economic downturn in the Nation's history, and would last until just before America's entry into the Second World War in 1941.

Whereas the "Roaring Twenties" was a time of major prosperity, the Great Depression was a time of despair and desperation. Thousands lost their jobs and savings. Banks foreclosed on farms, throwing multitudes of people into the streets. Desperate people do desperate things when their survival is at stake. Crime rates rose exponentially as many of the unemployed who couldn't find any sort of work turned to petty theft and more serious crimes just to be able to feed their families. The suicide rate rose sharply. Hundreds of people reportedly starved to death. Thousands left New England and the East Coast to escape the crime in the cities, and drought conditions in Oklahoma and Arkansas drove many farmers to the West Coast.

Out of this economic nightmare soon arose a new class of "motorized" bandits. Clyde Barrow and Bonnie Parker, "Pretty Boy" Floyd, Lester "Baby face Nelson" Gillis, John Dillinger, John "Red" Hamilton, Harry Pierpont, Homer Van Meter, among others, became prominent names on the front page of newspapers all across the country during the 1930's. These gangsters made effective use of automobiles in hitting banks and making fast getaways in even faster cars. Clyde Barrow preferred Ford's new Flathead V-8 and even wrote Henry Ford, telling him that he used them "exclusively" whenever he could "get away with one"[1]. John Dillinger and his gang liked the new 1933 and 1934 Ford Model 40, and also larger cars such as the 1933 Essex Terraplane 8, and the big Buick limousines, which could outrun anything the police had at that time. These gangs were also well-armed. They would raid National Guard armories and even police stations, stealing Browning Automatic Rifles and Thompson machine guns. They could outgun and outrun anyone who tried to stop them, and they could be over a hundred miles away to hit another bank in another state within hours. They seemed unstoppable.

While the nation's attention was diverted to the "big time" motorized bandits like Bonnie and Clyde, John Dillinger, "Pretty Boy" Floyd, and others, another even more ruthless gang had been lurking in the shadows. This new gang managed to avoid detection for years by carefully planning their crimes, and frequently changing tactics. They committed burglaries and robbed banks all over, from Missouri, into Kansas, Oklahoma, Minnesota, and even South Dakota. It wasn't until 1934 that Law Enforcement was finally able to connect the dots. These desperadoes came to be known as the "Barker – Karpis gang", and consisted initially of Fred Barker, Alvin Karpis, and Phoenix Donald, a.k.a. "William Weaver", and later Arthur "Doc" Barker, following his parole from the Oklahoma State Penitentiary at McAlester. The gang would eventually consist of over 25 members at various times between 1931 and 1935.

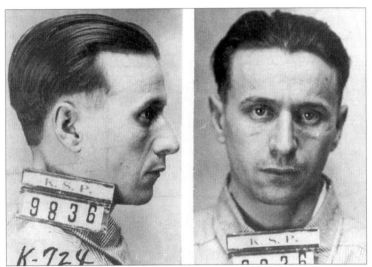

Frederick George Barker (Kansas State Prison photo)

Frederick George Barker was born in Aurora, Lawrence County, Missouri December 12, 1901, and was the youngest of his brothers. He, along with Herman, Lloyd and Doc, was part of the Central Park gang. Fred's first serious run-ins with the law seem to have begun around 1922. In September of that year, he very nearly joined his brother Lloyd at Leavenworth, but for a crime he didn't commit.

On September 1, three men robbed a mail courier of $14,200 that was to go to the bank in Picher, Oklahoma for the miners' payroll. On September 5, the police stopped a car in Ottawa County occupied by Fred, four other men, and two women. The car had matched the description given of the bandits' car, so they were all held "under investigation" but since the driver couldn't positively identify any of them, they were released. The real bandits' car was later found abandoned near Columbia, Kansas, and in October, four men, Ben Clement, C. Morgan Blalock, Joe Miller, and F. Dolson were arrested; two of whom confessed to the robbery. The other two stood trial shortly thereafter. Fred, however, was believed to have been involved in a number of burglaries in the Tulsa area, but the police had no proof, and weren't able to tie him to any of the thefts. But in October 1922, he was sentenced instead to 30 days in jail for vagrancy. [2]

On January 6, 1923, Fred and another young man crashed a Saturday night poker game going on in the back of Slim's Repair Shop located at 19 West Archer Avenue in Tulsa. The two men pulled their stick up, with Fred holding his pistol while his buddy gathered up the loot, which amounted to about $600. On Monday, police responded to a tip that Fred was in on the robbery, and was hiding out at a house on East Fourth Street. He was arrested, and on June 28, 1923, was sentenced to one to five years in the Oklahoma State Reformatory in Granite. He was paroled after only a short time, probably due to his mother's pleading and caterwauling with the courts. [3]

Fred Barker about 1931

After Herman was released from prison in 1925, Fred joined him and Ray Terrill's gang operating out of Radium Springs near Salina, burglarizing businesses, and robbing banks all over the area and in neighboring states. In July 1926, they were allegedly casing banks near Independence, Kansas when Fred and

Herman shot and killed a man, Charles Faurot, on the highway near Tyro, in Montgomery County. Another man, Everett Bible of Ocholala, Oklahoma, was identified by Faurot's girlfriend as the killer and was sentenced to prison. This may have been the first murder committed by Fred and Herman. It certainly wouldn't be the last. [4]

In July 1926, Herman had bought a new Nash Sedan from the Nash dealership in Tulsa, and a few months later, the gang was operating in Cowley County, Kansas where they burglarized several stores. On November 8th, Fred was caught burglarizing Dillon's Grocery in Winfield. Herman managed to escape, but he abandoned his car. Fred told the police his name was "Ted Murphy" and that he was from Miami, Oklahoma. The car's registration was traced back to Herman, and "Murphy" was identified as Fred Barker. Winfield Police Chief Fred C. Hoover contacted the Justice Department's Bureau of Investigation and informed them that the Barkers were close friends of the Sheriff in Mayes County, Oklahoma. He also informed them of his suspicions that Fred Barker and another fugitive, Elmer Inman, had been a frequent visitor to Ponca City, where Fred "Wentup" Tindle ran a roadhouse. Fred was tried and convicted of second degree burglary on March 5, 1927, and sentenced to five to ten years in prison. He was received at Kansas State Penitentiary in Lansing a week later on March 12. [5]

In 1930, Fred got a new cellmate. Alvin Karpis. Karpis had been transferred to the penitentiary from the Reformatory in Hutchinson, Kansas after guards found knives in his cell. He had begun his sentence at the Reformatory on February 25, 1926, for burglary. His nickname was "Old Creepy". A woman had commented that Alvin's dark, piercing eyes looked "creepy", and the nickname stuck. On March 9, 1929, Karpis and another con, Lawrence "Larry" DeVol, escaped. Karpis was recaptured just over a year later on March 23, 1930, and returned to the Reformatory. But after the guards found his knife collection, he was transferred to the prison.

Alvin Karpis as a teenager

Alvin "Creepy" Karpis was Canadian. He was born Albin Francis Karpowicz to Lithuanian immigrants John and Anna Karpowicz, in Montreal on August 10, 1908. He was the only boy out of four children. His eldest sister, Mihalin, was born in London, England. Emily was born in Grand Rapids, Michigan, and his baby sister, Clara, was born in Topeka, Kansas. Their father worked his fingers to the bone to provide for his family. They lived in a two-story farmhouse on Second Street, in Topeka, where Joseph raised cattle and chickens, and also held down a full time job as a sign painter for the Santé Fe Railroad. He was a stern disciplinarian, and expected Alvin to work hard.

He backed up his words with a bull whip if he thought the boy was slacking off too much. [6]

Larry DeVol and Alvin Karpis after their arrest in Kansas City, Kansas on March 25, 1930 (FBI photo)

Alvin and his sisters attended Branner Elementary School, and it was his teacher who began writing down his name as "Alvin Karpis", because it was easier for her to manage than "Karpowicz". The name stuck like glue, just like his later nickname "Old Creepy". While he admired his teacher, Alvin related that the greatest influence on his life was a street punk named Arthur Witchey. [8]

Witchey taught Alvin everything he knew about burglary,

shoplifting, and other crimes. He taught him how to study the routines of the police as they made their rounds, so he could avoid getting caught. They hit warehouses, and stole anything they felt they could turn a profit on. It didn't matter what it was.

Another thing Alvin loved were trains, and he would hit the boxcars and ride all over the country. He got caught in Florida once for riding on top of a train, and sentenced to 30 days working on a chain gang. But he was back in Kansas when he got caught burglarizing a warehouse. The judge sentenced him to five to ten years in the reformatory at Hutchinson. It was there that he met a convict named Lawrence James DeVol. [9]

DeVol had been in and out of jail since he was a young boy. He was born November 17, 1903 in Belpre, Washington County, Ohio to Hilem and Emma Lou (Shanks) DeVol, and was the second of three children. His older brother was Albert, and his younger brother was Clarence. His family moved to Tulsa's Second Ward, on Castor Street, when he was young. His father worked making candy at a confectionary but died in 1917. Emma moved the family to Black Dog Township, in Osage County, Oklahoma. A few years later he was back in Tulsa where her became involved with the Central Park gang.[10, 11]

DeVol got into his first big trouble with the law when he was only 11, and got sent to a reform school for being a delinquent. On August 19, 1927, he committed his first bank robbery with Harvey Bailey, Eddie Fitzgerald, and Harry Morris, at Vinita, Iowa. They made off with $70,000. On February 6, 1928, they robbed a bank in Ohio of over $225,000. Soon thereafter, DeVol was involved in a bank robbery in Kansas. He was arrested and sentenced to the Reformatory in Hutchinson, where he and Karpis soon met. DeVol taught him everything he knew, and on March 9, 1929, they and two other cons escaped by sawing bars in the reformatory garage. [12]

The two stole a car, guns, and some nice suits and took off across the Kansas prairie into Colorado, then headed South into

Oklahoma. Eventually, they took off to Chicago. It was there the law caught DeVol, and sent him back to Hutchinson. He was later transferred to the state penitentiary in Lansing, but was paroled a short time later.

Karpis' folks had moved to Chicago, so he dropped by to visit them for a while. His father lectured him about his criminal behavior, and convinced him to take a legitimate job. He decided that maybe his father was right, so he was hired as a assistant at Becker's Bakery on Chicago's North Side. He remained in Becker's employ until his business began to suffer as a result of the Stock Market crash. This was welcomed news to Karpis, and he took off back to Kansas City, where he teamed back up with DeVol. They hit clothing stores, filling stations, and various other businesses, but because of the Depression, their scores didn't amount to much. [13]

Then, on March 25, 1930, while driving through Kansas City, they were pulled over by some motorcycle cops and hauled to the police station. Karpis told them his name was Raymond Hadley. DeVol gave his name as Larry O'Keefe. After being roughed up pretty badly, they were finally identified and returned to Hutchinson. From there, Karpis was transferred to Kansas State Penitentiary. DeVol had taught Karpis a trick to shave time off his sentence. One of the main prison industries was mining coal, and prisoners could earn time off their sentences if they met a certain quota. Karpis paid some lifers to mine coal for him, and was able to be paroled earlier. [14]

Freddie and Creepy became close friends, and when Fred was paroled on March 30, 1931, he told Karpis how to reach him when he got out. Fred returned to Joplin, Missouri where he stayed with another ex-con, Jimmy H. Creighton, at 701 Byers Street. On May 2, 1931, Karpis was also released, and traveled to Tulsa to drop in on Fred's mother. But first, he paid a visit to Herman's widow, Carol, who told him how to find Ma's house. Alvin had first met Carol in 1929 through Lawrence DeVol when they were on the lam after escaping from Hutchinson. So when he was paroled, he dropped in on her at the Carleton Hotel in Sapulpa, where she was working. [14]

Carol knew her way around in the Oklahoma underworld, and helped him in finding contacts. She helped him in another way as well. Carol moved him into the Carleton, and took him to bed with her. Karpis said that up to this time, he didn't have much experience with women, but she taught him all of her tricks. Karpis described Carol as being about 5 feet 8 inches tall, with dark brown eyes, and black shoulder length hair. She was a beautiful, full-blooded Indian lady, and it was through her that he later met her niece, Dorothy Ellen Slayman, whom he would later marry. [15]

Arrie Barker was still living at 401 North Cincinnati Avenue, very near the corner of East Archer, and on the north side of the Frisco railroad. It was a dump. The place was little more than a dilapidated shack with a tarpaulin stretched on the roof. There was only an outhouse out back, and no running water or electricity. All she had for lights were coal oil lamps.[16]

When Alvin arrived he introduced himself. She was trying to nail a piece of screen wire on the window. She said "her man" wasn't here to help her, so he nailed the screen up for her. She told Alvin that Fred had told her to expect him. When he mentioned having spoken with Carol, her mood changed immediately. She angrily exclaimed, *"That Hussy! Why were you over there?"* It was obvious that she didn't care for Carol, despite her having to help Ma out and buy groceries for her when needed. But then, Ma didn't like any of her sons' women. Alvin changed the subject, and asked Ma if she would let Freddy know he was in town. He gave her a dollar, and she left to send Fred a telegram. [17]

Alvin went back to Carol's place. Fred had told him that George had left Ma and had gone back to Joplin, so he wasn't sure who Ma was referring to as "her man." Carol explained that he was a *"worthless bastard"* named Arthur Dunlop. She said *"He's too lazy to work, and too scared to steal."*[18]

The Barker home at 401 N. Cincinnati Avenue and East Archer Ave. Tulsa (The Tulsa Tribune, March 22, 1949)

Arthur W. Dunlop was something of a mystery. Very little is known about his family, other than on the 1930 he told the census taker that he was born in Michigan about 1867, and that his parents were Canadian. As for his appearance, he dressed well, but he had few other redeeming qualities. Despite all of that, Ma seemed to like him, so she kept him around. He was a sign painter by trade - whenever he was sober enough to actually do any painting. Most of the time, however, he just sponged off people and drank a lot. And when he drank, he got mouthy. What's worse, he would occasionally get rough with Ma. That would come to a screeching halt once Fred and Alvin returned to Tulsa. The two would grow to hate him, especially Fred, who always referred to Dunlop as *"the old bastard."* Dunlop was a royal pain in the ass, who sponged off Ma and everyone else. Whenever Alvin and Fred gave Ma money to go see a movie, they would have to pay Dunlop's way as well. [19]

On the night of May 13/14, Alvin and Fred, and a third man, most likely Sam Coker, robbed a clothing store and drug store in Caney, Kansas, about 63 miles due North of Tulsa. Coker had been convicted of bank robbery in 1924, and was sentenced to 30 years in the Oklahoma State Penitentiary, where he became friends with Arthur "Doc" Barker, and Volney Davis. He was paroled in the Spring of 1931, and teamed up with Fred to pull some new jobs. They surprised the Night Marshall, a Mr. Ross, tied him up and gagged him, then left him in a ditch by the side of the road. He was found at dawn by Alva Fuqua. Once he untied him, Marshall Ross said he saw three men but suspected others were involved.

Arrie "Ma" Barker and the
"old bastard" Arthur W. Dunlop

On May 16, Fred's old roommate Jimmy H. Creighton, was walking down the street in Webb City, Missouri when Coyne Hatten, son of wealthy businessman Amos Davis Hatten, came out of Morgan's Department Store and accidentally bumped into him. He apologized, but Creighton lost his temper and began a confrontation. He pulled a pistol on Hatten and shot him dead. When Creighton was arrested later that day, he claimed self-defense. During their search of his apartment, the police recovered two weapons that had been stolen from the Hastings, Nebraska, Police Department; a shotgun and a Police Special Colt .38 revolver that Creighton had used to shoot Hatten. He was convicted and sentenced to life in the Missouri State Penitentiary. [20]

On May 22, police raided a house at 6 East Haskell Street in Tulsa where they had a warrant to search for illegal liquor. The house was the residence of Carol "Hamilton", Herman Barker's "widow", and her niece Dorothy Slayman. Two men were there when the police drove up, and a gun battle ensued. The men escaped, leaving behind a large sedan that was later identified as having been used in a robbery in Kansas City. There were three bullet holes that had been filled with sealing wax. Chief Moore stated that he believed the men who escaped were implicated in the killing of a policeman in Webb City, Missouri the previous year during the robbery, and also suspected in a bank robbery in Hastings, Nebraska in February. They were also believed to have been responsible for a recent murder in Joplin. The men were possibly Alvin Karpis and Fred Barker. [21]

On the evening of May 31, burglars broke into Black's Jewelry Store in Henryetta, Oklahoma, stealing approximately $5,000 worth of jewelry and $300 in cash. On June 10, Alvin Karpis, using the alias George Heller, Dorothy Ellen Slayman, Fred Barker, his girlfriend Jo Ann Scott, Sam Coker, and Joe Howard were arrested by Tulsa police at the home of Mrs. Ernestine

Aiken, 519 S. Braden Street in Tulsa. [22]

Karpis was charged with the jewelry store burglary. Fred was taken to the jail in Claremore, but somehow managed to escape. Because of his arrest in connection with the jewelry store heist, his parole was revoked, and he was returned to McAlester to finish his sentence. Joe Howard managed to make bond, and then simply disappeared. Jo Ann Scott later pleaded guilty. Earnestine Aiken, said to be Dorothy Slayman's paternal grandmother, was charged with receiving stolen property, but the charges were dismissed for lack of evidence. [23]

On September 11, Karpis pled guilty to burglary, and was sentenced to four years. However, Ray had contacted his pal George "Burrhead" Keady in Tulsa. He told him to get the jewelry to Dorothy so that she could return it to Mr. Black in Henryetta. Dorothy returned it to the jewelry store, then went to stay with Harry Copeland and his wife at their rooming house in Arkansas City, Kansas. She remained with them for the next six weeks until Alvin was released. He was paroled on September 20 for making restitution, plus he was awarded time served for the three months he was in jail. On September 26, Karpis and Dorothy Slayman were married in Sapulpa using their true names, Alvin Karpis and Dorothy Slayman.[24] They rented an apartment at 23 E. Matthew B. Brady Street, at the corner of N. Boston Avenue.

Dorothy's mother and step-father, Lawrence J. and Elizabeth Richards, had moved back to Creek County, and were living in a small town called Keifer, about five and a half miles southeast of Sapulpa. They dropped in on them for a short visit, then drove to Wewoka, where they bought a brand new blue 1931 DeSoto Sedan from the auto dealership there.

Dorothy (Slayman) Karpis

On September 29 the newlyweds took off to see Alvin's family in Chicago. John Karpovicz and his wife were living at 1114 Richmond Street, and they were thrilled to meet Dorothy, and encouraged Alvin to go straight and settle down. About a week later, they went to stay with Alvin's sister Emily and her family at 1141 North Francisco Avenue, about four blocks from his parents' residence. Emily, who had married Phillip Newbold about 1924, had a daughter, Betty Jane, who was about six years old. Emily got Dorothy a job with her at Eastman Kodak. His sister Mildred had married Albert Grooms, and Clara had married an Italian, Bob Venrite (or Vineyard).

While Alvin and Dorothy were in Chicago, Fred made his way to Tulsa, loaded up Arrie and Dunlop in a maroon Chevrolet sedan he had bought, and moved to a cottage outside Thayer, Missouri. It was owned by Mr. Wellington McLelland, and Fred sent Dunlop with the money to rent it. Dunlop rented it under his own name, signing as "Mr. and Mrs. Arthur W. Dunlop". He told McLelland that he was a retired oil man. When McLelland met Fred and Alvin, Dunlop introduced Fred as his "son". The cottage sat on high ground on the east side of the creek, overlooking Thayer. The gang had an excellent view of the surrounding area. They rigged up a string on the gate to ring a bell inside to alert them of uninvited "guests".

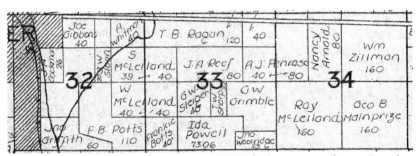

W. McLelland's land was just east of Thayer, and consisted of 80 acres, lying in Sections 32 and 33. This is the Ary Road area, today. (Plat Book, Oregon County, MO. Page 17) [24]

Alvin was getting bored of Chicago, and told Dorothy he would have to move South and team back up with Fred before they ran out of money. Dorothy wasn't happy at all about this, and did everything she could to talk him into staying in Chicago with her. He assured her that he would be back soon, and he headed to Thayer to meet up with Ma, Fred and Dunlop at the cottage. Once Alvin arrived, he and Fred teamed up with Phoenix Donald, a.k.a. "William Weaver", and Jimmy Wilson. Shortly after Alvin's arrival Dunlop identified him to McLelland as his "nephew".

On September 21, the gang broke into the Hildrith Chevrolet dealership in Monett, in Barry County, Missouri. Fred and Weaver broke in to steal a car for a bank job, and as they were opening the sliding door, they were surprised by the night watchman, Elisha L. Hagler. He was standing right outside the door with his gun drawn. Fred quickly turned on the headlights to blind him. He shot Hagler, then hit the gas and sped away. Fred cursed, *"That's what comes from stealing these goddamn cars all the time!"* The bullet severed the man's spine and he died on October 21. [25]

Astonishingly, once again, the wrong suspects were arrested. Two Arkansas men, James Langely and Rudolph Parker, were fingered by a security guard from another agency close to Hildrith Chevrolet. They were tried, convicted, and sentenced to life in the Missouri State Penitentiary. It wasn't until 1971, when Karpis published his autobiography, that Fred Barker was identified as Hagler's real killer.

Their next job would come off without a hitch. Fred had told Alvin *"I know a bank in Mountain View that'll be easy to take."* He said it would take four men. The plan was to break in and wait until the bank employees arrived. About 3:00 a.m. on the morning of October 7, they got inside the People's Bank in Mountain View Missouri, and waited. Two bank employees showed up just a few minutes before 9:00. The boys pulled bandanas up around their faces, and came out with their guns drawn. *"Don't move! We're robbing this place!"* One of the employees, a young lady, nearly fainted. The other one was forced to open the safe. Karpis and Weaver bagged up the money, and forced the two employees inside. They closed the safe but didn't lock it, and said. *"Don't come out for ten minutes!"* They quickly got into their car and sped out of town, and just in case anyone saw them and decided to give chase, they dumped roofing tacks on the road behind them. The haul amounted to over $14,000 in cash and securities. Not a shot was fired, and no one was hurt. It was Alvin's very first daylight bank robbery, and he was feeling the adrenaline rushing through his body. [26]

On November 8, Alvin and Fred drove down to Pocahontas, in Randolph County, Arkansas, to case the place for a possible bank robbery. They were surprised to find the Night Marshall, Albert Manley Jackson, watching them and writing down their license tag number. Fred quickly jumped out with his gun drawn, disarmed Manley, and forced him into the car. They drove out of town until they reached a quarry and ordered him to get out and start walking. Before Manley could turn around, Fred shot him four times in the back with a .45 automatic and they sped off back to Thayer. [27]

Jackson's body was found the next day by Mrs. Charles Johnson. They were driving down the road when one of their tires blew out. While her husband changed the tire, she got out and walked around to stretch her legs a bit. As she walked over to look at the quarry, she noticed something behind a rotten log. When she saw that it was a body, she screamed, and shouted for her husband to go to town and get help, and that she would stay with the body until he returned.

Two weeks later, two men, Lige Dame and John Decker, were arrested in connection with Jackson's murder. Dame confessed, and tried to implicate Pocahontas Chief of Police John Gordon Slayton in the affair. Dame and Decker were convicted, and in February 1932, they were sentenced to life in prison. However, years later, in 1971 when Alvin Karpis published his autobiography, he stated that Fred Barker was the real killer.

Night Marshall Albert Manley Jackson
Pocahontas, Randolph County, Arkansas

Sometime in the early winter of 1931, Fred, Alvin, and William Weaver began casing places to rob in West Plains. Of particular interest was the West Plains bank. Alvin made several visits to the bank, and drew up a layout of the interior. He also dropped by Prosecuting Attorney Floyd Bean's office next door to C. C. McCallon's clothing store, on West Main Street, posing as a typewriter repairman. Bean told him he didn't need any work done at the moment, so Alvin thanked him and quickly left. Suspicious, he made a mental note of Alvin's appearance, particularly his scarf. On the night of Thursday, December 17, Fred and Alvin broke into McCallon's place, and stole over $2,000 worth of clothing and other items. The following day, the West Plains Journal reported that the thieves who broke into McCallon's store had managed to gain entrance in the rear of the building by removing two bars from a window. The article pointed out, *"The stock was carefully selected as shown by the fact that only the winter shades were taken in the hosiery lines. Ties, gloves, sweaters and shirts were not taken in great piles but were selected carefully as to quality and the latest styles."*[28] The following day, Alvin and Fred ate breakfast at the West Plains Café, then headed over to Campbell's garage in the DeSoto to get gas and oil. They also had Cecil Campbell do a lube job, and wash the car. [29]

Howell County, Missouri Sheriff Calvin Roy Kelly
(Courtesy Toney Aid and West Plains Historical Society)

December 19th was a chilly Saturday, and early that morning while driving into town, Fred and Alvin picked up a young man, Robert Gross, who had been hitchhiking from his home in Paragould, Arkansas on the way to Springfield, Missouri. Once they got to West Plains, Alvin backed his blue DeSoto into Carac Davidson's shop on East Main Street to have two flat tires repaired. Davidson noticed some articles of clothing in the car that matched the description of some of the items McCallon said had been stolen from his store. That, and a feeling he had that something just wasn't quite right about the men, prompted him to excuse himself. He got to a telephone without the men noticing and called McCallon, asking him to come by the shop. When he arrived, Davidson looked up and saw Sheriff C. Roy Kelly across the street at the post office. [30]

West Plains, MO Post Office about 1931, across the street from Carac Davidson's garage. (Courtesy West Plains Historical Society)

Kelly had just come out of the post office and had stopped to light a cigarette when Davidson told him what was going on. Kelly went to his car to get his pistol and holster, and walked back across the street. McCallon was standing outside the shop with Bus Barrett. Kelly greeted Barrett, and walked into the garage. [30]

About that time, Dutch James from next door and one of his employees, Jess Thomas, joined Barrett and McCallon. Barrett whispered, *"Something's hot."* Kelly walked into the garage to talk to Fred, who was sitting in the passenger's seat. But before he could say a word, Fred pulled his gun and shot Kelly in the chest. Two more shots struck him in the left arm. Karpis bolted out of the garage and headed down the alley. He fell, got back up, and continued running until he was out of sight, not noticing that he had lost his scarf. A young man named Monroe Forbes and his friends were in the back alley shooting a game of craps when Karpis ran by loading a fresh clip into his .45. They watched as the man continued to run until they saw a red Chevrolet coupe pull up. He climbed in and the car sped away.[31]

Sheriff Kelly died instantly. Fred jumped behind the wheel, threw the DeSoto into gear, and roared out of the garage. He raced down East Main Street out of town towards Thayer. Dutch James ran to his car to get his .22 automatic rifle, and fired away at the fleeing car, hitting it several times, but without effect. [32]

From West Plains Gazette, May-June 1982. Pages 16 17.
Davidson's garage is the middle building with gas pumps.
(Courtesy Toney Aid and West Plains Historical Society)

As the crowd gathered, they noticed Robert Gross, who had come into town with the killers. They attacked him instantly, giving him a good beating before Barrett stepped in and got them to calm down. Gross was taken down to the jail, and explained that he had been hitchhiking from Arkansas to Springfield, Missouri when the two men picked him up and brought him into West Plains. Finally convinced that he was telling the truth, and had just been in the wrong place at the wrong time, they let him post bond and released him. [33]

Dutch James rushed over to Police Chief Bridges' house, woke him up, and told him to get dressed. *"They've shot Kelly! Let's go!"* he shouted. A city police officer, M. C. Stephens, led the posse, and the state authorities were notified. [34]

Late on Saturday night, Rush Cochran and Ed A. Kerr were out hunting near Thayer when they came across a blue DeSoto stuck in a ditch along the road between Thayer and Mammoth Springs, Arkansas, where it had been abandoned. They looked the car over and reported it to the police after noticing bullet holes. The car bore Oklahoma license tag number 121-020.[35] The authorities traced the registration and found that the car belonged to Alvin Karpis. It was the car he had bought in Wewoka, Oklahoma when he and Dorothy had gotten married three months before. Karpis had been in the area for quite some time, even seeing a physician, Dr. F. A. Barnes, who treated him for Gonorrhea both at the McLellan cottage, and at his office in town. He had been receiving his mail under the name George Dunn. [36]

Karpis insisted in his autobiography that it was Weaver and Fred, who had shot Sheriff Kelly. He claimed that Weaver had "borrowed his car" that day. However, Karpis' just story doesn't add up in light of eyewitness statements. First, witnesses in the alley saw Karpis get away in a red Chevrolet coupe, and it was known that Fred had arrived in Thayer driving just such a vehicle. Secondly, Floyd Bean had seen Karpis wearing the same red scarf that was found in the alley the day of the shooting. Lastly, Robert Gross, the hitchhiker who rode into West Plains with the boys, was certain that Karpis was driving the DeSoto, and the other man in the car he identified as Fred Barker. [37]

Phoenix Donald, a.k.a. "William Weaver" who Karpis claimed was the real killer of Sheriff Kelly in West Plains. FBI Archives

In his autobiography, Karpis stated:

"Freddie took her (Ma) with him in the jalopy to our friend Herb Farmer's place in Joplin, Missouri, where I was to meet them later. In the meantime, I decided to stick around on my own to see if the cops would find our place. I walked to a wooded bluff and hid myself. Less than three hours later, I saw two sedans pull into the yard. Each car held four or five guys, carrying weapons." [37]

"That was enough for me. I walked cross country, staying in the woods as much as possible. I was a stranger in that part of the state and didn't recognize the roads or landmarks. I kept

moving, and eventually I stumbled into a little town called Mammoth Springs, in Arkansas, waited until dark, and then broke into the Ford agency. Soon I was driving north in a brand-new Model A sedan, wearing one of those long white coats that garage attendants sometimes wore. The coat was a necessity because by now my clothes were a mess." [38]

The theft is proven by a letter from Floyd Bean, prosecuting attorney at West Plains, dated December 22, 1931 to the St. Louis Police. Bean advised them that a Ford Sedan, motor number 304471, had been stolen from the Mammoth Springs Motor Company, by whom they suspected was Phoenix Donald, a.k.a. "William Weaver".[39]

It didn't taken them long discover their hideout, but by the time the posse got there, the gang had made a hasty retreat. Half of McCallon's merchandise was still there, along with photos of Fred, his mother, Karpis, his wife Dorothy, other family members, and some others who weren't identified, letters, and various newspaper clippings. Among the personal effects was Arthur Dunlop's will, which he had executed in Tulsa on January 26, 1928, and which bore the signatures of John L. Ward, Mildred Turley, and S. O. Todd, as witnesses.[36] The newspaper clippings were articles detailing various crimes in Oklahoma and other places. A letter was found that Fred had written to his mother while he was still incarcerated at Kansas State Penitentiary. Also found was a layout drawn of the West Plains Bank. These items were turned over to Homer Rhinehart, Prosecuting Attorney in West Plains. [40]

Alvin and Fred had sent Ma ahead with Weaver to Herb Farmer's place in Joplin, telling him they would meet him there later. Meanwhile, Dorothy was tired of not seeing Alvin and being alone. So she bought a bus ticket from Chicago to West Plains on the very day Sheriff Kelly was murdered and went searching for her husband. Alvin had written her and mentioned staying at the Baltimore Hotel, and was receiving mail at the

Post Office under the name "George Dunn". When the desk clerk at the Baltimore was shown a photo of Karpis, he recognized him as Dunn. By the time Dorothy got off the bus in West Plains, the cops were already watching everyone coming and going. [41]

When she arrived, the first place she went was to the Post Office, and asked for any mail left for her husband, "George Dunn". The clerk handed her some letters, and then contacted the police. They wasted no time taking her into custody for questioning. At the hideout, the police had found some of the letters.[40] One of them was postmarked from Chicago, and dated December 10, 1931, addressed to George Dunn, General Delivery, West Plains. It was signed "from Father." It read:

"Dear R,

I suppose you've received the letter from last Monday. It was written when some of us were excited.

"The boys (police) that were over there asked P. if his wife's brother was out and also asked about Larry (DeVol). There is a reward of $500 out for him. We understand that they have nothing on you up here -but if they pick you up here – you know what they will most likely do in order to get out of you the information about Larry. But it seems to me that if they are out for him they'll do that no matter where you are.

" Things don't seem to be very bright here. I'm still out of work and can't do very much for anyone. I'm sorry for that. What do you think you'll do now? It's up to you. I'm just letting you know how things were around the holidays. They are worse than ever. Those boys will do anything for what they want – money and promotion."

Another letter, dated December 13, 1931, read:

"The boys were asking about you mostly to find out about Larry. There is a $500.00 reward out for him for murder. They think you are with him, I suppose. Joen (Joe Ann Scott) came clean at her trial and I'm glad she did although I don't care

anything about her personally. I wonder if she and Freddie will go together again." [42]

Copy of the wanted poster issued after the murder of Sheriff Kelly. December 1931

One thing was painfully certain for Alvin. He and Dorothy would never be together again, mostly because Alvin knew the authorities would be watching her every move in hopes of catching him. It tore him apart, but under the circumstances, he had no choice except to cut his losses and stay away. He wrote when he could, and sent money, but it would be four years before he ever saw her again. The last time he saw her, he gave her $500 she needed to take a secretarial course, and to file for a divorce.

Mrs. Lulu Victoria Kelly was appointed as Sheriff to finish the unexpired term of her husband. She and West Plains Chief of Police James A. Bridges issued a wanted poster as soon as Sheriff Kelly's killers were identified. It was distributed as quickly as possible throughout the region. A reward of $1,200 was offered for the capture of Alvin Karpis and Fred Barker. An additional reward of $100 each was offered for A. W. Dunlop and "old lady Arrie Barker, mother of Fred."

This was the first and only time that Arrie Barker was mentioned in a wanted poster. Since she had never been arrested, there were no fingerprint cards for her, nor mugshot photos. She had no known criminal record, despite J. Edgar Hoover's claims to the contrary. After her death, he defamed her character, claiming Ma Barker was the "brains of the Barker-Karpis gang".

Hoover (actually Hoover's ghostwriter, Courtney Ryley Cooper) wrote, *"The eyes of Arizona Clark Barker always fascinated me. They were queerly direct, penetrating, hot with some strangely smoldering flame, yet withal as hypnotically cold as the muzzle of a gun."* [43]

In his autobiography, The Alvin Karpis Story, Alvin stated:

"The idea that Ma was the brains behind our five years of holdups and crimes is strongly entrenched in North America. In books, kid's comics, detective fiction, and movies, and, for that matter, in every other entertainment outlet Ma has been described as a genius of crime for so long that nobody will ever believe what she was to us....a simple woman and the mother of Freddie and Doc. Ma was always somebody in our lives....She was somebody we looked after and took with us when we moved from city to city, hideout to hideout....... Her participation

in our careers was limited to one function. Whether she was aware of it or not, Ma made a nearly foolproof cover for Freddie and me and Doc. When we traveled together, we moved as a mother and three sons. What could look more innocent?"

Harvey Bailey told L. L. Edge, author of "Run the Cat Roads", much the same thing about Ma Barker. He stated: "The old woman couldn't plan breakfast. When we'd sit down to plan a bank job, she'd go in the other room and listen to Amos and Andy or hillbilly music on the radio."

CHAPTER 4:
SAINT PAUL: A REAL GANGSTER'S PARADISE

Harry Sawyer's Green Lantern Club at 545 N. Wabasha Ave.
was one of the top gangster hangouts in Saint Paul.

What is now the city of Saint Paul, Minnesota, owes its existence to an expedition in 1805 led by Lieutenant Zebulon Montgomery Pike to explore the headwaters of the Mississippi River. Pike was impressed with the high bluffs overlooking the convergence of the Minnesota River and Mississippi River so well that he made a treaty with the Ojibwa and Sioux tribes who lived there for 100,000 acres. He offered them about $200 worth of trade goods, as well as a promise to build a trading post. He built a small fort on the bluff overlooking the river gorge.[1]

In 1820, Colonel Josiah Snelling arrived to take command of the fort, and it was soon thereafter renamed Fort Snelling in his honor. In 1837, about seven miles downstream on the opposite side of the river, northeast of the fort, an old vagabond ex-fur trader, Pierre "Pig's Eye" Parrant, essentially became the "founder" of Saint Paul. He staked a claim at the mouth of a cave from which a creek flowed about 375 feet through a ravine down to the Mississippi River. Because of the cold, clear water, it became known as Fountain Cave. Here, in early 1838, Parrant built a cabin and established a saloon where he sold illegal whiskey to both the local Indians, settlers and soldiers. Later that year, several settlers living on the military reservation at Fort Snelling were evicted. They joined "Pig's Eye" Parrant, and established a small village that became known as "Pig's Eye Landing". However, in 1840, the Army, most likely growing tired of Parrant selling illegal booze to the soldiers and the Indians, mobilized a small force and evicted everyone at Pig's Eye Landing, forcing them further downstream. [2]

Fort Snelling at the end of the Civil War

In 1841, a newly ordained Catholic Missionary, Father Lucien Galtier, built a cabin on a bluff about three miles further downstream and northeast of Fountain Cave. This cabin would serve as a Mission, and was situated in present-day Kellogg Mall Park just off Robert Street North. He named the Mission "Saint Paul", and by the time the Minnesota Territory was organized in 1849, "Pig's Eye Landing" had been renamed "Saint Paul", after Galtier's Mission, and became the Territory's Capital, then the State Capital when Minnesota was admitted to the Union in 1858. [3]

Galtier's Mission at Saint Paul ministered to the scores of Catholic Canadians and the Irish immigrants who settled in the area.[4] Among the latter was the family of John and Catherine (Woulf) O'Connor, who had left Ireland and had settled originally in Louisville, Jefferson County, Kentucky. Their oldest son, John J. O'Connor, was born in Louisville on October 29, 1855. They arrived in Saint Paul in 1856, where their next son, Richard Thomas O'Connor, was born on June 21, 1857. Another son, Daniel O'Connor, was born in 1860. [5]

Saint Paul Police Chief John J. O'Connor

John J. O'Connor joined the Saint Paul Police Department about 1880, and served on the force until June 1, 1900, when the new Mayor-Elect appointed him as Chief of Police. O'Connor had a reputation as being tough, in his younger days, there wasn't a single man who could beat him in a fight. His nickname was "Big Fellow", and he was most certainly lived up to that name. He stood six feet, three inches, was loud and boisterous.

However, he was also a no-nonsense man with keen organizational abilities. He completely reorganized the police department, and made it more efficient. Under his guidance, they busted up the crime wave that had terrorized Saint Paul for much of the previous four years. [6]

Behind the scenes, however, he and his brother Richard quietly put together a plan whereby criminals could come to Saint Paul, pay a bribe, and stay without being bothered so long as they didn't commit any crimes within the city limits. Saint Paul would be a safe haven for them. A Sanctuary City. This plan became known as the Layover Agreement. It actually worked to make Saint Paul a safer place to live, but surrounding regions suffered as Saint Paul-based bandits committed robberies in other towns and cities, and then fled back to their safe haven. Chief O'Connor finally retired in 1920, but his Layover System survived for over a decade after his death in 1924. [7]

Corruption ran deep within the Saint Paul Police Department, and filling the vacuum left by O'Connor was an Irish gangster named Daniel P. "Dapper Dan" Hogan. Hogan had settled permanently in Saint Paul in 1909 after leaving California, where he had been arrested in 1905 and sentenced to a term in San Quentin Prison. He arrived in Saint Paul in 1909, where he flourished in his newfound profession – organizing criminal gangs into an effective machine to laundry money and fence stolen goods using Saint Paul as a safe haven. By the 1920's, with help from his corrupt friends within the police department, he had established himself as the Godfather of organized crime in Saint Paul, running his bootlegging and other criminal operations out of his restaurant, the Green Lantern, at 545 North Wabasha Avenue. Hogan worked with his cronies in the police department and in city government to continue the Layover Agreement, so long as they paid a protection fee, and didn't commit crimes within the city limits. [8]

Daniel P. "Dapper Dan" Hogan
Saint Paul's "Godfather"

Dapper Dan's reign came to an end on the morning of December 4, 1928, at his home at 1607 West Seventh Street. As he got into his car and turned on the ignition, a bomb that had been planted underneath the vehicle exploded, critically injuring him. He died about eight hours later. No one ever learned who planted the device, but his business partner, Harry "Dutch" Sawyer, was the prime suspect. Sawyer took over the Green Lantern – and Hogan's control of the Saint Paul underworld. [9]

Harry Sawyer was born in Lithuania as Harry Sandlovich, the sixth of nine children born to David and Gertrude (Polsky) Sandlovich, in March 1890. His family immigrated to America and settled originally in Lincoln, Nebraska. He later moved to Minnesota, but became involved with criminal elements there and his parents disowned him. In early 1920, Sawyer was arrested for his role in an Omaha, Nebraska bank robbery in which over $115,000 was stolen. He made bond, but jumped bail and fled to Saint Paul, where he became Dapper Dan

Hogan's partner. He had cronies in the police department who helped him shelter fugitives from all over the country. He also took an active role in planning and organizing robberies, murders and other crimes for the many gangs who took up residence there.

Harry Sandlovich (Sawyer)

After the murder of Sheriff Kelly in West Plains, Alvin, Fred, Ma, Weaver, and Dunlop arrived in Joplin and immediately went to their friend Herb "Deafy" Farmer's house. Farmer had been the Barkers' friend and neighbor for the years when they lived in Joplin and Web City, and he had a lot of contacts. One of these contacts was Harry Sawyer himself. Herb called Sawyer and said he needed a favor. He explained the situation to him and soon, Sawyer found a place for them to stay. They rented a house from Mrs. Helen Hannegraf at 1031 South Robert Street, in West Saint Paul, with Dunlop and Ma passing themselves off as "Mr. and Mrs. George Anderson and their boys". The Hannegrafs owned three houses at 1025, 1031 and 1035 South Robert Street, and Helen lived next door at 1035 with her son Nick, who owned a speakeasy called Drover Tavern and Restaurant near the Armour meat-packing plant in South Saint Paul's Packing House District. [10]

Barker hideout , 1031 Roberts St.,, W. Saint Paul MN (Photo source: Placeography.org)

The neighbors described the "Andersons" as very nice, friendly and polite people. Fred and Alvin passed themselves off as musicians, claiming they were members of an orchestra and were playing at resorts at the lakes around Saint Paul and Minneapolis. This accounted for why the neighbors often saw them carrying violin cases when they left the house. However, the boys weren't packing violins, but guns. And they used their new digs to plan their next robberies. Sawyer helped them find places to knock off, and he also paid Alvin to run errands for him. One day, Sawyer sent them to deliver a package to one of his employees, William Alfred "Pat" Reilly. Pat Reilly was Sawyer's bartender at the Green Lantern, and when Alvin knocked on the door, a beautiful sixteen year old girl answered. She said Pat wasn't there but he could come in and wait. Meanwhile, she played records until he returned home. Alvin couldn't keep his eyes off her. [11]

Dolores Delaney

When Reilly walked in the door, he immediately got the wrong impression. *"What the Hell is going on? Are you trying to make my sister-in-law?"* Defensively, Alvin answered, *"Why ask me such a thing as that?"* then said he had a parcel from Sawyer. Reilly explained, *"Every guy wants to make her. But we've got a rule. Nobody gets in her pants until she's seventeen."* The girl was Dolores Ellen Delaney, Helen "Babe" Reilly's baby sister. She was the youngest of the three Reilly girls. The other sister was Margaret Jean, who was married to Eddie Crompton, a singer who was into the rackets. "Jean" Crompton would later become the girlfriend of Dillinger gang member Tommy Carroll. Alvin was completely awestruck by Dolores, and he dropped by frequently to see her. After a few weeks, it was obvious that Dolores wanted to be with him, and the feeling was mutual. They spoke with Sawyer, and then with Pat and Helen, who gave their ok. The two were together for the next three years, except for when Alvin was out with the gang knocking off banks. She would also bear him a son, whom she named Raymond Alvin Karpis, in 1935. [12]

Soon, it was time to pull more jobs. Alvin, Fred, Weaver, and three others are believed to have been the gang that hit Pine River, Minnesota, about 165 miles northwest of Saint Paul. During the early morning hours of December 29' 1931, men claiming to be on official business for Sheriff F. E. Little of Brainerd, the bandits arrived at the home of Frank Marshall and forced him to direct them to the Constable's home. He resisted and they knocked him cold. When he came to, they forced him to go with them to the Horrigan drug store, which they robbed. They also sacked a hardware store, and other businesses and homes. They locked their hostages in a basement, then fled town South back towards Brainerd and Saint Paul.[13]

On January 5, 1932, Alvin, Fred and four other men raided the town of Cambridge, Minnesota, about 50 miles north of Saint Paul. In Isanti County. They arrived about 3:00 a.m., where they broke into a car dealership. They were surprised by the night watchman, Mark Dunning, whom they took hostage. They then surprised elderly Night Marshall Frank Whitney, who had just turned 68 the previous September. He didn't put up any fight. The men stole a large four-door Buick Sedan, took Dunning and Whitney as hostages, then ransacked the town. They looted four stores of about $3,000 in cash and merchandise, then headed south out of town where they released the two men. They drove off back to Saint Paul, but by the time Whitney got to a phone, the men were long gone.[14]

Karpis was getting frustrated at these nickel and dime jobs. He was in on a lot of smaller jobs with other gangs, but he wanted in on the big time scores. He soon would be. New Year's Eve would prove to be a pivotal time for Karpis and the Barkers. Harry Sawyer and Pat Reilly were pulling out all the stops at the Green Lantern for what was probably the largest gangster's New Year's Eve party ever held in the country.

Fred, Ma, Alvin, and Dunlop were there that evening, and became acquainted with nearly every one of the Midwest's most notorious criminals, including Harvey Bailey, Thomas James Holden, Francis "Frank" Keating, Frank "Jelly" Nash, August "Gus" Winkeler, who worked for Capone, and the crime boss of Minneapolis, Isadore "Kid Cann" Blumenfeld. Nash was still on the lam after escaping from Leavenworth on October 19, 1930. This gala introduced the Barkers and Karpis to the Big Hitters of organized crime. Despite the fact that Fred and Alvin did jobs together after getting out of prison, most historians agree that what is know today as the Barker-Karpis gang was actually born on December 31, 1931 at 545 North Wabasha Avenue, Saint Paul, Minnesota.[15]

Things would be fairly quiet for much of February and March, as the gang was getting organized to pull off some large jobs, They would need more people. Alvin contacted his old pal Lawrence DeVol, who joined the gang, along with some other new members. One of these new guys was a former Cicero, Illinois motorcycle cop named Phil Courtney who used the nickname "Bernard Phillips". "Big Phil", as he was known, was hired by Capone to follow his beer trucks to scare off hijackers. Karpis wasn't very happy with Courtney, especially after his big Buick, which he had let Courtney borrow, had been found burned near Balsam Lake Wisconsin on March 7, 1932 with the bodies of two women, Margaret Perry, a.k.a. "Indian Rose" Walker, and Sadie Carmacher, inside. The photo of the burned out car was on the front page of the Saint Paul newspaper and Karpis recognized it immediately. It was the car he had stolen in the Cambridge job. [16]

Rose had just gotten out of prison for serving six months for Grand Larceny, and Sadie was a prostitute friend of hers. They showed up at the Green Lantern and started running their mouths about things that certain people took notice of. One of these things involved the Cambridge robbery, and that they knew who was involved. They knew Cambridge authorities were offering a reward, and they wanted it. However, they told the wrong people, especially John Peter "Jack" Peifer, who ran a club called the Hollyhocks, and he knew every gangster and crooked cop in Saint Paul.[17] Peifer was born in Leitchfield, Meeker County, Minnesota on December 11, 1891 to Peter and Barbara Peifer. He moved to Saint Paul by 1930, moving up the criminal corporate ladder to become one of the city's "fixers" for the area crime bosses.

Word got around quickly, especially when these two bimbos got stupid and went to the Saint Paul police station. They repeated their story to the police about how they knew Cambridge officials were offering a reward for information about the bandits, and that they knew who the bandits were. Another mistake these two made was in trying to set up a trap to rob an underworld banker. This banker had handled the bonds from the Denver Mint robbery years before. When he found out these two girls were tailing him, he contacted Sawyer to have them bumped off.[18]

John Peter "Jack" Peifer

As soon as Alvin saw the picture of the burned out car in the newspapers, he went over to the Green Lantern to tell Sawyer about it. Sawyer said, *"He shouldn't have left the car there like that."* He then told Alvin about the banker. Contacts at the police department leaked the information to Sawyer and Peifer about their whereabouts, and Peifer contacted them at their hotel under the premise of arranging for them to meet the Cambridge police. Courtney and Peifer drove over to meet them, in Alvin's Buick and picked them up. It was the last time they would ever be seen alive. When their bodies were found in the burning car, it was determined that they had been shot to death. Their faces had been dowsed with acid before the car was set on fire. Saint Paul Police Chief Thomas A. "Tom" Brown took over the investigation, insisting that no one from Saint Paul was involved, and the story was hushed up and swept under the rug. But everyone knew the score. They had caught the proverbial "one way ride". A short while later, Sawyer mentioned the banker. He was mad as Hell. *"That son of a bitch. He guaranteed fifty-thousand dollars to have those broads killed, and nobody's seen a goddamned cent!"*[18]

Another new member of the gang was a Chicago thug, Thomas James Holden. Holden had been involved in the Evergreen Park, Illinois, job on September 10, 1926 with Frank Keating where they stole $135,000 from a U.S. Mail train. They were caught and convicted, and sent to Leavenworth in 1928. They both escaped on February 28, 1930, and were involved in some major bank stickups with Harvey Bailey, Vernon Clate "Verne" Miller, Frank "Jelly" Nash, and George "Machine Gun" Kelly.

Soon, they were planning their first big robbery, set for March 29, 1932. The target was the North American Branch of the Northwestern National Bank at 1223 N Washington Avenue, in Minneapolis. DeVol suggested they steal a big fancy car for the holdup, so they stole a Lincoln Limousine. Holden drove into an alley behind the bank and stayed with the car while the other four men walked into the front lobby. Courtney quickly took over the lobby while Barker, Karpis and DeVol moved in to clean out the teller cages. While Barker and DeVol moved in on the huge walk-in vault, they noticed Courtney flirting and talking with a pretty young switchboard operator, while a teller a few feet away took advantage of the situation and shoved about $10,000 into his own pockets. [19]

As they got ready to leave, DeVol looked out the window and yelled, "Watch it. The cops are unloading at both ends of the street!" The cops headed towards the front door as Karpis and the gang headed out the back. Holden had caught a detective off guard and had disarmed him. They piled into the Lincoln and took off. Not a shot was fired. It went off without a hitch. When they got back to their hideout on Robert Street and counted the loot, it came to about $75,000 in cash, $6,500 in change, and $185,000 in bonds. It was the most money Karpis had ever seen in his life. [20]

The Minneapolis job made life a lot more bearable for a while, and the boys were chomping at the bit for more scores like this. Things were going fine except for the tensions flaring up between Fred, Alvin and the "old bastard" Dunlop. He was a lush, and continued being an pain in the ass. Alvin had already had to take a .38 pistol away from him after he got drunk and started waving it around. He was more a danger to himself than anyone else. But anytime they took Ma to a movie, Dunlop had to tag along as well. He was a leach, never worked, and was an out and out ingrate. Fred hated him, and told Alvin the "old bastard" was wearing out his welcome really fast. The only reason they tolerated him was that Ma liked him.

The worst thing about Dunlop was that when he got drunk, he got mouthy. And while he and Nick Hannegraf's brother Pete were at the Drover Tavern getting plastered, Dunlop ram his mouth about the gang's activities. Nick then happened upon a copy of *True Detective Magazine*, and was shocked to see photos of the neighbor boys, identifying them as the two men wanted in connection with the murder of Sheriff Kelly in West Plains, Missouri. Nick showed the magazine to Helen. It was still early morning, and the sun had not yet come up, so they quickly and quietly walked out to the garage where the boys had their cars parked, wrote down their license plate numbers, and went back inside. [21]

Nick got in his car and drove to the police station and spoke with Chief Inspector James P. Crumley. He showed him the photos in the magazine and said that his neighbors looked just like Alvin Karpis and Fred Barker, and that they were renting the house next door from his mother. Crumley kept stalling. Nick got tired of waiting and went to speak with Detective Fred Raasch and showed him the photos. He insisted that they raid the house so they could catch the gang while they were asleep.

Instead, Raasch directed him to a bench in the Bureau of Records, and told him they'd be with him shortly and look into it. Hours passed until Helen called for him, and said the people next door had already cleared out. Crumley, it turned out, had told Chief Brown about the boys being seen on Robert Street. Brown panicked, and rushed to his office to call Harry Sawyer. As soon as Sawyer hung up the phone, he called the boys and told them that they needed to get out of town fast, because someone had fingered them. He told them he would stall things long enough for them to make tracks. They cleared out within minutes, leaving behind clothes, guns, ammunition, a camera, and they also forgot to turn off the gas burner on the stove. They grabbed what they could, loaded Ma and the *"old bastard"* Dunlop, and Ma's little black and white dog, got in their cars, and took off northeast out of town towards Webster, Wisconsin. [22]

Fred and Alvin suspected Dunlop was to blame. He had gotten plastered at Drovers Tavern and had run his yap to Pete.

In fact, he had been bragging about all the jobs the boys had been in on. They cornered *"the old bastard"*, and demanded answers. He sheepishly admitted he may have said the wrong things while he was drunk, and said he was sorry. Then Nick found that detective magazine and recognized them in the photos. This was the last straw. They told Ma that Dunlop had to go, and that she'd be better off without him. She reluctantly agreed. They told her they were going to give Dunlop some money and drop him off at a hotel somewhere in Chicago and leave him there. So they made him get in the car and took off.

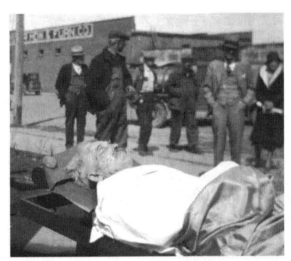

Body of Arthur W. Dunlop, found April 25, 1932 at Lake Franstead, Webster, Wisconsin (Courtesy MNHS)

Dunlop never reached Chicago. On April 25, the nude body of an elderly man was found on the edge of the water at Lake Franstead, near Webster, Wisconsin. He had been shot several times, and it appeared an attempt was made to dump the body in the lake, but because the shoreline was too boggy, he was left lying at the edge. It was the *"old bastard"*. Fred and Alvin couldn't risk leaving him alive to run his yap, so they shot him and dumped his body at the lake. When Alvin wrote his autobiography in 1971, he denied killing the old man, and instead claimed Jack Peifer killed him as a favor. [23]

Ma and the boys went to Kansas City, Missouri to lay low for a while. Once they were settled, Alvin and Fred decided to check out some of the bars in town. They found one at the Pickwick Hotel that looked like a nice, out of the way place, where no one would recognize them, and dropped in for a bit. An older fellow was sitting by himself at a table, and saw them as he came in. He needed someone to talk to, and motioned for the boys to come join him. He bought a round of drinks, and he and Alvin talked for hours. This made Fred nervous, though, and he sat at the bar, watching them. After a while the two men were pretty well plastered, and began arguing about politics. The old man stared at his drink, and said, *"Young man, you don't know a thing about politics!"* Alvin replied, *"You don't know who I know in politics!"* Finally, Fred grabbed Alvin by the arm and led him out of the bar, and back home. Ironically, Alvin's new drinking buddy was none other than Judge Harry S. Truman, who would, in 1945, become *President* Harry S. Truman! [24]

The new place they found was in a nice neighborhood on Jefferson Street, called the Longfellow apartments, These are huge mirror-image twin high rise apartment buildings, with the front entrances facing each other on either side of a walkway leading out to the street. The one on the left was, officially, the Robert Lewis Stevenson building.

According to FBI reports, they were identified as the "Longfellow Apartments" in the Country Club District. Here, they laid low, from about late April or May to about July 1932, while the authorities were investigating Dunlop's murder. They were soon joined by Lawrence DeVol, Frank Keating, Tommy Holden, Phillip Courtney, and Harvey Bailey. Out of all of these new gang members, Harvey Bailey was a legend. He has been called the "Dean of bank robbers". He joined the Chicago Outfit in the early days of Prohibition, running bootleg whiskey out of Canada to Chicago for John Torrio and Al Capone.

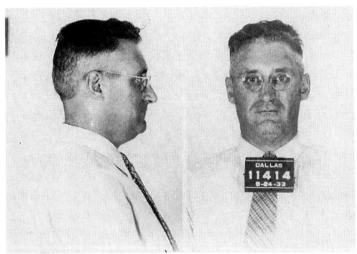

John Harvey Bailey, September 24, 1933 (FBI photo)

Bailey was a meticulous planner. He would carefully research an area before he robbed a bank, getting local maps, and carefully planning his escape routes ahead of time. His first bank robbery was in 1920, and he was probably the mastermind of the Denver Mint robbery in December 1922, in which over $200,000 was taken. Allegedly, Bailey's biggest job (although he denied being there) was on September 17, 1930 with the robbery of the Lincoln National Bank in Lincoln, Nebraska, in which his gang made off with $2,678,700 in cash and bonds. Bailey robbed over 20 banks throughout his criminal career, and he would teach the Barker-Karpis gang well.

The gang's next big job was to rob the Citizens National Bank in Fort Scott, Kansas, on June 17, 1932. As with his other robberies, Bailey helped them plan everything ahead of time, even exploring the roads to choose their best escape route. For this job, they had stolen a big Hudson Sedan and parked it behind the bank. Holden remained with the car while the others made their way inside. Things ran smoothly as DeVol and Courtney entered the bank first, followed by Fred, Bailey, and then Karpis. Two tellers hit the floor and one of them tried to push an alarm button. Karpis kicked his hand. He and Bailey kept their guns trained on everyone while the others crammed cash into their bags. As luck would have it, a courier from the local electric company showed up to make a deposit. They took it also for an extra $800. [25]

Robert Lewis Stevenson Building
4804 Jefferson Street, Kansas City, Missouri
Barker-Karpis gang hideout approximately May - July 1932
Photo by Christopher Williams

It was then that things began to go wrong. One of the employees had managed to trip an alarm, and the street outside began to fill up with cops headed straight for the bank. They grabbed the loot, and each man grabbed a girl as a hostage and headed for the Hudson, making the girls stand on the running boards. No one fired a shot out of fear of hitting one of the girls. Holden hit the gas and sped out of town.

A short distance out of town, one of them noticed a motorcycle cop tailing them. Holden floor-boarded the accelerator and outran him. The girls were holding on for dear life. Once the gang once they knew they were in the clear, they released the girls, and continued on their way. The take amounted to $47,000. On the same day as the robbery, one of Fred's prison buddies, Jess Doyle, was released from Kansas State Penitentiary. To celebrate, the gang used some of the proceeds from the robbery to throw a big party for him. Doyle had been sent to prison on a jewelry theft charge. His help would come in handy on future jobs.

Jess Doyle Mugshot

Once again, their luck held out when three men were arrested in Rich Hill, Missouri and charged with the robbery. Ed Davis, Jim Clark, and Frank Sawyer were escapees from the Oklahoma State Penitentiary in McAlester, and they were in a stolen Buick. The police found pistols and weapons in the back seat, but none of the money was found. No matter. Bank employees and passersby during the robbery mistakenly identified them as the bandits. They were charged and later convicted.

Things were pretty hot after the Fort Scott robbery, so the boys decided to lay low. This proved to be a smart move on their part, because on July 7, Federal agents learned that Bailey, Holden, Keating, and Phillips were playing golf at the Old Mission Golf Course in Kansas City, Missouri. Phillips managed to get away, Warned by Phillips that Keating, Holden and Bailey had been grabbed, the gang fled back to St. Paul and rented a summer cottage near White Bear Lake. There they settled down to plan new jobs and recruit new talent, including Frank Nash, who had escaped from Leavenworth, and Earl Christman, who had recently gotten out of the penitentiary in Indiana.[25]

Karpis paid $5,000 to a crooked attorney, J. Earl Smith, to get Bailey acquitted, but he was convicted anyway, and sentenced to ten to fifty years in Kansas State Penitentiary for bank robbery. On August 16, the day after the trial, Smith received a call and told his wife he would be gone about 20 minutes. He never returned. Smith's body was found at the Indian Hills Country Club near Tulsa. He had been beaten badly before someone put a bullet in his head. It was rumored Smith had been drinking before the trial, bungled Bailey's defense, and was murdered in retaliation for losing the case. Bailey was received at the penitentiary the very next day.[26]

The next robbery took place at the Cloud County Bank in Concordia, Kansas on July 25. This time, Fred and Alvin brought along Jess Doyle and Earl Christman. This robbery went without much trouble at all, and the gang made off with about $250,000.[27]

On August 18, the gang hit the Second National Bank in Beloit, Wisconsin. The job was a quick one, and they were in and out so fast few of the startled bank employees knew exactly how many bandits there were, but believed they saw six men. A. B. Cox was the only customer in the bank at the time, and when he started for the door, one of the men knocked him down.

Cloud County Bank, Concordia Kansas
(Courtesy Cloud County Historical Society)

They ordered Bank President B. P. Eldred to open the vault, but when he refused, they cursed and pistol whipped him until he opened it. After filling their bags full of money, they ordered six of the women inside to carry them out to the car. The ladies were Lola Peebles, Emily Menhall, Louise Wolfram and Mrs. Louise Anderson, all employees of the bank, and Elizabeth Evans, a customer, and Ruth Wolfram. On the way out, they disarmed Desk Sergeant Fred Stockwell, the only policemen there. Emily Menhall, one of the employees, was stepped on by one of the bandits, but wasn't badly injured. After they loaded the bags into the car, the gang made them ride on the running board of their automobile, three on each side. When they were safely away, they let the girls off on the side of the road in front of the Salvation Army. But before pulling away, one of the men kissed Emily as she stepped off the running board. The loot amounted to about $50,000. [28]

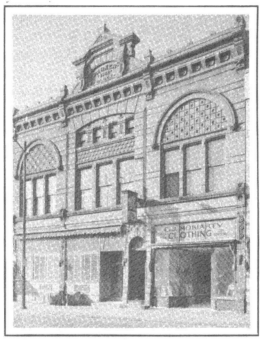

Second National Bank of Beloit, Wisconsin about 1925
(Courtesy Beloit Historical Society)

After the Beloit job, Fred and Alvin decided to prowl around South Dakota for a while. On September 1, the gang hit the First National Bank of Flandreau, South Dakota, just over the state line from Wisconsin in Moody County. For this job, they dressed like the local farmers in order not to arouse any suspicion. Holden had stolen a Chevrolet and he dropped two of the boys off a bit north of the bank, and then dropped another two off a block or two south. As the four converged and prepared to go inside, Holden pulled up and parked.

As the robbery began, Sheriff Charles Gray was across the street from the bank, speaking with the furniture dealer, Will Davis, who reported that his car had been stolen early that morning. Davis had seen the four men go into the side door of the bank, but didn't think much of it, and obviously didn't notice that it was his own car parked in front. The gang quickly made their way inside and pulled out their guns. Fred hit the teller cages and the vault and scooped up $7,400 in cash and $2,600 in bonds. Once they were finished, they forced one of the bank employees, Miss Alma Weide, to go with them as a hostage. They made a clean getaway, and headed West, leaving Miss Weide at the city limits. A few miles out of town, they dumped roofing nails across the road to slow down anyone chasing them. [29]

CHAPTER 5:
DOC COMES HOME

Arthur Raymond "Doc" Barker

Arthur Raymond "Doc" Barker was born June 14, 1899 in Aurora, Missouri, and was about five years old when George and Arrie moved to family to the Joplin-Webb City area of Jasper County, Missouri. Just like his brothers, he became a royal pain in the ass to his neighbors and to the police, getting into trouble for petty theft, burglary, and other minor offenses. And each time he got into trouble, his mother would storm down to the police station, throw a tantrum, and get him off the hook.

It wasn't until the family moved to Tulsa that he and his brothers really began to get into more serious trouble. Doc was a follower, and he joined right in with his brothers and their buddies in the Central Park gang. On June 24, 1918 he stole a car from in front of the Tulsa Post Office. Unbeknownst to him, it was a government car being used by a U. S. Mine Inspector named Scott. On July 4, former Sheriff James Wooley was driving about three miles southeast of Tulsa, where he saw a group of boys trying to pull a car out of a creek. Suspicious, he got to a phone and called the police. It was the missing Government car. Doc was arrested and taken to jail. No further mention was made regarding the other boys, so it is assumed they happened along, saw that Doc was stuck, and were trying to help pull him out. Doc was taken to court for car theft on July 18, and fined $1,000. However, since the car was U.S. Government property, he was charged with a Federal crime. He was still incarcerated in Tulsa on September 12, 1918 when he filled out his Draft Registration. He gave his name as "Arthur Raymond Barker", and states he was "in prison" at the Tulsa County Jail. [1]

Tulsa police delivered him to the U.S. Court in Joplin, but he escaped. Surprisingly, the following year he was listed in the 1919 Tulsa City Directory, as a "student", living at "502 S. Trenton" (actually 702 S. Trenton).[2] According to Joel Gazis-Sax, in his article *"Doc on the Rock"*, Doc had actually trained for a job as a glass blower for a company that made glass chimneys in Fort Smith, Arkansas and Tulsa. Whether or not he actually worked in that capacity is uncertain, and if so, it was short-lived. Either in late 1919 or early 1920, Doc was arrested by the Joplin police and returned to Tulsa. [3]

He was enumerated as "Raymond" Barker on January 28, on the 1920 Oklahoma State Census for Tulsa County, age 19. He was in the Tulsa jail, and his occupation was listed as a truck driver for the Tulsa city water works (most likely Crystal Springs Water Company). On February 18, 1920 he escaped once again and soon joined up with a band of hooligans led by Robert V. "Bert" Prince. [4]

Bert Prince and his wife Bernice were the proprietors of "Hotel Prince" at 119½ East 2nd Avenue. His gang would rob the homes of wealthy Tulsa residents and then fence the stolen goods through Prince, who also worked for the Carlton Hotel in Sapulpa. The police made repeated booze raids on Hotel

Prince until they finally succeeded in getting it closed. Other members of this gang included Claude "Slats" Chamberlain, Joe Morris, and also most likely Volney Davis. [5]

On January 15, 1921 Doc and Ray Terrill tried to break into the bank in Coweta, Oklahoma, but were caught and taken to jail in Muskogee. Doc gave his name as "Claude Dale", and Terrill gave his name as "G. R. Patton". Terrill already had a reputation as an escape artist, so it was decided to transfer them both to a more secure location. They were taken to McAlester. Meanwhile, Ma Barker argued with the courts, and finally had a judge order his release on June 11, but Ray Terrill was sentenced to three years for burglary, and was released on parole on March 1, 1923.

On August 25, 1921 Doc borrowed a couple of pistols from a friend, saying he planned to rob a couple of rich Jews. One of the pistols was an old .45 Smith & Wesson and the other one was a .38 Colt. Late that night he had a change of plans. Instead, Doc, Volney Davis, and Howard Carpenter were dropped off at Woodward Park on 21st Avenue by R. J. "Chigger" Bates. As soon as Bates was out of sight, they walked quietly East towards the new Saint John's Hospital, then under construction on the northeast corner of 21st and Utica Avenue. The first floor of the hospital had already been completed, and it was there that the construction office was located.

The intent of these men was to break into the office and crack the safe. Doc was packing the .45 and Volney carried the .38. They had managed to get the safe open, but before they could get away, the night watchman, Thomas J. Sherrill, walked in on them. Mr. Sherrill was about 74 years of age, and before he could draw his pistol, he was shot twice. Doc shot him in the head with the .45, and Volney shot him in the abdomen with the Colt, then quickly fled the area with Carpenter. Sherrill was found dead early the next morning.

Over two months passed before any progress was made in

finding Mr. Sherrill's killers. Frustrated with the Tulsa Police Department, Mrs. Sherrill and her son Jimmy hired a private detective, Walter Duckett. Working with Tulsa County Investigator F. J. Hays, he was able to determine the type of weapon the .45 slug removed from Sherrill's brain had been fired from. [6]

As it turned out, the bullet was of a peculiar shape, with a slender thread. After doing some checking with local gun shops, it turned out only one type of pistol was known to have existed in Tulsa County at the time. It was a rare type of Smith & Wesson .45 Revolver owned by C. A. Bingley, who resided on the corner of 12th and Main Street. Duckett and Hays contacted Bingley, who admitted to owning the pistol, but he said it had been stolen shortly before Mr. Sherrill was killed. [7]

Several days later, they arrested Sylvester Gilliard, who worked for Bingley with the Admiral line, driving a Jitney, which is a small bus similar to a taxi, with low fares. Gilliard admitted stealing the pistol, but told the police that he had loaned them to Howard Chamberlain. It was Chamberlain who had, in turn, loaned the pistols to Doc Barker and Volney Davis. Chamberlain and another man, Joe Morris, were subsequently arrested, and it wasn't long until they began to sing like canaries. They said Doc and Volney Davis were the actual shooters, and in October, Doc was arrested and charged with Sherrill's murder. Davis was arrested a bit later. On January 14, 1922, Arthur "Doc" Barker was convicted and sentenced to serve a life sentence in the Oklahoma State Penitentiary at McAlester. He was spared the death penalty only because one juror refused to support him being sentenced to die. George and Arrie were present at his sentencing, and upon hearing the verdict, Arrie wailed hysterically, and had to be carried out. George was devastated. Volney Davis was also convicted of his role in the crime, and likewise received a life sentence. [8]

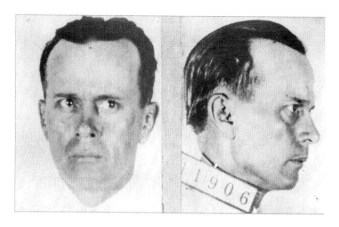

Arthur "Doc" Barker in 1922, McAlester, Oklahoma

Alvin Karpis said in those days, every man had his price. This was especially true of elected officials, and others in places of authority, including policemen and judges. Oklahoma certainly had its share of corrupt people looking for a little extra cash on the side, such as the Barker boy's buddy Q. P. McGhee in Ottawa County. Several State Senators were on the take as well. This worked out to the Barker-Karpis gang's benefit many times. Ma longed for her boys to come home, and she asked Alvin if he could help get Doc released. By this time, Herman was dead and Lloyd was in the Federal Penitentiary, and Doc had been at McAlester for ten years. Alvin told her he knew a guy in Leavenworth, Kansas, Jack Glynn, who was a crooked private investigator with a lot of political connections. Karpis contacted him, and on September 10, 1932, Glynn helped get Doc paroled from McAlester. The only condition the courts gave to granting Doc parole was that he was never to set foot in Oklahoma again. George Barker was living in Neosho, Missouri at the time, so when Doc was released he went there for a short visit. Afterwards, he went to join Ma, Fred and Alvin in Saint Paul. Glynn's efforts to spring Lloyd from Leavenworth, however, were unsuccessful. [9]

State Bank & Trust, Redwood Falls, MN
(Courtesy Redwood Falls Historical Society)

Ma was happy as could be to have two of her sons home with her, and they threw a big homecoming party for Doc. Arrie wasn't known to drink much, but for this occasion she would make an exception, and she got good and plastered to everyone's amusement. Doc would play an important role in the gang, and they were planning even bigger jobs.

Their next robbery would be the State Bank & Trust in Redwood Falls, Minnesota, located about 130 miles Southwest of Saint Paul. The bank was located in the 100th block of East 2nd Street. Fred, Alvin and Doc planned out their moves carefully for this job. Jess Doyle, who had participated in the Cloud County robbery, and Lawrence DeVol was in on this heist as well.[10]

They spent several days in town watching everyone, especially the police, and realized that wearing suits as they normally did would arouse too much suspicion. This was a farm community, and they needed to blend in. So, they all dressed in overalls. They parked their car behind the bank, and at 9:15 a.m., Alvin, Doc, Fred and Doyle made their way inside, while Doyle acted as lookout. They drew their guns, and quickly took control. They forced the employees, A. F. Hassenstab, Mona Leavens, G. R. Engeman, E. R. Whiting, and H. F. Peterson to get on the floor. [11]

Alvin, Fred and Doc quickly emptied the cages and the safe into bags, while Doyle held watch over the people on the floor. and headed out the back door into the alley. One of the bank customers, Matilda Buchholz, was employed next door at Fox Millinery. As she watched the gang carrying the loot out to the car, she told another customer, *"If we had a gun we could shoot them."* Doyle was just around the corner out of their sight and overheard her. Amused, he suddenly poked his head around the corner of the doorway, startling them, and grinned widely. He asked *"Oh, you wouldn't shoot us, would you?"* [12]

Once they were finished, the gang grabbed two of the bank employees, Hassenstab and Miss Leavens, as hostages, and headed out of town. They made Hassenstab stand on the running board on one side, and Miss Leavens on the other, holding them tightly by the arm. The gang headed South, and once they were safely out of town, they let the hostages go. After a couple more miles, they threw thumb tacks across the road to impede anyone who tried to catch them. The tacks did the job, leaving several of their pursuers stuck on the side of the road with flat tires. It was a clean getaway, even despite the Sheriff taking off in his airplane in hopes of spotting them from the sky. The loot amounted to $30,850.79 in cash and another $4,000 in traveler's checks.[13]

The Redwood Falls robbery went off without a hitch, and

without any gunshots fired, or anyone getting hurt. This was the way they liked for things to go. Bloodless. Fast and Smooth. Get in quick and get out quicker. However, the next job wouldn't be so bloodless. Their initial plan was to rob two banks on the same day. The targets were the bank at Breckinridge, Minnesota and the Citizens National Bank across the Red River in Wahpeton, North Dakota. Deciding not to take too many risks, they chose to hit the bank in Wahpeton, just across the state line.

The gang had been casing both towns for several days, and decided the bank in Wahpeton looked like it would be a cake walk. Another routine robbery. Fred parked the car in the alley behind the bank, and Jess Doyle stood watch outside. Alvin, Fred, Doc and DeVol moved in fast with machine guns, and took charge. It took less than ten minutes to scoop up the cash, but one of the tellers had managed to trip a silent alarm. As they made their way out the back door, Doyle yelled that the cops were closing in on them from both ends of the alley. Any delusions they had had that this was going to be easy quickly evaporated. Doc and Fred rushed back in and grabbed two of the girls as hostages; a book keeper, Miss Ruth Whipps, and a customer, Miss Doris Stock. [14]

As they rushed out to the car and out of the alley with the girls, the policemen held their fire. But just as soon as they headed down the street, all Hell broke loose. The cops began shooting at their tires. By the time they got to the edge of town, the back of the car was riddled with holes and the tires were completely shredded. They had no choice but to keep going on bare rims.[15]

Just as they veered around a corner, they nearly ran over a posse that was just getting organized to go after them. The men scattered, but one of them was armed with a high-powered rifle, and began shooting up the rear of the car. Seemingly oblivious to the poor ladies standing on the sideboards, the men opened up with another volley. Miss Stock caught a round from the rifle which broke her left leg. She screamed in agony, nearly falling off the car, but DeVol grabbed her around the waist and told her to hang on. Miss Whipps suffered minor buckshot wounds in her arms, left shoulder, chest and face. The boys quickly grabbed the girls and pulled them inside the car to keep them from being killed.

About two miles out, they reached their initial destination. It was a prearranged turnoff point across a bumpy field, then across a dry creek bed, then in front of an old school building. They rolled to a stop beside the school, and Karpis grabbed his medical bag. One of the gang picked up Miss Stock and laid her down carefully on the ground. Miss Whipps sat beside her. Karpis told Miss Stock to lay still while he pulled out a syringe, and gave her a quarter grain of Morphine in her leg, and did what he could to give the girls some first aid. He told Miss Stock, *"Don't blame us! Blame that trigger-happy bastard with the rifle!"* They left the girls at the school and drove away. [16]

The car was shot to Hell and was beginning to fall apart. They noticed an old Essex sedan at a run-down house about a mile further down the road. Some kids were playing outside when they pulled into the yard and an elderly man came out. Alvin asked, *"Will that car run?"* He replied, *"Yeah, it'll run. It doesn't have hardly any brakes, and there's a short in the wiring, but it'll run some."* [17]

The farmer looked at their car and saw that it was all shot up, and asked, *"What's this all about?"* Alvin replied, *"We just robbed the bank in Wahpeton, and we need that car to get out of here fast. We're taking yours and leaving ours, and we'll give you some money to square it."* As DeVol started pulling money out of the bag to give him, the old man smiled and said, *"So you robbed the bank did you? Well, I don't care. All the banks ever do is foreclose on us farmers."* He went back inside and brought out the keys. They handed him the money, thanked him, and took off in a cloud of dust. Once they got back to their hideout they divided the loot. It came to about $7,000. Considering nearly getting themselves killed, and getting one of the girls seriously wounded for such small change, it didn't seem quite worth it.[18]

National Bank of Wahpeton N.D.
(Currently, the Red Door Art Gallery)
Photo Courtesy of the Red Door Gallery

While the Barker-Karpis gang was lying low, Lawrence DeVol and three of his pals hit the bank at Amboy, Minnesota, taking about $1,892 (some reports state $4,400). Witnesses reported that four young gunmen held up the bank, and cursed continually, and ordered them to lay on the floor. The leader of the bandits gang examined the dally cash book before proceeding to rob the cashier's drawer and then the safe in the vault. They warned, *"We'll blow your brains out if you don't stay put on the floor!"* [19]

The only people in the bank during the robbery were Herbert Dredge, assistant cashier; Miss Lulu C. Nuoffer, stenographer; Mrs. H. I. Hoffman, John A. Starkweather, and two customers, Russell Johnson and Merrill Anthony. Three of the bandits rushed into the bank., while the fourth acted as lookout in front. *"Now you all, get 'em up quick or we'll wipe you out! This is a hold up!"* The leader was wearing overalls and a bandana around his face, and when he looked at the cash book, it recorded only about $500. [20]

Singling out the assistant cashier, he asked, *"Where's all the dough? You've got to have more than this!"* He stuck a pistol into Mr. Dredge's ribs, and ordered him to open the safe in the vault. After DeVol was handed $700 more from the safe, he walked towards his accomplices, pointed to Mr. Dredge, and told them to *"Give him the works," "He's got more money."*[21]

"But we haven't got any more money In the bank!" Dredge insisted. The bandits then made a more thorough search, and not finding any more money, the leader asked *"Is the coast clear?"* They answered yes, and he told said *"let's go."* But before he ran from the bank. he ordered his victims, *"Stay on that floor and don't dare get up right away."* They got into their car, and headed east towards Mankato, about 25 miles away. Someone had managed to write down the license tag number without being seen. The car bore Minnesota license plates with the number B160-448. Upon investigation, it was learned the tags were registered to Lizzie Godsiedson of Austin, Minnesota. She had reported that her tags had been stolen three weeks previously, and she received a duplicate tag on September 30. A short time later, Lawrence DeVol was identified as one of the bandits. [22]

The gang knew they needed more men, and Doc Barker suggested they try to spring Volney Davis from McAlester. In fact, he insisted. Davis had also been sentenced to life for his role in the murder of Thomas J. Sherrill in Tulsa in 1921. The Oklahoma prison system had some rather unusual practices, among them granting leaves of absence from prison for good behavior. Karpis knew a guy in Saint Paul, whom he described as a "big operator", and paid him $1,500 to spring Davis. On November 3, 1932, Volney Davis walked out of McAlester on a two year leave of absence. He was to return on July 1, 1934. But he never darkened their doors again and rejoined the Barkers in Saint Paul. [23]

Volney Davis and his girlfriend, Edna Murray, a.k.a. the "Kissing Bandit".

Soon thereafter, Volney learned that his girlfriend, Edna Murray, known as the "Kissing Bandit", had escaped from the Women's Prison in Jefferson City, Missouri where she was serving a 25 year sentence for robbery. on December 13, 1932, she and another inmate, Irene McCann, who was serving time for murder, sawed the bars off the windows of their cell and escaped. Edna was born Martha Edna Stanley in 1898 near Marion, Kansas to Nicholas Drew "Charles" and Louie Nettie (Waddell) Stanley. Her family had moved to Chase County,

Kansas by 1900, then to Oklahoma.[24] She was a teenager when she married her first husband, a Mr. Paden. In 1915, they had a son, Preston Leroy Paden. It isn't clear when Edna first met Volney Davis, but it was possibly while he was still with the Central Park gang in Tulsa before he and Doc Barker were sent to prison for the murder of night watchman Thomas J. Sherrill. Edna was working as a waitress at the Imperial Café in Sapulpa at the time. [25]

Edna married again to "Diamond Joe" Sullivan, about 1923 but he was soon in prison and was executed in 1924. She then married a stick-up man named Jack Murray. In 1925, they robbed Rev. H. H. Southward in Kansas City, Missouri, taking his wallet, trousers and shoes. Edna then offered him a kiss, earning her the nickname, the "Kissing Bandit."[26]

For this crime, she and Jack were sentenced to 25 years in the Missouri State Penitentiary in Jefferson City. Two years later, on May 27, 1927, she escaped. Edna was apprehended in Chicago on September 10, 1931 and returned to prison. She escaped a second time on November 8, 1931, but was captured later that same day. Then on December 13, 1932, she escaped a third time. Her talent for prison breaks earned her another nickname; "Rabbit". Soon, she and Volney Davis were back together, and they settled in Aurora, Illinois. [27]

On December 16, 1932, the Barker-Karpis gang robbed the Third Northwestern Bank in Minnesota. They had first hit the North American Branch of the Northwestern National Bank on March 29, without anyone getting hurt or killed. This time, things would get ugly. Third Northwestern Bank was an unusually designed building, being triangular with large glass windows. The odd shape of this building was no doubt determined by its location. Both Hennepin Avenue and Central Avenue run diagonally, and intersected immediately in front of the bank, with 5th Avenue bordering the rear.[28]

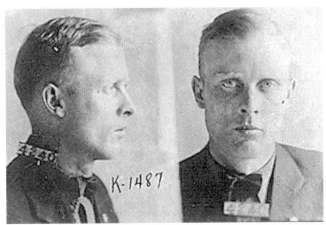

Ex-Sheriff Vernon Clate "Verne" Miller

Another big time operator, an ex-Sheriff gone bad, Vernon Clate "Verne" Miller, would be with them for this robbery. He was tough as nails and a cold-blooded killer. Miller was born August 25, 1896, supposedly in South Dakota, but more likely in Woodbury County, Iowa. His parents, Charles and Emma Miller, had divorced when he and his siblings were young, and they were farmed off to other relatives. Vernon and an older sister, Aubrey, were living with Rachel Marlin and her son Louis W. Marlin in Concord, Woodbury County, Iowa in 1900. Audrey was eight years old and Vernon was four at the time of the census. [29]

Miller quit school after the fourth grade, and when he was 16, he lied to an Army National Guard recruiter in North Dakota, giving his age as 21. He served one year with the North Dakota National Guard, and moved to Huron, Beadle County, South Dakota, where he got a job as a mechanic for a car dealer, Guy Richard. He was still working there in 1916, when Mexican bandit Pancho Villa attacked the New Mexico town of Columbus on March 9, 1916 during which several people were killed. The attack created an international incident resulting in President Woodrow Wilson ordering Brigadier General John J.

"Black Jack" Pershing to lead a military expedition into Mexico to arrest or kill Pancho Villa and his Villanista bandits. Miller was recalled to the National Guard and sent to an Army camp in Mercedes, Texas. This "Punitive Expedition", as it was called, wound down by the end of January 1917, and Miller had been promoted to 1st Sergeant. [30]

However, Verne would return to active duty two months later, after it was learned that a German telegraph to Mexico had been intercepted, asking Mexico to join Germany's side in the European War. The Germans hoped that a Mexican attack on the U.S. would prevent American troops from being sent to France. The entire country was furious and demanded that Congress declare war on Germany. On April 6, 1917, President Wilson asked Congress for a Declaration of War against Germany and the Central Powers. [31]

On June 7, Verne married Mildred Brown, and just over a month later, on July 15, he was again called back into the Army. He reported to the 1st Regiment, North Dakota National Guard, which was then transferred to Camp Greene, North Carolina where it was renamed the 164th Infantry Regiment on September 29. They were sent to France in April 1918. By the end of the war, Vernon C. Miller had become a war hero. He had been wounded twice, then injured in a gas attack on his position. He was awarded the Croix de Guerre for bravery, although actual proof of this hasn't been found, mainly due to a fire at the National Personnel Records Center in Saint Louis, Missouri on July 12, 1973. 80 percent of military records for the period November 1, 1912 to January 1, 1960 were lost. [32]

When Miller returned to Huron, South Dakota he was greeted with a hero's welcome, and became a Patrolman with the Huron Police Department on March 19, 1919. He ran for Beadle County Sheriff the following year, winning by just eleven votes, and was sworn in on January 4, 1921. He soon gained a reputation as a tough lawman, but some felt he was too brutal and trigger-happy. Then in 1922, Miller's dark side began to emerge. His wife was suddenly called to Rochester, New York when her aunt had become seriously ill, but while there, Mildred also fell dangerously ill and was admitted to the hospital. Miller left to be with her. A while later he telegraphed the office to say that he was going to stay a few more days, then take time off to go to the Government Sanitarium in Washington DC to be treated for the effects the gas attack he had suffered during the War had caused to his lungs. However, he never returned, and when the Sheriff's Department checked on him at the Sanitarium, they learned that he never arrived. Meanwhile, Beadle County auditors found that $6,000 was missing from the Sheriff Department budget. A warrant for Miller's arrest was issued on suspicion of embezzlement. [33]

Miller was finally tracked down and arrested without incident at a hotel in Saint Paul, Minnesota. He was returned to Huron to stand trial, plead guilty, then sentenced to two to ten years in the South Dakota State Penitentiary. Miller soon won the trust of the warden, who appointed him as his personal chauffer. After 18 months, Verne Miller was paroled and walked out of prison a free man. But he didn't stay out of trouble for very long. [34]

Government agents were mucking about in South Dakota investigating bootleggers, and indicted Miller on five counts of violating Federal liquor laws. His father Charles Miller, and his uncle Clarendon Miller, got him released by coughing up $1,500 to pay his bail. He fled the state and went back to Saint Paul. Soon Miller was making some high-level contacts with several key underworld figures, and he became a freelance hitman for several gangs. On May 31, 1930 Miller blasted three gangsters with his Thompson at the Manning Hotel in Fox Lake, just outside Chicago, in retaliation for the murder of one of his friends, Eugene McLaughlin. [35]

Miller returned to Saint Paul and joined a gang led by Thomas

Holden and Frank Keating. They hit the bank in Wilmar, Minnesota on July 15, 1930, taking $140,000. On August 13, Miller got into a heated argument with Frank "Weinie" Coleman, Mike Rusick and Sammy "Jew" Stein. He accused them of double-crossing the gang over the Wilmar robbery, and shot them dead. He then dumped their bodies at White Bear Lake, northeast of Saint Paul. He, Holden, and Keating then hit the bank in Ottumwa Savings Bank in Iowa. Larry DeVol and his brother Eddie also took part in this robbery. They made off with $30,000. After Frank "Jelly" Nash escaped from Leavenworth on October 19, he joined them and Harvey Bailey on April 8, 1931 in robbing the Central State Bank in Sherman, Texas of $40,000. On October 20, 1931, Miller, Holden, Keating, Charles Preston "Charlie" Harmon, and Frank Webber, robbed the Kraft State Bank in Menomonie, Dunn County, Wisconsin of $100,000. A bank clerk managed to sound an alarm, and an armed civilian shot Webber as the gang made their escape. Charlie Harmon was shot badly as well. The gang had taken a young bank clerk named James D. Kraft, the son of William F. and Lena (Radke) Kraft, and grandson of the bank's founder, as a hostage. Miller killed the young man, and his body was found near the bodies of Harmon and Webber.[36]

Alvin and Fred had planned the Northwestern job carefully, and this time, there were seven of them; Doc, Fred, Alvin, DeVol, Weaver, Doyle, and Miller. They parked the big Lincoln limousine they'd used in the March robbery, just outside. Doyle stayed with the car. Two of them moved quietly inside from the Central Avenue entrance, and the others entered through the Hennepin entrance, while DeVol, armed with a Thompson, stood guard out front. Fred, Weaver and Miller sprang into action. Miller forced the bank customers to lay face-down on the floor while Fred and Weaver ordered the tellers to open the vault. One teller claimed he couldn't get it open, but Miller promptly pistol-whipped him. The teller managed to trip a silent alarm, and soon two police officers were on the way to the bank. As soon as Officers Ira Evans and Leo Gorski pulled up, DeVol opened up on them with the Thompson. Miller promptly busted out a window and began spraying the police car with bullets. Evans was killed outright, but Gorski was mortally wounded, and died two days later. [37]

The take was $22,000 in cash, and $100,000 in securities. They jumped into their car, and sped away. During the gunfire, one of their tires had been punctured, and it fell off the rim at Snelling avenue. They finally pulled into Como Park, where they had earlier stashed a green Chevrolet Sedan. While they were switching tags on the cars, a car slowed down so the driver could see what was going on. It was a salesman named Oscar Erickson. Thinking he was trying to write down their tag number, either Fred or Miller pulled out his pistol and shot Erickson twice. His passenger quickly took over the car and drove to the hospital, where Erickson died later that afternoon. These two men were merely innocent bystanders who were in the wrong place at the wrong time. [38]

The gang made plans to spend the winter in Reno, Nevada, to give time for all the dust to settle in the wake of the robbery. Fred made arrangements for Ma to stay with some friends in Chicago while they found a place to stay in Reno and then had her fly out to join them. They met her at the airport a few days later. Alvin and Dolores caught a plane out as well, but it was grounded at Cheyenne, Wyoming due to the weather but they finally made it to Nevada. Fred had found a house to rent 138 West Pueblo Street that was nice and quiet. Here, they could kick back and relax awhile. [39]

Two days after the robbery, on Sunday morning, December 18, officers were called to a loud party at an Apartment building in Saint Paul. Lawrence DeVol was drunk and belligerent, and had crashed the party. Ironically, he gave his name as "Lawrence Barker". The other people at the party had thrown DeVol out earlier, but then he pulled a gun from his coat. Officer George Hammergren knocked on the door of another apartment, and a man sitting in the living room pointed to the bedroom, and said *"The guy you're looking for is in there!"* The officers fought with DeVol and disarmed him, and then placed him in their car. However, as one of the officers left to call Police Headquarters, DeVol attacked Officer Hammergren and bit him in the wrists. Hammergren pulled DeVol from the car and fought him some more to get him under control. DeVol got loose and bolted down the street, but Hammergren caught him and knocked him in the head with his pistol. [40]

Something just didn't smell right about this situation, so they went back to the apartment where DeVol had been. That's where they found over $1,700 still in wrappers marked "Third Northwestern Bank", along with another $10,000 in stolen securities. DeVol was identified as being one of the main leaders of the gang that robbed Third Northwestern, and admitted to killing the two officers. On January 10, 1933, DeVol pled guilty to second degree murder and sentenced to Minnesota State Prison in Stillwater. Three other men, Clarence DeVol, Lawrence's brother, Robert Newbern, and Leonard Hankins, were also arrested. Hankins was found guilty of first degree murder, and sentenced to life. Clarence DeVol and Robert Newbern were found not guilty. [41]

On March 4, 1933, Franklin Delano Roosevelt was sworn into office as the 32nd President of the United States. He was the first Democrat President since Woodrow Wilson ended his term in 1921. Soon after he took office, a great many men from Tennessee contacted a prominent Democratic Senator, Kenneth D. McKellar, stating their interest in becoming agents with the Division of Investigation. McKellar supported their efforts, and contacted Hoover. However, Hoover, being a dictatorial pompous ass, snubbed him. Furious, McKellar contacted United States Attorney General, Homer Stille Cummings, who was technically, Hoover's boss, to voice his concerns. When After Cummings raked Hoover over the coals, the Director retaliated by firing three agents from the Tennessee office of the Division of Investigation. McKellar was furious. Hoover's arrogance would come back to haunt him, since McKellar, a powerful Democrat who had been in the Senate since 1917, was the Chairman of the Appropriation Committee's Justice Department subcommittee, which controlled the purse strings to Hoover's department. Hoover essentially bit the hand that fed his department, and his attitude would hamper his ability to get proper funding for the Division of Investigation, and as a result, hamper his ability to effectively hire more agents to go after criminal gangs. McKellar never forgot the incident, and he would rub Hoover's nose in it. [42]

After Alvin and Dolores arrived in Reno, he had a cabbie drive them to a club he knew called the Rex. When he walked into the back room, he was relieved to see Ma, Fred, Doc, Weaver and Doyle. He told them about DeVol, and they decided to lay low for a while.

Reno was a good change of pace. They had the time of their lives going to the casinos, hanging out at the Rex, and meeting other people in their line of work. One of these contacts was a young fellow who was on the lam after escaping prison in Illinois. As it turned out, he grew up in the same area of Chicago where Alvin had, but they'd never before met. The two became good friends, and Alvin would often eat dinner with him and his wife and children. When Alvin became ill, his new friend hooked him up with a doctor who performed a tonsillectomy for him. This young man looked much younger than he really was, with smooth boyish features. His name was Lester Joseph Gillis, who would soon become known by his alias "Baby-face" George Nelson. [43]

Two guys, William J. Graham and James McKay, ran the gambling rackets out of their Casino, called The Willow, which was located inside Reno's notorious Stockade red light district. The Willow also operated as a brothel. Prostitution was legal in Nevada, and The Willow was one of the two main brothels in Reno. The other one being The Cottage. Graham and McKay made sure Gillis and his family were taken well care of, but Gillis was getting antsy, wanting to make some connections elsewhere. Alvin gave him some names of people he knew back east who could probably use him. [44]

Finally, in February 1933, it was time for the gang to return to the Midwest and get back to work. By this time, Verne Miller and his girlfriend Vivian Mathis, had moved to a nice house at 6612 Edgevale Road in Kansas City, Missouri. Alvin wanted him to join the gang for another job they had planned, but he declined, as he had business elsewhere. The job was to knock off the bank in Fairbury, Nebraska. This had to be done carefully. They knew those Nebraska farmers were tough as nails, so they took extra time in planning this robbery.

First National Bank, Fairbury, Nebraska. Old Postcard Photo

Earl Christman would help them on this job, and they also recruited a veteran gangster, Frank "Jelly" Nash, who had escaped from Leavenworth over a year and a half earlier. Nash had a lengthy criminal career beginning in 1913 for robbing a bank in Sapulpa, Oklahoma. He was given a life sentence, but convinced authorities that he wanted to join the Army and fight in France during the First World War. As soon as he signed the enlistment papers, he was shipped off to Boot Camp, and then to France. He saw combat in the bloody fighting in Belleau Wood just a few months before the Armistice in 1918. [45]

By October 1919, he had joined the Al Spencer gang, and earned the nickname "Jelly" from his knowledge of using nitroglycerin in blowing safes. In 1924, he was arrested and sentenced to 25 years at Leavenworth Penitentiary in Kansas. In 1930, Nash had been promoted as the deputy warden's chief handyman. On October 18, 1930, he was sent on an errand outside the prison. He never returned, but fled to Chicago instead. [46]

By March 1933, Nash was in Hot Springs with his girlfriend,

Frances Luce, and her daughter. Verne Miller had tried to warn him that Hot Springs was crawling with feds, but he paid no attention. He and Luce were married there on March 26. The gang needed experienced stickup men for this robbery, and Nash's experience was just what they were looking for, so Miller contacted him to see if he were interested. They had rented an apartment in Kansas City, Missouri, and began studying all of the roads between there and Fairbury. Nash agreed to get in on the job, so about March 30 – April 1, he drove up to Kansas City to go over the plans.

Fairbury is situated in Jefferson County, Nebraska, just across the Kansas state line. The First National Bank, on the corner of 5th and E Streets, was the only bank in town, and situated on the northeast corner of the courthouse square.

In early April just before the Fairbury robbery, Alvin drove down to Joplin to see Herb Farmer. When he arrived at Herb's house, he saw that he had company. Three people were there and he knew one of them, Mickey Carey, who had served a lengthy sentence at Leavenworth on a narcotics conviction. The other two were a young couple in their early 20's whom Alvin had never seen before. They looked like sharecroppers, but there was a look in their eyes that bothered him. [47]

Carey told Alvin, *"These people here have some Browning automatic rifles, and want to know if anybody would like to buy them."*

Alvin replied, *"What would anyone want with those damned things?"*

The young couple just stared. It was obvious they didn't much like what he'd said. They both just stared a hole through him, like coiled rattlesnakes ready to strike. The girl especially. She just stared at him with her beady little eyes. Neither of them spoke a word.

"Well, I'm sure they're useful if you're caught in a building, but if

you try running with one of those things in your hands, well, you're likely to shoot yourself all to Hell."

A few minutes later, Carey and his two friends left, and Alvin asked Herb who they were.

He said, *"Goddamned Texas screwballs. That's Clyde Barrow and his girlfriend Bonnie Parker. They've rented a house in Joplin, and sure as Hell they're going to be shooting up drugstores and every other damned thing around here. I don't like it!"* He was right.

Bonnie and Clyde, Buck and Blanche (Caldwell) Barrow, and W. D. Jones had rented a garage apartment at 3347 ½ 34th Street at the end of March, and on April 13, five police cars pulled up with a liquor search warrant, as they were suspected of being bootleggers. They were also suspected of having burglarized a business in Neosho earlier that week. A violent gun battle ensued that left two police officers, Newton County Constable J. W. Harryman, and Detective Harry McGinnis, shot to pieces. Both men were killed instantly. The Barrow gang escaped.

Apartment in Joplin where the Barrow gang escaped, leaving two policemen dead. (Photo by Blanche Barrow)

Apartment as it appears today. (Photo by Christopher Williams).

By April 4, everything was ready to go. With Karpis were Doc and Fred, Earl Christman, Jess Doyle, Volney Davis, and Frank Nash. They arrived in Fairbury early just as the bank was opening for the day. The shades were drawn on the east side of the building to block the early morning sunlight. They provided perfect cover. No one inside saw them walk past towards the front. Jess Doyle drove the car, and dropped two of them off on one corner of the block, and another pair off on the opposite corner. Fred was with Christman, Doc was with Davis, and Karpis was with Nash. [49]

They barged quickly into the bank, and yelled, *"This is a stickup!"* One of the tellers thought it was all a joke, and burst out laughing – until Karpis slapped him across the face and knocked him down. No one was laughing then. They kept their guns drawn and went to the teller's cages and cleaned out the cash drawers. Outside, they heard people yelling, *"Robbers! Robbers!"*, and knew all Hell was about to break loose. [50]

When Karpis heard the commotion he rushed outside to check on Doyle. He wasn't in the car. He was standing by a corner of the building holding .45's in both hands. He yelled, *"The Goddamned machine gun is jammed!"* A crowd of men were slowly approaching the bank with rifle, and began firing at them. Karpis got the Thompson to fire – and then couldn't stop it! The trigger was stuck, and it spewed bullets over the heads of the crowd. They fled for cover. The gun didn't stop firing until the entire 100 round drum was empty. He grabbed a 50 round drum, reloaded it, and tossed it back to Doyle. [51]

Meanwhile inside, Nash's machine gun also wasn't working. He had loaded it backwards. Karpis fixed it, and Nash began firing towards the courthouse. Then a man came running from the courthouse firing a Luger at them. Fred shot him in the legs, and he went down. Christman was hit badly, and Karpis dragged him to the car and got him in the back seat. Everyone piled into the car and they brought out two girls as hostages. They made one of the girls stand on the left running board, and the other girl on the right side, and took off down the street with guns blazing. As they got outside of town they dumped boxes of roofing nails out onto the road just in case anyone was tailing them. They released the two girls ten miles out of town. From there, they went straight to Verne Miller's place in Kansas City, where Miller called a doctor for Christman. But there wasn't much the doctor could do, and he died two days later. They took his body to a secluded place out in the country and buried him in a dry creek bed. The take from the Fairbury robbery amounted to $37,000 in cash, and another $39,000 in World War One liberty bonds. It had come at a high price. One man dead, and six bystanders wounded, two critically. [52]

Verne Miller's house at 6612 Edgevale Road in Kansas City, Missouri, where Earl Christman died. (Photo by Christopher Williams)

Once things settled down, Fred decided he wanted he wanted to find a steady girl. There was one particular lady whom he fancied and he asked Verne Miller to contact her for him. She was Paula "fat witted" Harmon, the widow of Charles Preston Harmon, who had been killed during the robbery of the Kraft State Bank in Menomonie, Wisconsin on October 31, 1931.

Paula was born Paula M. Brannan in Demorest, Habersham

County, Georgia on February 11, 1904 to David Byrd and Annie Alexander (Ellis) Brannan. Her family moved to Port Arthur, Jefferson County, Texas about 1907, where her other siblings were born. English Fred Brannan was born in 1905, David Byrd Brannan, Jr. was born in 1908 and Wesley Wright Brannan was born in 1910. On March 8, 1921, Paula married Dennis J. Wood, but they were divorced the following year. In 1925, she married Charlie Harmon after he was released from the State Penitentiary in Huntsville, Texas. They were arrested in 1926 along with James Ira Harmon and Leota Graham in connection with the robbery of the post office in Underwood, Iowa, but released soon thereafter. [53]

After Charlie's death, she worked briefly in Chicago as a prostitute, but soon left for Lake Charles, Louisiana, where she married Doyle Benson on July 18, 1932. The marriage didn't last, and she went back to using her previous married name of Harmon when she was arrested in Houston, Texas for loitering on March 5, 1933. [54]

Fred wanted Paula to come up to Kansas City to see him. She agreed, and they hit it off pretty well. But Paula had a lot of bad habits. Her worst habit was drinking. Charlie's death had taken a heavy toll on her, especially mentally, and she had turned to booze for solace. It was her boozing and her mental problems that earned her the nickname "fat-witted".

Charles Preston "Charlie" Harmon (L), a member of the Holden-Keating gang, was killed December 2, 1931 during the robbery of the Kraft State Bank in Menomonie, WI.
Paula became Fred Barker's girlfriend in April 1934 , shortly after the Barker-Karpis gang robbed the bank in Fairbury, NE.

Fred's dalliance with Paula, whom the gang also referred to as "Paula the drunk", would cause a lot of friction and headaches for them. By this time, Ma Barker was living in the Commodore Apartments in Kansas City under the name "Mrs. Gordon". When he finally got up the nerve to take Paula to meet her, the meeting didn't go over very well at all. That would be the only time Paula would ever meet Ma Barker. Poor Fred just never had much luck with women. But then, Ma didn't care for any of her boys' girlfriends, and they rarely brought them around whenever they dropped in to see her.

CHAPTER 6:
KIDNAPPING BECAME BIG BUSINESS

Charles Lindbergh III, infant son of Charles Lindbergh, Jr.

On March 1, 1932, Charles Lindbergh III, the infant son of aviator Charles Lindbergh, Jr., was kidnapped from the Lindbergh's' home in Hopewell, New Jersey. Lindbergh became a national hero in 1927 by being the first to fly solo across the Atlantic Ocean. He had taken off in his Ryan monoplane, named "The Spirit of Saint Louis", from Roosevelt Field on Long Island. He arrived in Paris 33 ½ hours later, to win the Orteig prize of $25,000, and upon his return home, was greeted by President Calvin Coolidge, who awarded him the Distinguished Flying Cross. [1]

When "Lucky Lindy's" wife, Ann, went in to check on little

Charlie, she discovered him gone and a ransom note for $50,000 was left in his crib. The kidnapper had used a ladder to reach the second story window. The crime shocked the Nation, and offers of assistance came in from all over. Even Chicago gangster Al Capone, then in prison for tax evasion, offered to help find the child. On April 2, another ransom note arrived demanding $70,000, and contained instructions for delivering the money. The Lindberghs followed the kidnapper's instructions to the letter, and shortly thereafter, they were told the child could be found on a ship off the Massachusetts coast named "Nelly". But after an exhaustive search, no such ship was ever found. [2]

Richard Bruno Hauptmann, convicted and executed for the kidnapping and murder of the Lindbergh baby.

Another search for the child was begun near the Lindbergh home, and on May 12, the baby's body was discovered less than a mile away. Little Charles had been murdered the night he was kidnapped, and buried in a shallow grave. The entire Nation was heartbroken and outraged, and a massive manhunt got underway. Congress rushed legislation through to make kidnapping a Federal crime, and it was signed into law by outgoing President Herbert Hoover on June 22, 1932. But it wouldn't be until September of 1934 that any progress would be made. In New York, a man had used a ten dollar gold certificate to pay for gas, and the station manager had written the man's license number down in the certificate's margin. The certificate was found by a teller at a bank in Manhattan.

Authorities traced it back to the gas station, where the manager informed them that he had suspected the man who used it might be a counterfeiter. The tag number was traced to a blue Dodge Sedan in the Bronx belonging to Bruno Richard Hauptmann, a German illegal alien with a known criminal record back in Germany. After searching Hauptmann's garage, another $14,000 of the ransom money was found, and he was arrested. After eight handwriting experts testified that Hauptmann's handwriting closely matched that in the ransom notes, he was convicted and sentenced to death. Hauptmann was electrocuted in New Jersey State Prison's electric chair, "Old Smokey", on April 3, 1936. [3]

The new kidnapping legislation gave the Division of Investigation jurisdiction over investigating these crimes if they involved the victim being taken across state lines; a very loose interpretation of the of the Interstate Commerce Act, and very similar to the Dyer Act, which made auto theft a Federal crime if a stolen car was driven into another state. The latter was used as justification for the Division of Investigation to go after John Dillinger after he escaped from the Lake County Jail in Crown Point, Indiana, driving Sheriff Lillian Holley's 1933 Ford Sedan across the Illinois state line to Chicago, where it was later found.

On July 6, 1932, Saint Paul's new reformist Mayor William Mahoney appointed demoted Police Chief Thomas A. Brown to Chief Detective, and replaced him with Thomas E. Dahill, who wanted to do away with the corrupt O'Connor layover agreement. He made it clear that he intended to clamp down on the city's criminal element.[3] He stated, *"Gangsters and would-be gangsters aren't wanted here, and we intend to drive them out!"* Sometime in August, Clarence DeVol, brother of Lawrence "Larry" DeVol, and William Weaver, got into a drunken brawl at the Green Lantern. Dahill had them arrested. They were released on $500 bond each, but skipped town. Harry Sawyer was livid over Dahill's disregard of the layover agreement not to bother crooks. When he saw one of his informants, Detective Fred Raasch, he told him he could have handled the situation, and if Dahill was going to violate the agreement, he just might do the same and cause some big time trouble in Saint Paul.[4]

When Franklin Delano Roosevelt was elected President, he made it known that the Volstead Act would be repealed once he took office. This would spell the end of Prohibition, and with it, the end of the speakeasies, and the lucrative trade of illegal booze that had arisen as an unintended consequence. Those who had gotten rich off illegal booze would have to find other means to keep their coffers full. Their involvement in the liquor trade would continue of course, but they would soon get more into illegal narcotics, prostitution, protection rackets, gambling, labor racketeering - and kidnapping. [5]

Shortly after the Fairbury robbery, Jack Peifer contacted the gang, and asked them to come up to the Hollyhocks to discuss a new job. Peifer had taken a liking to them, and made sure they had plenty of jobs to do. He especially wanted them for this job, so when Fred and Alvin got to the Hollyhocks, Peifer began going over the backgrounds of two other major players who would be involved. They were gangsters who worked for Capone's Chicago Outfit ; George "Shotgun" Zeigler and Byron Bolton. Both men had played key roles in Chicago's infamous Saint Valentine's Day massacre in 1929. [6]

Peifer told an interesting story about Zeigler. He was born Fred Samuel Goetz in Chicago on February 14, 1897 to German immigrants Samuel T. and Ottillie (Bensel) Goetz. He graduated from the University of Illinois in 1918 with an engineering degree, and then joined the Army. He served in the final months of the First World War as a 2nd Lieutenant with the U.S. Army Aviation Branch. After coming home from the war, he was working as a lifeguard at Beach Park, Illinois when something happened to derail his life. [7]

In 1925, he was accused of raping a young girl named Jean Lambert. He vehemently denied the charges, jumped bail and vanished. He surfaced a few years later using the name "George Zeigler", and was working with the Chicago Outfit. During the Saint Valentine's Day massacre, Peifer told Fred and Alvin that it had been Zeigler's idea to use Cadillac sedans painted as Chicago police cars, and to use men dressed like Chicago cops. Their intended target was Capone's arch rival, George "Bugs" Moran. Moran's men had been meeting at a garage at 2122 North Clark Street on Chicago's North side. [8]

Byron Bolton rented an apartment in the building on the opposite side of the street from the garage, and he watched through his window for the men to show up. The plan was to use the fake cops to corner Moran and his men inside, then kill them. Bolton waited until he saw the assassins enter the building behind Moran's men and left. The hit went as scheduled, though their main target, Moran, didn't show up. Whether he smelled a trap or was just late getting there is uncertain. But in the end, seven of his top people were dead. He told the press, *"Only Capone kills like that!"* [9]

Fred Samuel Goetz
a.k.a. "Shotgun George Zeigler"

The hit squad included George Zeigler, Fred "Killer" Burke, August "Gus" Winkeler, Ray Nugent, and Bob Carey. Jack McGurn was suspected of being involved, but he claimed he was with his girlfriend, Louise May Rolfe, at the time of the murders. She would be subsequently assailed by the newspapers as his "blonde alibi". Their victims were John May; one of Moran's mechanics, Adam Heyer; Moran's business manager, Albert Kachellek; one of Moran's hired killers, Albert Weinshenker;

owner of a club called the Alcazar, Reinhart Schwimmer; a friend of Moran, Weiss, and O'Banion, and Peter and Frank Gusenburg. The Gusenburg brothers were Moran's top hired killers. [10]

John Peter "Jack" Peifer's club, the Hollyhocks
Saint Paul, Minnesota (Photographer unknown)

Winkeler was from Saint Louis, and began his criminal career while running with a gang known as Egan's Rats, and he was also a wheelman for mob boss William "Dinty" Colbeck, who was sent to prison in 1925. When Gus left the City Workhouse, he met a girl named Georgette Bence at her family's boardinghouse, and they were married. Soon thereafter, the couple moved to Chicago, as did two other former Rats members, Fred "Killer" Burke, and Byron Bolton was also known as Brian Carter. He was also from Saint Louis, and had been a childhood friend of Winkeler's. Bolton often used the alias "Monty" Carter, but was generally known as Byron Bolton. While in Chicago, Burke and Winkeler became lieutenants for

Capone's outfit. During the Saint Valentine's Day massacre, Winkeler was the wheelman for the assassins.

Peifer and Bolton were friends, and in 1932, Peifer had been speculating on the wheat markets and had used some of Bolton's money. The investment failed, and they nearly went broke. They were now in dire financial straits, and since Peifer had done a lot of favors for Karpis and for the Barkers, he asked them to do this job as a way to return the favor. At least that is what Peifer told them. [11]

Alvin and Fred said they'd be glad to help, however, they still didn't know what the job was! Finally, Peifer stopped beating around the bush, and asked, *"How would you boys like to work a kidnapping?"* They looked at each other. They had no experience with snatching anyone, and realized that this would be risky, since the Lindbergh Law now made kidnapping a Federal crime if the victim was taken across state lines. Peifer continued. *"I figure we'll go for $100,000 ransom. I'll take ten percent, and the other $90,000 will be split between you guys, Bolton, Zeigler and maybe a couple of more guys."* [12]

It sounded like too sweet of a deal to pass up, especially since they were nearly broke, so they agreed. However, they needed to know who the *kidnappee* would be! Peifer told them he wanted to snatch a rich guy named William A. Hamm, Jr., President of Hamm Brewery Company in Saint Paul. Hamm had made a fortune after the Roosevelt Administration passed a law allowing breweries to make and sell beer with an alcohol content of 3.2 percent. He was one of the richest men in Saint Paul, so the gang knew that $100,000 would be a drop in the proverbial bucket for the Hamm family. After meeting Bolton and Zeigler, they decided to hire two more men, Doc Barker and Charles Fitzgerald. Peifer promptly rented a cottage called "Idlewood" northeast of Saint Paul, along the east side of White Bear Lake at 5500 East Bald Eagle Blvd. They used the cottage as their headquarters during this operation, and studied Hamm until they knew his habits, and his daily routine in the minutest detail. [13]

Idlewood, the Barker gang hideout at White Bear Lake, MN

William Hamm, Jr. was born September 4, 1893 in Minnesota to William Hamm, Sr., and Marie (Scheffer) Hamm. His grandfather, Theodore Hamm, had founded the Hamm Brewing Company in about 1864. It had previously belonged to Andrew F. Keller, who wanted to expand his business. He borrowed the money from Hamm, using the brewery as collateral. But when Keller defaulted on the loan, Hamm took over the brewery, and by 1885 he was brewing over 40,000 barrels per year with 75 employees. The business continued to grow, with a bottling works and refrigeration by 1895. [13]

In 1896, the business was incorporated with Theodore as President, and his son William Hamm as both secretary and Vice-President. When Theodore died in 1903, William then became President of the company. When William Hamm, Sr. died in 1931, William Jr. then became CEO of Hamm Brewing Company. Hamm had become one of the richest men in Saint

Paul, and Peifer knew he had a lot of ready cash on hand since most all of the over-the-counter cash beer sales just in the Twin Cities alone added up to a huge chunk of change. And this didn't include the distribution sales outside of the area. [14]

William Hamm, Jr.

William Hamm Jr's residence at 668 Greenbrier (MNHS)

The gang spent most of May and early June planning the

kidnapping. They drove to Saint Paul each day to case the Brewery and keep tabs on Hamm's routine. The Theodore Hamm mansion was situated on a hill overlooking the brewery, but William lived at a house his father William Sr. had built for his mother, located just a short distance from the Brewery, at 668 North Greenbrier Avenue. Every day at noon, Hamm would walk from the brewery to his house. He was a creature of habit, which would work perfectly to the gang's advantage. He would leave work every afternoon about 6:00 p.m. for home. [15]

Hamm's Brewery in Saint Paul, Minnesota. The Theodore Hamm mansion can be seen on the far right in the distance. (MNHS)

It was decided that they would snatch him as he left his office. The gang stole a huge black 1932 Lincoln KB limousine and Alvin dressed up like a chauffeur. Doc Barker, Byron Bolton and Charles Fitzgerald would accompany him. Fitzgerald was an older man in his sixties, and would play the role of a businessman when he greeted Hamm along the street and invited him to the car. Doc and Bolton would stand at a distance with their guns in case something went wrong. Once they got out of town, they would switch cars. From there, they would take Hamm to a safe house belonging to the Postmaster, Edmund C. Bartholmey, at 222 York Avenue in Bensenville, Illinois, just outside of Chicago. He was completely trustworthy, and using his house to hold Hamm was a stroke of genius, as no one would ever suspect the City Postmaster of being involved in a kidnapping! [16]

Edmund C. Bartholmey and his house where William A. Hamm, Jr. was held captive.

On May 30, they learned that eleven convicts had escaped from the Kansas State Penitentiary in Lansing. Among them was their old pal, Harvey Bailey. Frank Nash had managed to smuggle four .38 caliber pistols into the prison hidden in a bale of material used to make whisk brooms. During a prison baseball game, Bailey and Wilbur Underhill took Warden Kirk Prather and two guards, L. A. Lawes and John Sherman, as hostages. Once outside, they split up. Bailey, Underhill, Ed Davis and Jim Clark, stole a car belonging to the prison farm superintendent, Woodson, and escaped with the hostages into Oklahoma. They gave them $5.00 each and released them unharmed near Welch, in Craig County, then sped off. The other escapees were Lewis Bechtel, Bob Brady, Kenneth Conn, Frank Delmar, Clifford Dobson, Frank Sawyer and Billy Woods. [17]

Most of these men were captured or killed soon afterwards, but Underhill and Bailey robbed several banks together until August, when Bailey was recaptured in Paradise, Texas, along with George "Machine Gun" Kelly and his wife. Underhill was known as the "Tri-State Terror", and had been serving a life sentence for the murder of Wichita, Kansas police officer Merle Colver. On August 30, 1927, Colver had been the officer who killed Porter Clay Meek, an accomplice of Herman Barker. The law finally caught up with Underhill on December 30, 1933, when he was mortally wounded in a shootout with police near Shawnee, Oklahoma. He lingered on for a few days and died January 6, 1934. [18]

Everything was ready to go on June 15. Just before noon, Alvin parked the limousine on Minnehaha Street across from the Brewery and waited. Sure enough, Hamm came out right on schedule. Fitzgerald called out to him. *"Mr. Hamm"*, he said as he reached out to shake the man's hand. *"I wonder if I might speak to you on a rather important business matter."* Hamm nodded as Fitzgerald guided him over to the Lincoln, and into the back seat. Alvin got behind the wheel, and Doc and Bolton took their seats. Fitzgerald continued, *"I don't like to do this Mr. Hamm, but I'm going to have to ask you to get down on the floor because I don't want you to see where you're going. I hope you don't mind."*

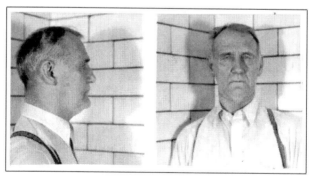

Charles J. "Big Fitz" Fitzgerald

Alvin noticed in the rearview mirror that Hamm didn't suspect anything was amiss. He seemed more puzzled than anything.

But he complied with this strange request as Alvin drove away down the street. *"Please don't try to look out, Mr. Hamm. I'll tell you when you can look up."* Twenty minutes later, they reached the second car where Zeigler and Fred were waiting with the ransom notes that Zeigler had typed out. [19]

There were four notes in all, and they asked Hamm to sign each of them. They asked $100,000 be paid and assured that if the instructions for delivery of the ransom money were followed, that Mr. Hamm would be released quickly and unharmed. He read each one and signed them. Doc then took a box of cotton balls from a glove compartment, pressed them against Hamm's eyes, and covered them with a pair of dark glasses. They were now on their way to Bartholmey's place. The abduction had gone off smooth as silk. [20]

Once Hamm was secure upstairs at the Postmaster's house, they took certain precautions to prevent him from identifying them once he was released. First of all, he had Bartholmey send his wife and children out of town, and had him sleep on the couch downstairs. The only time he was to go upstairs was to use the bathroom. In Hamm's room, they boarded up the bedroom window, and positioned the table so that Hamm would sit with his back to the door. It was hot upstairs with the window boarded up, so Alvin brought him a fan. He also brought him magazines and newspapers and made him feel at home as best he could. A day or two after snatching Hamm, Karpis picked up a newspaper and the headline sent shivers down his spine. [21]

On June 17, two days after the kidnapping, Frank Nash had been killed in a bungled rescue attempt at the Union Station in Kansas City, Missouri. Verne Miller had repeatedly warned Nash that Hot Springs was crawling with federal agents, but he refused to listen. Soon, agents got a lead from Thomas Holden and Francis Keating, who had been arrested with Harvey Bailey at the Old Mission golf course in Kansas City on June 7, 1932.

They informed the agents that Nash was living in Hot Springs with his new wife, and on June 16, agents Frank Smith and F. Joseph Lackey, along with McAlester, Oklahoma Police Chief Orrin "Otto" Reed, arrested him at a gift shop without incident. They then drove him to Fort Smith, Arkansas. From there, they caught a train to Kansas City, Missouri. Before boarding the train, the agents called Reed E. Vetterli, the Special Agent in Charge of the Kansas City Missouri office of the Division of Investigation, and asked him to meet them at Union Station the following morning. [22]

The failed attempt to rescue Frank "Jelly" Nash during the infamous Union Station Massacre in Kansas City, Missouri left five men dead – including Nash himself.

As soon as Nash was picked up, his wife Frances called Louis "Doc" Stacci in Chicago, who then notified Frank Mulloy at his tavern in Kansas City. Herb Farmer in Joplin and Verne Miller were also notified. Miller contacted John Lazia, Kansas City's mob boss, for approval, but he didn't want his people involved because it was too risky. However, Lazia recruited Charles Arthur "Pretty Boy" Floyd and Adam Richetti, who had just arrived in Kansas City after escaping an altercation in Bolivar, Missouri instigated by Richetti. [23]

Richetti had lived in Bolivar and had family there. So when

their car broke down, it was towed to a garage owned by Richetti's brother. When Sheriff William Killingsworth dropped by for a visit, as was his habit, Richetti recognized him. Richetti panicked, grabbed a Thompson from the car, and pointed it at Killingsworth. Floyd tried to diffuse the situation, but they wound up commandeering a car and took Sheriff Killingsworth as a hostage. They took another hostage named Walter Griffith – and his car – near Clinton, Missouri before releasing both men unharmed at Lee's Summit, Missouri just southeast of Kansas City. Lazia put Floyd and Richetti in contact with Miller. They agreed to meet at Miller's house to discuss the details, and both men agreed to help. [24]

The train arrived at Union Station at approximately 7:15 a.m. Lackey, Smith and Reed were met by S.A.C. Vetterli. Accompanying Vetterli was Special Agent R. J. Caffrey and two Kansas City police officers, W. J. Grooms and Frank Hermanson. After carefully surveying the area for anything amiss, the men escorted Nash through Union Station and towards a car in the parking lot. Caffrey was driving a 1932 Chevrolet two-door Sedan, and the Kansas City officers were in a Plymouth. [25]

Nash had started to crawl into the back seat, but Caffrey said, *"No, you'd better sit up front where we can keep an eye on you."* So Nash sat down in the front seat, and slid over behind the steering wheel so that the passenger side front seat could be lowered to let Joe Lackey, Smith and Reed into the back seat. Once they were in, Reed reached up and pulled the front seat back into position. Caffrey then closed the door and walked around to the driver's side. As he did so, he saw two armed men approach. They yelled *"Get 'em up! Get 'em up!"* Lackey had borrowed Reed's 1897 Winchester pump shotgun to guard Nash. The shotgun had a hair trigger, and before Lackey could get out to confront the men, it discharged. The blast blew the back of Nash's head off. As he tried to chamber another cartridge, it fired again, blowing a huge hole in the windshield and struck Caffrey, who was standing in front of the car, killing him instantly. [26]

Thinking they were being shot at, Miller yelled, *"Let 'em have it!"* They opened up on the lawmen. Lackey and Smith ducked down to the floorboard as the gunmen opened up with their Thompsons. Lackey was shot in the back and paralyzed for life. Reed was killed. Smith was uninjured. Vetterli was seriously wounded. Grooms and Hermanson were standing outside, between both cars, and were shot dead where they stood. Vetterli managed to crawl away from the vehicles. Miller ran over to Caffrey's car, and seeing Nash dead, yelled, *"They're all dead! Let's get out of here!"* They piled into their car and fled the scene. [27]

The incident was dubbed the "Kansas City Massacre" and it sent shockwaves throughout the country. Hoover was livid. Four of his agents were dead, and he swore he would track down the killers. This event would pave the way for what Hoover wanted more than anything: To transform his Division of Investigation into a National crime fighting force that could move across state lines. After it was all over, Miller and his cohorts had failed to free Nash. If anything, they had gotten him killed. They had stirred up a hornet's nest, and the heat would be on like never before. The feds weren't the only ones riled up, however. Every underworld boss in the Midwest was now out for blood – specifically Miller's, because Hoover would now be turning the heat on them as well. He and Vivian fled Kansas City for Chicago.[28]

Karpis was horrified. He knew Hoover's boys would be everywhere as thick as flies on a carcass, leaving no stone unturned. No one would be safe. He knew extra measures would have to be taken from this point forward if they were to avoid getting caught. The main thing now was to remain calm and make the arrangements for the ransom money to be delivered. [29]

About 2:00 a.m. on the morning of June 16, an anonymous call was made to William Dunn, Hamm's vice president, informing him that Mr. Hamm had been kidnapped and that instructions would be sent within a short time detailing how the money was to be prepared. The police were not to be involved in any way. When Dunn notified Hamm's mother, telling her Hamm had been kidnapped, she insisted the police be called. So Saint Paul Police Chief played along with them and had a wire place on Dunn's phone. Being Peifer's inside man at the Police Department, he was indirectly involved in the plot himself. He kept the gang informed on the police department's every move.

One of the kidnappers spotted a taxi driver near the Lowry Hotel and asked how much he would charge to deliver a letter to Mr. Dunn's resident at 1916 Summit Avenue. He the handed the driver the letter with the money, plus a $2.00 tip. About twenty minutes later, the cabbie pulled up to his house and handed it to him. The letter gave instructions for the money to be paid in denominations of $5.00, $10.00 and $20.00 bills, and said further instructions would follow soon. [30]

The next note gave instructions for a Hamm's Brewery truck to make the money drop along a certain specified stretch of Highway 61. Fred Barker and Zeigler drove to Saint Paul to get ready to meet the truck, but then Peifer called them with bad news. They were NOT to meet the truck. Chief Brown had phoned him to let him know that some cops were setting up a trap, and were in the back of the truck with a machine gun hidden under the tarpaulin. They returned to Bensenville empty-handed. [30]

About 11:00 p.m. on the night of Friday, June 16, another note was left in a phone booth at Rosedale Pharmacy, a place frequented by Mr. Dunn. An employee received a call, supposedly by Dunn, telling him he'd left a letter in a phone booth, and asked the employee to bring it to him. The employee found it and delivered it. It was much more terse. The note stated that unless the demand for $100,000 was met and instructions followed carefully, without the knowledge of the police, the sum would be raised to $150,000. New instructions for delivering the money would be sent soon.[31]

The next note was left in a car owned by L. J. Sullwood, an associate of Mr. Hamm. He received an anonymous call advising him that the note was in his vehicle. Sullwood went out to his car, found the note, and immediately took it to Mr. Dunn. It instructed Dunn to remove the doors and the lid of the rumble seat from his Chevrolet Coupe. The money was to be placed in a satchel, and he was to drive to Saint Paul on Highway 61 no faster than 20 miles per hour, and watch for a car flashing its headlights. Upon seeing the signal, he was to leave the satchel by the road and drive on towards Duluth at no more than20 miles per hour. This time, the instructions were followed to the letter. He was told that once the ransom was paid, he would receive word on where to pick up Mr. Hamm. [32]

On June 17, Dunn drove slowly down Highway 61, and just before he reached Pine City, he saw two cars. One of them flashed its headlights five times. That was the signal to drop the money. He did exactly as instructed, and continued to drive slowly north towards Duluth. [33]

The whole thing went as planned without a cop anywhere in sight. The idea of having Dunn remove the car doors had been Zeigler's. With the doors removed, there was nowhere for a cop to hide. They picked up the satchel and headed back to Bensenville. Hamm would be going home soon. Meanwhile, Karpis was worried about not offending their guest. He couldn't find any Hamm's Beer, so grabbed what he could find and removed the labels. While Hamm was drinking, Karpis asked, *"Can you tell by the taste if it's your beer?"* He laughed and replied, *"Good question!"* He sniffed the beer, and said, *"I always tell people Hamm's is the best but, to tell you the truth, I don't know what the hell brand this is!"*[34]

While Karpis was with Hamm, he heard Zeigler's car pull up in the driveway. He rushed downstairs and opened the door. Fred and Zeigler were grinning like possums as they brought the heavy satchel inside. Zeigler said, *"You'd better round up some Hamm's beer. I have a feeling that it's going to be my favorite brand for a long time!"* When Bartholmey walked in and saw the money, he fell onto the sofa, speechless. They whooped and hollered like they were at a Holy Roller camp meeting.

Now would come the hard part; releasing Hamm without getting caught. The feds were all over Kansas City, but they were also crawling around the Twin Cities area as well. They had to change plans for dropping Hamm off. Karpis went upstairs, smiled, and said, *"Mr. Hamm, you're going home, Sir!"* He asked him to go take a bath, and while he was getting into the tub, Karpis replaced four twenty-dollar bills from Hamm's wallet with four twenties from the kidnap loot. That way, if the bills had been marked, they would know it if they showed up in Saint Paul, because it would be front page news in the papers.

Karpis had Hamm put the cotton balls back over his eyes under the dark glasses, and led him out to the car. It was about 6:00 p.m. and already dark. Doc and Bolton rode with Karpis for protection as they headed out. The original plan was to drop Hamm off back in Saint Paul, but because the feds were there in force with twitchy trigger fingers, he instead drove to a small place called Wyoming, Minnesota. He had grown to respect Mr. Hamm, and thought he was an alright guy. He had been a model prisoner and had given them no trouble at all. Before letting him out, he said, *"I'd like for you to wait here about ten or twenty minutes before you make a phone call. I'd appreciate it if you gave us that much time."* Hamm replied, *"I doubt if I could ever identify any of you fellows."* [35]

Karpis pulled over and let Hamm out of the car. Once he was out, he hit the gas and headed back towards Illinois. When they got to Elmwood, Bolton pointed out a house with a beautifully manicured lawn. *"That's Zeigler's place!"* He was impressed. Zeigler was a man of many talents; one of them being a professional landscaper under another one of his several aliases. He let Bolton out at his house, and drove on to Chicago. Karpis and Doc went to Fitzgerald's apartment in the North Side of Chicago the following day to discuss how to split the loot. The one thing they were concerned about is whether or not the cops had recorded the serial numbers. They played it safe and assumed the money was marked. Peifer said that instead of taking his ten percent, he would take only five percent. His other five percent would cover the fee to have the money laundered in Reno. Karpis flew out to Reno, exchanged the money, and returned to Chicago. The gang then split it up in equal shares. [36]

William Hamm Jr. (at left) after being released by the Barker-Karpis gang (Courtesy Minnesota Historical Society)

As luck would have it, on July 19, just over a month after the

Barker-Karpis gang kidnapped Hamm, Gangster Roger Touhy was involved in a wreck in Elkhorn, Wisconsin. With him was a union boss named Eddie "Chicken" McFadden, and two bodyguards, "Gloomy Gus" Schafer and "Wee Willie" Sharkey. When the police searched their car they found a small arsenal of firearms that included a pistol converted to full automatic. The men were arrested and turned over to Captain Gilbert, who worked for the Cook County, Illinois State Attorney's office. From there, they were turned over to Special Agent in Charge Melvin Purvis, of the U. S. Bureau of Investigation's Chicago office. [37]

Touhy and his friends were subsequently charged with the kidnappings of both William Hamm, Jr. and Jake Factor, who had been kidnapped in April but released unharmed on July 12, after his wife had paid the kidnappers $70,000 in ransom. On August 12, Touhy, McFadden, Schafer and Sharkey were indicted by a federal grand jury in Saint Paul, Minnesota for the Hamm kidnapping. They were acquitted on November 23, but instead of releasing them, the prosecutor decided to charge them in Chicago for the Factor kidnapping. Sharkey was devastated. When he was returned to his cell, he hanged himself. [38]

On September 6, latent fingerprints were found on the ransom notes using a new technique. Scientists had known for some time that when an individual handles anything, perspiration from their fingers leave behind traces of sodium chloride. The Hamm ransom notes were brushed with a solution of silver nitrate, which reacted to the sodium chloride from the fingers of everyone who had handled those notes, revealing their fingerprints! After excluding the prints from those who had handled the notes after they were left by the kidnappers, they were then compared with the prints of suspects believed to have been responsible. They discovered the prints belonged to Alvin Karpis and Doc Barker. This was the very first time the technique was used to solve a crime. [39]

OK Oil Tycoon Charles F. Urschel

George Kelly   *Kathryn Kelly*   *Albert Bates*

Meanwhile, on July 22, Oklahoma oilman Charles F. Urschel, his wife and another couple, Walter Jarrett and his wife, were playing Bridge at Urschel's home at 327 NW 18th Street in

Oklahoma City. Two armed men interrupted their game and kidnapped Urschel and Jarrett while their wives watched helplessly. The kidnappers were George Kelly and Albert L. Bates. Kelly's real name was George F. Barnes, Jr., born in Chicago on July 17, 1900, to George F. Barnes Sr. and Elizabeth (Kelly) Barnes. When he was a young boy, his family moved to Memphis, Tennessee. While Kelly had a good family background, he got mixed up with the wrong crowd, getting into trouble for bootlegging. His wife divorced him over the bootlegging, and he moved West. Bates was born in 1893 and had been in trouble since he was a youngster. He joined the Army in 1911, but deserted. He was arrested and sentenced to 15 months at hard labor in the military prison at Alcatraz Island. After a stretch in the Colorado State Penitentiary, he was released in July 1930, and met George Kelly soon thereafter. [40]

George began using the name George R. Kelly, and resumed bootlegging. He was arrested in New Mexico in 1927. In 1928, he was arrested for smuggling whiskey into an Indian reservation in Oklahoma. This conviction landed him in the Federal penitentiary in Leavenworth, Kansas until 1930. While there, two of his mentors were Harvey Bailey and Frank "Jelly" Nash, and after his release in June 1930, he was involved in several bank robberies with Bailey. In 1932, he and Albert L. Bates robbed banks in Denton, Texas, Colfax, Washington, and Tupelo, Mississippi. [41]

It was about 1930 when George walked into a honky-tonk in Fort Worth, Texas where he said he met the prettiest redhead he had ever seen. Her name was Kathryn Thorne. Kathryn's real name was Lera Cleo Brooks. She had been born in Saltillo, Lee County, Mississippi on March 18, 1904 to James Everett and Ora Lillian (Coleman) Brooks. She hated her real name, and when she was older, she went by the name "Kathryn". The family moved to Brown County, Texas by 1910, and then to Pottawatomie County, Oklahoma by 1920. Her parents divorced soon thereafter, and by 1930, her mother had remarried to an influential leader of the Democrat Party in Wise County, Texas, Robert G. "Boss" Shannon. Kathryn married the first time when she was 15 to Tony B. Fry, by whom she had a daughter, Pauline, born in 1919. They later divorced, and she married twice more; the last time to an illiterate bootlegger named Charlie Thorne. Amazingly, despite his illiteracy, he managed to write a suicide note and was found dead with a bullet in his head. Thorne was obviously murdered, but the death was ruled a suicide. The money from a previous robbery and Thorne's money from bootlegging amounted to a small fortune, and Kathryn lived the good life before marrying George Kelly in Minneapolis, in September 1930. [42]

It was Kathryn who bought George his trademark firearm, a Thompson machinegun, from a pawn shop in Fort Worth, Texas in 1933. He practiced his marksmanship with the weapon at Shannon's farm, and Kathryn began referring to him as "Machine Gun Kelly". Growing tired of robbing banks, and seeing the success the Barker-Karpis gang had with getting $100,000 ransom for William Hamm, Jr., the Kelly's decided to turn to kidnapping. The plot to snatch Urschel had been Kathryn's idea, but when Bates and Kelly broke into the Urschel home, they couldn't identify him. So they blindfolded Urschel and Jarrett, and took them both. Once Urschel identified himself, they released Jarrett along the side of a road, and gave him cab fare to get home. Urschel was taken to Robert G. Shannon's farm just outside of Paradise, Texas, and was held in a small shed on the property. [43]

It was here that they held him prisoner for a little over a week, demanding $200,000 ransom. What they didn't count on was the Charles F. Urschel had a photographic memory. He made mental notes of everything he heard and felt along the road on the way to the Shannon farm. Once there, he made sure to leave as many fingerprints in his room as possible. He also listened carefully to everything that was said, airplanes that flew over, passing traffic, anything that he could identify later to help the authorities nab his captors. Another thing they didn't count on was that Urschel's father was a close personal friend of President Franklin D. Roosevelt. When FDR found out about it, he pulled out all the stops to help Hoover track down the culprits. The kidnapping shocked the Nation. [44]

Nine days later, after the ransom was paid, Urschel was released outside of Norman, Oklahoma. The details he gave to the Feds led them to the Shannon farm. They rushed to Paradise, Texas and found Harvey Bailey asleep on a cot. Unfortunately for him, Kelly had repaid him for a loan with some of the ransom money, which he had on him when the agents showed up. Robert and Ora Shannon, their son Amon and his wife, along with Bailey, were arrested. George and Kathryn, however, weren't there. Neither was Albert Bates. George and Kathryn were eventually captured in Memphis, Tennessee on September 26, where Kelly supposedly shouted, *"Don't shoot G-Men!"* Bates was arrested a short time later in Denver for passing stolen checks. [45]

George, Bates and Kathryn would be given life sentences for the kidnapping. Harvey Bailey was taken to Dallas for safe-keeping until he could be tried. However, he managed to escape from the Dallas jail, stole a car, and fled to Ardmore, Oklahoma. After a lengthy car chase through the streets of Ardmore, Bailey wrecked the car and gave up without a fight. He would receive a life sentence for his alleged part in the Urschel kidnapping. He denied having anything to do with until the day he died. Bailey was released in 1965, went straight, and eventually married the widow of Herb Farmer in Joplin. He died in 1979. George Kelly died of a heart attack in prison in 1954. Kathryn and her mother were paroled in 1958. Ora Shannon died in 1980, and Kathryn died in a Tulsa nursing home in 1985. [46]

George "Machine Gun" Kelly and his wife during their trial for the kidnapping of Oklahoma oil tycoon Charles F. Urschel

The Barker-Karpis gang was in South Saint Paul by August, where they planned to rob the Post Office. The job involved robbing two postal workers as they carried payroll from the Post Office to Swift and Company. The job seemed easy enough, but was complicated by the police who shadowed the employees. Another problem was Freddie. He was off his game and was unusually jumpy. Everyone was set to go on Wednesday morning, August 30, 1933. They arrived early at the Depot Café to drink a few beers, wait, and watch. [47]

Just past 9:00 a. m., two young postal messengers for Stockyards National Bank, Herbert Cheyene and Joseph Hamilton, arrived at the South Saint Paul Railway Station to pick up the payroll for Swift and Company. They were accompanied by Officer Leo Pavlak. The payroll had arrived from the Federal Reserve Bank in Minneapolis. Once they picked it up, Officer Pavlack escorted them back along their usual route through an alley to the Post Office, which was only a block in front of the Railway Station. Once there, they divided the payroll into envelopes, placed the envelopes into money bags, and set out for Swift and Company. The process didn't take very long, as they were ready to go by about 9:45.

As Pavlak, Cheyene and Hamilton exited the Post Office, a black sedan with a siren blasting loudly roared up to the curb and came to a screeching halt. Thick black smoke belched from the rear of the car as three armed men piled out. Doc Barker raised a shotgun at Pavlack, yelling "Stick 'em up!" Pavlak did as he was told and raised his hands as high as he could. Doc then yelled for the messengers to drop the money bags and scram. They promptly obeyed, and dived underneath a nearby delivery truck to take cover. As Doc threw the money bags into their car, a police car roared around the corner towards them. Doc shot Pavlak in the upper chest, nearly blowing his head off. The officer was dead before he hit the ground. [48]

Officer Leo Pavlak,
South Saint Paul Police Department

Fred Barker, already on edge, panicked and opened up at the car with his Thompson. It careened wildly out of control, jumped a curb, hit a building and then came to rest in the middle of the street. It's driver, Officer John Yeoman, was slumped over the steering wheel. Fred rushed over to the car, pushed Yeoman away from the steering wheel, stole his Thompson, then shot the officer again. Yeoman was lucky to survive.   As the bank guards and more cops opened fire on them from the Post Office and surrounding buildings, Fred opened up on them, firing wildly, blowing out windows all along the street, spraying other cars, and even hitting a streetcar that just happened to come along during the robbery. [49]

Charlie Fitzgerald took a slug in the hip and went down close to Pavlak. He was barely able to crawl to the car as the gang made their escape. Once in the car, Fitzgerald was given a shot of Morphine and a shot of whiskey to help ease the pain. Once they were out of town, they found an underworld doctor in Calumet, Illinois to treat him. The doctor said that because of Fitzgerald's age, it was a serious wound that would take some time to heal. He would be out of action for months. They got away with about $33,000. In addition to Fitzgerald's share of the loot, it was decided they would give him a percentage of what they took in their other jobs until he was back on his feet, as a type of "gangster health insurance" plan.[50]

In September, Zeigler contacted the gang to see if they would be interested in a robbery in Chicago that he had in mind. The job involved robbing some post office messengers while they were carting bags from the Post Office to the Federal Reserve Bank on Jackson Boulevard. Alvin said he might be interested, so he rode with Zeigler to scout things out. They parked along Jackson and watched. Shortly after 11:30 p.m., they saw two messengers leave the post office with a pushcart full of bags. They were escorted by two plainclothes police officers to the bank, and once there, the doors were opened to let them in. Once they were finished, the officers escorted them back to the post office.[51]

Alvin asked, "Why do you think there's money in the bags?" He replied, "It's obvious. They're being escorted by the cops." That made sense, he thought, but this part of town was crawling with the police, not to mention the feds. They would have to plan this job out carefully. Alvin told Zeigler they would need a safe house to head to after the robbery. Zeigler said he knew just the place. It was a property for sale, cheap, just a short distance north of Elmhurst, on the outskirts of Chicago. It was a fairly small place with a dance hall, and it also had a garage with upstairs apartments. It sounded good, so they went to check it out. After a bit of haggling, the owner agreed on a price, and they bought it.[52]

Five men would be needed for this caper. They counted Harry Campbell out, since he was unfamiliar with the area. So that left Alvin, Byron Bolton, William Weaver, Doc and Fred Barker, and Zeigler. Alvin bowed out of this one and let the others carry it out, since he would do all the planning. Doc came up with an idea that Alvin liked. He said they could use a second car blowing out black smoke like they did in South Saint Paul. But they'd leave the second car parked in the street to impede traffic while they drove away in the first car. [53]

Alvin and Zeigler came up with a 1933 Hudson four-door sedan and a 1933 Dodge DP four-door sedan, most likely through Joe Bergl, a used car dealer in Cicero. His shop was at 5346 Cermak Street, right next to Ralph Capone's Cotton Club. Bergl was a master car armorer, and he worked his magic for a great many underworld figures in Chicago, including Al Capone himself. In 1929, he had fitted Capone's 1928 Cadillac Town Sedan with thick steel plates inside the doors and installed bulletproof glass. Another nice touch were gun portals in the front and back windshields. For the Barker-Karpis gang, he worked his magic again. He installed bulletproof glass and a hidden panel in the driver's door activated by a button in the glove box. When the button was pushed, it opened the portal so that a gun could be fired through the door. The Hudson was then painted up to look like one of the State Attorney's cars, with one headlight red and the other green, as well as a red star on the spotlight. Anyone seeing this car at night would think it was one of Chicago's Secret Six off to raid some gang hideout. The Dodge was fitted with a smokescreen device similar to what they had used in South Saint Paul.[54]

The next phase was planning their escape route. Alvin got into his car and drove for hours through the streets, checking the traffic and various landmarks. He then poured over maps until he put together a good plan. He went over it with the gang, and they liked what he had come up with. Once they grabbed the loot, Doc would block traffic with the Dodge and start the smokescreen and jump into the Hudson. From there, the plan was to drive a block West on Jackson, then turn North for a block, cut through an alley, then turn left onto Adams. From there, they would drive through the loop, across the river, cross Canal Street, and then head West on Adams, and on to Elmhurst.[55]

Everything was ready to go on the night of September 22. They parked, waited and watched. Right on cue, they saw the messengers and the plainclothesmen come out of the post office. As they reached the sidewalk, the Hudson to a stop beside them. While Zeigler and Fred jumped out to disarm the cops and take the bags, Doc pulled the Dodge across Jackson Blvd to block traffic. He pulled the lever and the car began belching out thick, black smoke. He then ran to the Hudson as the other two threw the bags in, and off they went. The whole thing took less than three minutes. They were all smiles as they turned right off Jackson Blvd towards their next turn. But then all Hell broke loose.[56]

Just as they were gloating over the success of their latest heist, a reckless driver in a Ford tried to cut around a corner at Adams and Halsted, and despite Fred's best efforts, he couldn't avoid a collision. What's more, this was the worst possible place to have a wreck. It was one of Chicago's skid row areas, and it was swarming with cops. Before they could get out of the Hudson, Bolton looked up to see three cops on foot patrol running over to the crash. He panicked, poked his Thompson out the window, and started blasting. One of the officers, Miles Cunningham, was hit with six .45 rounds and killed instantly. As Doc grabbed his 380 and stuck his hand out the window to fire, one of the rounds from Bolton's gun hit his right ring finger, peeling the skin off and taking a diamond from Doc's favorite ring with it. Doc howled in pain as they grabbed their guns, ammunition and the mail bags, commandeered a passing Buick, and sped off; leaving the Buick's previous occupants on the curb wondering what had just happened. [57]

As they made off with the Buick, Doc looked at the gas gauge, and noticed that it read less than a quarter tank. They would run out of fuel and get caught for sure unless they grabbed another car and continued on West Adams until they reached Ashland, and turned South. At the intersection of 48th and Ashland Avenue, they hijacked a brand new Ford Sedan, ejected the passengers and told them to scram, loaded the mail bags, guns and ammunition as they had before and took off again. They finally got back on course back to Elmhurst. It had been a close call, but they managed to get away. However, they were worried about the Hudson. They were just sure the cops would find their fingerprints or some other piece of incriminating evidence they had left behind in the rush to get away. As it turned out, however, by the time the cops reached the Hudson, the bums had already picked over it like vultures, destroying any prints they might have left. The only thing they had left was a shortwave radio. The cops did find a phone number on the bottom, and it was traced straight to Joseph Bergl. [58]

When the gang reached their hideout in Elmhurst, they

couldn't wait to open the mail bags. They were horrified at what they found. As they opened each bag, all they found were canceled checks. There wasn't one red cent in any of them. Their shock turned to anger. Zeigler's hunch had been a bust, and it had cost them plenty. All the work Bergl had done on both the Dodge and the Hudson had not been cheap, and now they had lost both cars. It was money down the drain. In addition, they had killed a cop. Now the Chicago Police Department would out in force with the feds not far behind.[59]

LEFT: *Federal Reserve Bank in Chicago under construction in the 1920's. Other photos from the Chicago Tribune dated September 22, 1933, page 1: Top: 1933 Dodge DP Sedan Smokescreen Car. Bottom left: Smokescreen Device. Bottom Right: Officer Miles A. Cunningham. Murdered at the intersection of South Halsted and West Adams by Byron Bolton during the Barker gang's escape.*

Federal Reserve Bank under construction in the 1920's, and Chicago Tribune account of the robbery, September 23, 1931, Page 1.

Alvin was pretty sore at Zeigler, and told him, *"What a*

goddamn score that was!" Zeigler was still in shock. He was scared as well. He replied, *"I'm afraid to talk to anybody right now!"* When Alvin got back to Chicago, Fred was mad as Hell. He and Fred decided to take off to Reno, but they would stop in Saint Paul first to see Harry Sawyer. When they arrived at the Green Lantern, Sawyer confronted them. [60]

"That was a bad caper!" Alvin tried to be evasive, and asked what he meant. Sawyer yelled, *"Come off it! Everybody knows you guys pulled at Reserve Bank job in Chicago. And I want to tell you something! A couple of years ago, some other guys went on that caper and got just what you got – a bunch of worthless checks! If you had asked around, you would have found it was just no damned good!"* [61]

After the massacre at Union Station, Verne Miller and Vivian Mathis fled Kansas City for Chicago. Afterwards, Vivian left for Brainerd, Missouri and Miller headed east to New York. In August, he dropped in on another contact, Al "Silvers" Silverman, who agreed to help him evade the authorities. Silverman helped set him up with a new alias as an optical salesman named "Stephen J. Gross", gave him a new 1933 Ford and set him up at the Greenbrier Hotel in White Sulfur Springs, West Virginia.[62]

The following month, on September 26, George "Machine Gun" Kelly and his wife were arrested in Memphis, Tennessee. Kelly presumably yelled, *"Don't shoot, G-Men!"* as they barged in on them. The feds then moved Miller to the top of their "Most Wanted" list. He knew it was time to move again. Silvers contacted him again early in October. He and a friend, Abraham Chait, looked into getting Miller a new driver's license under the name "Frederick J. Glaubach". Another one of their friends, Herman Borenstein, took the driver's test for Miller. Once he had the license, they gave him the keys to a 1933 Ford V-8 Coupe, and off he went again.[63]

On October 9, Gus Winkeler got out of his car to enter the beer distribution office of Charles H. Weber, at 1414 Roscoe Street in Chicago. As he walked towards the door, a green delivery truck slowed down. Three men in the truck fired shotguns, hitting him with six slugs. He was rushed to a local hospital, and after calling for a priest, died about a half-hour later. His last words were *"The end of a gangster"*. His body was transported to Donnelly Funeral Home, at 3840 Lindell Boulevard in Saint Louis. Long lines showed up for the viewing, and the Funeral Mass was held at Saint George Catholic Church at 4980 Heege Road. He was buried at Park Lawn Cemetery in Lemay, Missouri next to his parents. Georgette was completely distraught, and on October 22, she turned on the gas in her Chicago apartment trying to commit suicide. However, Bonnie Burke, Fred "Killer" Burke's wife, arrived just in time to save her life.[63]

No one knew who the killers were, but it was believed to have been a mob hit by Frank Nitti's boys. Nitti didn't like Winkeler because, first of all, he had been a close friend to Capone. Secondly, he had become a stool pigeon for the feds. Nitti had to shut him up. Another thing that Nitti didn't like about Winkeler was that he had been in the rackets just as the Touhy gang had been. Alvin had known some Touhy men in Long Beach, California. In fact, he had warned them to be careful since the Syndicate men didn't care for robbers. This warning almost got Alvin killed as well. [64]

While in Chicago, Alvin was called to a Syndicate hangout, the Motion Picture Operators Union. When he walked into the office, there were three of the Chicago Syndicate's top bosses: Frank "the Enforcer" Nitti, Phil D'Andrea, and William J. "three-fingered Jack" White. They mistakenly thought he was a member of the Touhy gang because he had tipped them off. They demanded an explanation. [65]

"I didn't want any of my friends getting killed. They were just burglars. Not rackets guys", he said.

Nitti replied *"There was one guy among you who was in the rackets."* White then cut in, smiling, and asked, *"Can you guess which one?"* They were all smiling and looking at each other, which made Alvin nervous. He had no idea what they were talking about, and he had a feeling he might not leave this office alive. After a long silence, White answered. *"It's Verne Miller! We want to know where he is!"* [66]

Alvin responded that he hadn't seen Miller since the Fairbury job in Nebraska, then said *"I didn't know you were hot at him!"* Nitti stood up and sat on the edge of his desk. No one was smiling now. They all just gave Alvin that cold stare, like a rattlesnake ready to strike its prey. Nitti told him, *"Everyone's hot at that bastard!"* Finally, D'Andrea cuts and said, *"We're going to give you a pass!"* Alvin breathed a sigh of relief as the meeting ended. Satisfied that he had told them the truth, he was allowed to leave. His knees felt like gelatin. [67]

Towards the latter part of October, the feds were prepared to spring a trap for Miller, using information they had received from Gus Winkeler. They knew Vivian was in Chicago staying at the Sherone Apartment Hotel at 4423 N. Sheridan Road, so they assigned agents to watch for him. They also brought in two informants from Huron, South Dakota, who could identify Miller on sight. On Halloween night he showed up to see Vivian, but he spotted them and a gun battle broke out. In the confused melee that followed, they lost track of him and he escaped. Mathis and another woman, Bobbie Moore, were arrested and taken to jail.

On November 6, Herman Borenstein, Abraham Chait, and Al Silverman were indicted on conspiracy charges, but Silverman was never found – until November 20, when he was found dead. He had been stripped naked and beaten to death. His body was wrapped in a mechanic's robe and dumped on the side of a road near Somers, Connecticut.[67]

On November 29, the same day Mathis and Moore were sentenced to a year in jail for harboring a fugitive, Verne Miller's naked body was in a ditch near Detroit by Vernon Northrup as he was driving to work. Miller also had been beaten and strangled to death, wrapped in a mechanic's robe, and dumped at the intersection of Cambridge Road and Harlow Avenue. When Alvin found out about Miller's death, he knew all too well that this had been a mob hit.[68]

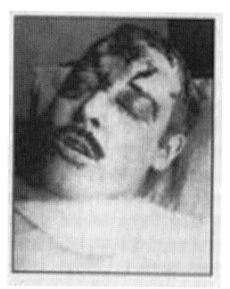

Vernon C. Miller's body was found near Detroit

Miller's body was returned to White Lake, South Dakota, amidst a great deal of controversy, since the National Chapter of the American Legion forbade the Beadle County post to participate, saying it would be an embarrassment to the organization. But American Legion Post 7, for all practical purposes, told the National organization to go to Hell. Post members, family, and members of his old Army unit during the Great War, escorted his flag-draped casket from White Lake to Huron and gave him a funeral with full military honors. He was laid to rest at Riverside Cemetery. Folks in Huron still honored the Verne Miller they remembered. Not the cold-blooded killer-for-hire, but Verne Miller the war hero, and the tough, no-nonsense lawman. Not even his estranged wife had any ill feeling towards him. They had been separated since 1929. She said, *"I don't believe all the things they say about Verne. Because he became involved in a few scrapes nearly every major crime in the country was laid to him. He was wonderful to me and I have nothing against him."* [69]

The Barker-Karpis gang took another vacation to Reno in November 1933 along with Harry and Gladys Sawyer. On December 2, they all left together in what the feds later described as an "automobile caravan" back to Saint Paul. On Christmas Day, they all met at the Sawyers' farm. Karpis was there with Dolores, Ma, Fred and Doc were there, along with George Zeigler, Harry Campbell, William Weaver, Myrtle Eaton, Volney Davis and Edna Murray. After all the gifts had been exchanged, and they were quite thoroughly stuffed to the gills with the huge meal Gladys had prepared, Harry got the boys together to tell them about a new job he had planned. They were always careful not to discuss such matters in front of Ma Barker, so they went into another room. This job, Sawyer said, would be their biggest yet.... [70]

CHAPTER 7:
1934: THE BREMER KIDNAPPING AND
THE END OF THE GANGSTER ERA

Edward George Bremer

Once Harry had shut the door to his office, he let the boys in on the new job he had planned. He wanted Alvin and Fred to pull off another kidnapping. The target this time would be a banker for whom Sawyer had an intense dislike named Edward George Bremer, President of the Commercial State Bank in Saint Paul. The boys had no idea what Harry's beef was with Bremer, but in time, he figured just maybe old man Otto Bremer,

Edward's uncle, had been the one who had handled laundering the Denver Mint bonds back in December 1922, and possibly the banker who had Sawyer bump off those two girls in Alvin's Buick — then welched on paying for the hit. Whatever the reason was, Sawyer was adamant. *"I want him snatched."* He assured them it would go as smoothly as the Hamm kidnapping, except this time the ransom would be $200,000. Alvin didn't like this at all. He knew that Bremer's father, Adolph Bremer, was a close personal friend to President Franklin D. Roosevelt, and that if they grabbed Bremer, the local cops would be the least of their worries. FDR would turn Hoover's G-Men loose like bloodhounds. But Harry said, *"The feds won't get involved unless they can prove you took him across state lines."* [1]

The Bremer family was one of the most important, and one of the richest, families in the Twin-Cities area, if not in the whole country at that time. Old man Adolph Bremer and his brother Otto had come to America from Germany, about 1886. After moving to Saint Paul, Otto Bremer became a stock clerk with a hardware business, then became a bookkeeper with the National German American Bank, and worked his way to the top. Adolph married Marie Schmidt, the daughter of Jacob Schmidt, in 1897. [2]

Jacob was the founder of Schmidt Brewery Company. He was born in Bavaria in 1846 and came to America about 1867. He worked for several breweries in both New York and Milwaukie, Wisconsin until finally settling in Saint Paul, where he eventually became Master Brewer for his friend Theodore Hamm, founder of Hamm's Brewery Company. He finally decided to go into business for himself, and purchased a half-interest in Edward Drewery's old North Star Brewery. After moving to a new location, he established it as Schmidt's Brewery, and turned it over to Adolph and Otto when he retired in 1899. When Jacob died in 1911, they took control of the company. Otto's fortunes in Saint Paul's banking industry continued to flourish until the

Bremers were one of the richest families in the area. And during the election of 1932, they poured an estimated $350,000 into Franklin D. Roosevelt's election campaign.[3] They were well connected to some of the most powerful political leaders in the country. Kidnapping Bremer would be much more complicated and dangerous than the Hamm kidnapping had been.

Sawyer kept needling the boys to do the job. In fact, he wouldn't let it go. He begged and pleaded with until finally, Alvin gave in despite his better judgement. *"Don't worry about the cops. My contacts in the police department will keep me informed. We'll know their every move"*,[4] he assured them. Alvin still didn't like it, and had a gut feeling that this could be their undoing. They moved ahead cautiously, taking extra special care, and giving more time to the planning. He would also need more men, so Alvin and Fred brought in Zeigler, Doc, Volney Davis, William Weaver, and Harry Campbell. [5]

Edward George Bremer was born in Saint Paul November 8, 1897 and married Emily Elizabeth Esswein, the daughter of Henry A. and Mathilda "Tilly" (Rosenkranz) Esswein, in Saint Paul in May 1923. Emily was just a few years older than Edward, having been born in Saint Paul December 23, 1894. His father-in-law was a well-to-do part owner of the grocery supply company Ornes-Esswein & Company in Minneapolis. Prior to 1904, he had built his wealth as a hardware dealer. The Bremers had an 8 year old daughter, Emily Elizabeth, born May 28, 1925, whom he drove to school every morning. [6]

Just as they had done in preparation for the Hamm kidnapping, they studied the Bremers in the minutest detail, and continued to watch his every move. Sawyer arranged for them to rent an apartment at the Dale Apartments at 628 Grand Avenue, where a woman identifying herself as "Mrs. B", rented a first floor flat on December 7, paying for the first month's rent in cash. On January 7, she paid for another month's rent [7]. Here, they planned the kidnapping. One detail that concerned them was that Bremer traveled with a bodyguard who was with him constantly. After the Hamm kidnapping, he had become frantic to the point of paranoia that he would be the next one kidnapped, so he hired a bodyguard. Also, Bremer was a fairly young man, 35 years old, and stood about six feet tall. He was muscular and weighed about 200 pounds. If he and his bodyguard put up a fight, it would be hard to pull it off. The risks were many. This wouldn't be as easy as when they snatched Hamm.

1930 model 3 Cell LIGHTMASTER flashilight, as probably bought by Alvin Karpis at F. & W. Grand Silver Store, at 67 7th Street St. Paul.
Image Source:
Courtesy Flashlight Museum
FllashlightMuseum.com

Alvin had another idea the gang liked. It involved using flashlights to use as signal lights during the money drop. The intermediary used to deliver the money would have to be signaled in some fashion. So Alvin visited several hardware store in Saint Paul, until finally dropping by the F. & W. Grand Silver Store, at 67 7th Street. Here, he found a special Blake Brand 3 Cell flashlight, for which he also bought red filmolens filters manufactured by Bell & Howell. He purchased four (some accounts state three) of them along with some Eveready brand batteries. For some unknown reason, these flashlights had "A Merit Product" stamped on the rear caps.[8] Next, they needed to place to take Bremer once they had him, so Byron Bolton contacted Elmer Farmer in Chicago. Farmer then called Zeigler, who found a house in an area that the gang knew quite well by now – right back in Bensenville, Illinois. This house was a little more than a rundown shack at 180 May Street, owned by a man named Herman Bauke – just blocks South of Bartholmey's house at 222 York Avenue. Bauke had rented his house to Harold Alderton in January, and it was Alderton who made arrangements with Zeigler to stash Bremer there. Just as before, Zeigler had the safe room windows boarded up, and prepared everything for the arrival of their new "guest". [9]

Now, all they had to do was determine when and where to grab Bremer. After watching him closely, they knew that he was a creature of habit. He always took the same route every morning from their home 92 North River Boulevard, right on South Cretin, then left onto Goodrich to Summit School, and then on to work. The original plan had been to grab Bremer and his bodyguard in a nearby park, but then all of their carefully laid plans were hit with the proverbial monkey wrench one morning when Harry Sawyer called to tell them that Bremer had just fired his bodyguard. Tom Brown had convinced him that the Saint Paul police would protect him, and that the bodyguard would be unnecessary, so he dismissed him. The gang had to revise their plan, and decided to grab him right after he dropped Emily off at school.[10]

Federal agents reenact the Bremer kidnapping (FBI Photo)

Now, Bremer would be driving alone to drop Emily off at school. They would stop him at the intersection of Goodrich and Lexington, just about a block and half east of Summit. By the morning of January 17, they were ready. Fred and Zeigler parked their Lincoln along the side of Lexington about half a block north of Goodrich and waited as Bremer pulled up to the stop sign. Before he had a chance to pull through the intersection, they quickly raced in front of him and stopped. Alvin then pulled out from his hiding place on Goodrich and parked behind Bremer's car, boxing him in. Volney Davis and Doc jumped out of the back seat of Alvin's car and rushed both sides of Bremer's Lincoln. As Doc opened the driver's side door, Bremer punched him. He wasn't a pushover as Hamm had been, and gave them a good scrap until Doc pistol-whipped him. [11]

Doc had given Bremer a good lick with his pistol, and the blood gushed down his face and all over the car. Dazed, They quickly shoved him into the back seat, then Doc jumped behind the steering wheel and drove off, following Zeigler's Lincoln. Alvin followed closely behind them South to a field on Edgecombe Road. Once there, Zeigler had typed three ransom notes and had Bremer sign them. He was still groggy from the bump on the head Doc had given him, making it difficult for him to see, but he finally managed to sign them. Once he was finished they blindfolded him and transferred him to Alvin's car. Zeigler and Fred headed to Saint Paul to deliver the ransom notes while Alvin, Doc and Volney headed to Bensenville with Bremer.

Once the ransom notes were delivered, Zeigler had everyone clear out of the flat they had rented at the Dale Apartments. Surprisingly, no one noticed them moving out. They left all the lights on and left the door standing open. All that was left behind were a few beer bottles. Since the kidnappers had made an anonymous call the following morning from a nearby phone, the Division of Investigation spoke with the landlord and took the bottles to be fingerprinted for possible clues as to the identity of the tenants.

Zeigler was the one who made the anonymous call to Bremer's friend Walter Magee. He said, *"We have Bremer. If you go to your office you'll find a note. Bremer's car can be found near the Snelling Water Tower."* Magee quickly rushed to his office and found the note. He immediately the Bremers and Special Agent in Charge Werner Hanni of the Division of Investigation's Saint Paul office. Chief Dahill at the Saint Paul Police Department was also notified, as were Chief Tom Brown and Inspector Charles Tierney. They met Magee, Otto Bremer and Adolph Bremer at the Ryan Hotel. [12]

Edward Bremer's 1932 Lincoln (St. Paul Daily News Photo 1934)

The kidnapper's note demanded $200,000 ransom. It was to be paid in five dollar and ten dollar non-consecutive, older bills placed in two suit cartons. The money was not to be marked. Once they had it together, they were to place an ad in the Minneapolis Tribune stating *"We are ready, Alice."* Dahill immediately ordered the phone lines of the Bremers and their business associates, as well as Magee's business and home phone lines, tapped. Adolph Bremer then contacted the Minneapolis Tribune to place the ad demanded by the kidnappers, beginning with the morning edition of January 18.

A diligent search for Edward Bremer's Lincoln was initiated in the area mentioned by the man who called Magee. It was finally located off Edgecombe Road, in an area that was out of view of area residents. Evidence of a struggle was seen immediately. There was blood on the steering wheel, shift lever, left door sill, on the back of the front seat, and the right front seat was soaked with blood. There was also a considerable amount of blood on the floorboard. The car was quickly taken to Walter

Magee's garage to be examined for evidence. [13]

It didn't take long for the local newspapers to find out about the kidnapping. Across the top of the Saint Paul Dispatch, the headline "**EDW. G. BREMER KIDNAPED; Secrecy Veils Second Major Seizure Here**." was emblazoned across the top of the Thursday, January 18, 1934 edition. Almost from the very beginning, the chief suspect was another well-known criminal named Verne Sankey. In June 1932, Sankey, who had tried and failed at farming in South Dakota, joined with Gordon Alcorn to kidnap Haskell Bohn, the son of a Saint Paul millionaire. They received $12,000 ransom. In early 1933, they struck again, this time kidnapping Charles Boettcher, a millionaire in Denver, Colorado. Sankey held Boettcher at his turkey farm in South Dakota and released him after receiving $60,000 ransom.   But Sankey had nothing to do with the Bremer job. Regardless, it indirectly resulted in his arrest at a barbershop in Chicago on January 31, 1934. He was promptly returned to South Dakota to stand trial for the Boettcher kidnapping. Just in case he tried to escape, he was held for safekeeping at the South Dakota State Penitentiary in Sioux Falls. But on February 8, Sankey used his necktie and hanged himself before he could be brought to trial. His partner Gordon Alcorn, meanwhile, had been also been arrested using the alias "William Thomas", and returned to South Dakota to stand trial. He was convicted and sentenced to life. [14]

The newspapers sensationalized the kidnapping, especially after the details were leaked about the blood found in Bremer's car. Rumors abounded that he had been murdered, and when President Roosevelt heard the news, he assured the Bremers that he would help in any way he could. The President even mentioned the kidnapping in one of his famous "fireside chats", during which he said the crime was *"an attack on everything we hold dear."* Federal agents soon swarmed all over Saint Paul with Roosevelt's blessing. The Governor of Minnesota also sent the State Police to assist in the investigation. Because of the rumors that he had been killed, search parties were sent out throughout the area where the car had been found looking for Bremer's body. Hoover expected Hanni to keep him updated constantly on developments, which he failed to do in a timely fashion, and was also careless in submitting evidence properly. In frustration, the Director fired off a letter to the Saint Paul office on January 19: [15]

"Mr. Werner Hanni   *1/19/34*

"It is difficult for me to understand why you neglected, in a case of such significance as the present one, to fully advise me concerning same. You are instructed that any developments and all information received in connection with this case, or any other important matter, must be immediately submitted to the Division by telephone or telegraph."

"I am now in receipt of the ransom note, together with your letter of transmittal, which I assume is the letter you referred to in your conversation with Mr. Cowley last night, advising that full details were being submitted by air mail. I note, however, that the letter contains no information, it merely being a letter transmitting the ransom note. I also note that the ransom note was not enclosed in a cellophane container. The matter of sending ransom notes to this Division in cellophane containers was also discussed at length at the conference of Special Agents in Charge and there is no excuse for your failure to so transmit this letter. I also note you're your conclusion to the effect that there is no possibility of developing latent fingerprints from this note, and I assume that your conclusion to that effect is your excuse for not transmitting this note in a cellophane container. I submit that fingerprint experts here at the Division's headquarters are in a far better position to determine the possibility of developing latent prints from notes of this kind and

are the sole judges, and will not arrive at any such conclusion until after a thorough and careful examination of the note has been made. It is also noted that the note purports to have been written by the victim and that you have submitted no specimens of his handwriting. It is requested that you immediately obtain as many specimens of his handwriting as possible and submit them to this Division by registered air mail, special delivery."

"In conclusion, I must add that I am entirely dissatisfied with the manner in which you have handled this case and I must insist that my instructions be complied with hereafter. [16]

Very truly yours,

Director "

On January 20, a bogus letter was addressed to the Minneapolis Postmaster from a man claiming to have been one of the kidnappers. It had been postmarked 9:00 p.m. on the 19th. In the letter, he claimed Bremer had been accidentally killed in Anoka County, and was in a snow bank. The letter had been mailed from the Union City Mission in Minneapolis. When the Postmaster opened it, the note read: [16]

"For a federal officer. Hear this. Very sorry, but Ed. Bremer is now resting in Peace. – Was by accident bumped off – body near Anoka Minn, will not be found until after snow gone. Contact are off. Please forgive us -all a mistake By one of our gang been drunk. Please tell Walter Magee – St. Paul. One of the gang." [17]

The Postmaster immediately called the Division of Investigation and handed it over to them. After a careful investigation it was finally determined that the letter was in fact one of several fake ransom notes sent to the authorities. These bogus letters were a great hindrance to the investigation, as more man-hours had to be spent investigating them.

Newspaper article showing (L) interior of house where Bremer was held. He memorized the wallpaper pattern seen through the center door.

(FBI file photo. Bremer Kidnapping Files. The Vault)

Meanwhile in Bensenville, Alvin Karpis wasn't having much fun. While Hamm had been a very pleasant and likeable fellow, Bremer was an intolerable ass, and he was getting on everyone's nerves. Fred wanted to shoot him, but he knew he couldn't. He whined and complained constantly. When he arrived at the house on May Street, he asked how much ransom they expected for him. When Alvin told him $200,000, Bremer exclaimed, *"You're crazy! My father would never pay that much for me!"* Had the feds back in Saint Paul heard his remark, they would have most likely agreed with him. During their investigation while interviewing people who knew him, it became clear that Edward George Bremer was arrogant, selfish, and short-tempered, with very few real friends. Even many of his own family didn't like him. In fact, some of them were probably glad he was gone. Alvin could hardly wait for the day when he'd be rid of him also. [18]

One day, Bremer said, *"You've got the wrong man! I know a guy in Saint Paul who has a quarter of a million dollars in a safety deposit box to be used by his wife in case he's kidnapped. You should have grabbed him instead! That would have been an easy score for you guys!"*

Then, he startled Alvin by mentioning Harry Sawyer and Jack Peifer. He said he was a good friend of theirs and that they would vouch for him. He told Bremer he didn't know them. But in the back of Alvin's mind, he wondered if just "maybe" that's another reason why Sawyer wanted Bremer snatched. Old man Adolph Bremer had been supplying beer to speakeasies all over Saint Paul and Minneapolis throughout Prohibition, and especially to Harry Sawyer at the Green Lantern, and Jack Peifer at Hollyhocks. The fact that Prohibition was about over signaled that the Bremers were fed up with doing business with them. They had hurt their business!

In the meantime, the gang had problems with some of the shenanigans Magee and old man Bremer had pulled. First of all, Magee had gone straight to the police, despite their demands to the contrary. Of course their inside man, Tom Brown, told them immediately. Secondly, the Bremers wanted to reduce the ransom by half. This didn't set well with the gang, so Zeigler typed off another note to them. He threatened to kill both Edward Bremer and Magee if their demands weren't met. The Bremers then demanded proof that Edward was still alive.

At 6:00 a.m. on the morning of January 20, Dr. H. T. Nippert received a phone call instructing him to go to the vestibule of his home and see what he could find there. After the caller hung up, he hurried downstairs, and found that someone had thrown a Lavoris mouthwash bottle through the window in his front door. In addition to the bottle was an envelope on the floor addressed to him. Upon opening the envelope, he found two other envelopes inside. One was addressed to Walter Magee, and the other was addressed to Mrs. Edward Bremer. Dr. Nippert immediately left to Adolph Bremer's home to deliver them. In the envelope addressed to Magee was a note which read:

"Chas. Magee

You must be proud of yourself by now. If Bremer don't get back his family has you to thank. You've made it almost impossible but we're going to give you one more chance – the last. First of all, all coppers must be pulled off. Second, the dough must be ready. The money must not be hot because it will be examined before Bremer is released. If Dahill is so hot to meet us, you can send him out with the dough. Third, we must have a new signal. When you are ready to meet our terms place a NRA sticker in the center of each of your office windows. We'll know if the coppers are pulled or not: Remain at your office daily from noon until 8:00 p.m. Have the dough ready and where you can get it within 30 minutes. Will try to be ready for any trickery if attempted. This is positively our LAST attempt. Don't duck it. "

Another note was in Edward Bremer's handwriting, and stated:

"Mr. Chas. Magee,
I have named you as payoff man. You are responsible for my safety. I am responsible for the full amount of the money. E. G. Bremer."

Another note in Bremer's handwriting was addressed to Dr. Nippert. It stated:

"Dear Doctor,
I am enclosing herewith two letters which please deliver for me at once. Deliver them both to my father at the house – 655 West 7th Street, or at the office, wherever he may be – it is very important that they be delivered right away as it means a lot to me. Be sure however not to say a word to anyone else that you have been given these letters to deliver. The reason I am writing

to you is because I know you can be trusted not to say anything - Edward G. Bremer."

The two additional notes which Bremer mentioned were addressed to Walter Magee and to Mrs. Bremer. The first stated:

"Dear Walter;
 I'm sorry to have to call on you but I feel you were the old standby. Assure Emily and Pat that I'm allright. I knew you would use your head & work on this all alone – no police. The people that have me have given the impression that you are not working alone. Walter, please do. I know you will for me. I've been told that the reason the first plan was not gone through with was because you were working with the police. Again I say please work all alone & I am sure everything will come out allright. Be sure – no strings allowed here. You & You alone. These people are going to give you a new plan. Work according to these directions & again I say – alone – no police – just you.
   -   Edward, E. G. Bremer"

The other note stated:

"Dearest Patz.
 Please don't worry. I hope everything will come out allright. Tell Hertzy to be a good little girl. Her daddy is thinking of her all the time and to see you or her again is all that I want. I suppose you are worrying about the blood in the car. I have a cut on my head which bleed a lot but it has been dressed & is allright now. Tell Pa too not to worry. I am treated nice & the only thing I have to ask is to keep the police out of this so that I am returned to you all safely.
 Yours, Ed."

After reading the part of the note which stated: *"if Dahill is so hot to meet us, you can send him out with the dough,"* Chief Dahill was convinced they had a crooked cop on their hands, leaking information to the kidnappers and to the press, and he had a suspect – Tom Brown, head of the city's Kidnap Squad. The Division of Investigation had given Dahill a brand new high-powered rifle a short time before, and he was showing it off to Charles Tierney, his Chief of Detectives, and Brown. No one else was in the office. Dahill picked up the rifle, aimed out the window, and said *"I'd love to have those guys in my gunsights now!"* [19]

The leaks to the press made Dahill look like a fool in the eyes of the Division of Investigation, but after meeting privately with "Pop" Nathan, they both agreed that the Saint Paul Daily News was privy to far too much information.

On January 23, 1934, Hoover sent out this memorandum:

"Mr. Nathan telephoned from St. Paul to give me the latest developments in the Bremer kidnaping case. In regard to the notes which were sent out last night, Mr. Nathan stated that the family seems to think there is a possibility that the kidnapers will demand the original notes when the pay-off is made and therefore would like for them to be returned by this Division by air mail as soon as possible. I advised Mr. Nathan that this would be done.

Mr. Nathan advised me that it had been ascertained that information had been given to the press by Tom Brown, connected with the Police Department' that, however, Chief Dahill will take no action against him because of his political connections. Chief Dahill repeated to Mr. Adolph Bremer and to Mr. Magee that he believed Brown was responsible for giving the information out, and further stated that Brown was responsible for the Hamm and the Bremer kidnapings. However, he had no proof for this statement. The Bremer family states it will continue to deny that they have any notes for six months.

Mr. Nathan stated the morning papers in St. Paul are carrying a story to the effect that a bottle was thrown into the doctor's residence and indicates a contact is about to be made. Mr. Nathan was of the opinion that because of the occurrence last night, the Bremer family will discontinue giving confidential information to Chief Dahill. I instructed Mr. Nathan to immediately call upon Mr. Bremer again, inform him of our distress at this occurrence, and assure him that anything given this Division will be kept strictly confidential.

I mentioned to Mr. Nathan the article by Mr. Cullen last night indicating that our Agents are contemplating discontinuing their "watchful waiting." Mr. Nathan said that of course there is no basis for such a statement.

I read to Mr. Nathan a memorandum addressed to the Attorney General by Mr. Keenan relative to making a statement to the Paramount News, as well as the Attorney General's notation thereon to me. I inquired of Mr. Nathan if there is any basis for the statement in the memorandum to the effect that investigation is being obstructed by reporters and photographers. Mr. Nathan advised me that your Agents are not hampered by reporters, and that nothing was mentioned in the kidnapers' last note about newspaper people. Mr. Nathan agreed with me that a statement of the character suggested by Mr. Keenan for Paramount News would be undesirable.."

The following day, Dahill met in his office with Tierney and Brown, discussing the kidnappers' ransom notes. The bottle mentioned in Hoover's memorandum had actually been a Lavoris mouthwash bottle. Only he, Special Agent Nathan, Tierney and Dr. Nippert knew what sort of bottle it was. But in Brown's presence, Dahill said it was a "milk bottle." Sure enough, the very next day, the Saint Paul Daily News reported that a "milk bottle" had been thrown through the Doctor's window! Again, the only people in the office that morning besides himself were Tierney and Brown. Dahill contacted Special Agent Nathan, and the two went to speak with Adolph Bremer. Mr. Bremer was dumbfounded when they told him about their suspicions. It had been he who had helped Brown become Chief of Police a few years earlier. Dahill removed Brown from the Kidnap Squad at once, and turned the investigation over to the Division of Investigation took complete control. The Bremers also refused to work with the Saint Paul police department, and dealt directly with Special Agents Hanni and Nathan. The leaks suddenly ceased. [20]

Nothing was heard again from the kidnappers for several days. Things were ominously quiet until the morning of January 22, when Mr. William P. Behrens, of Behrens-Whitman Coal Company arrived at his office at 972 West 7th Street in Saint Paul. His bookkeeper, C. A. Stahlman, had arrived earlier that morning to open the office, and discovered an envelope that had been slipped under the door. When he picked it up, he noticed that the address had been typed, and it was addressed to *"Walter Magee or Adolph Bremer."* Stahlman handed the envelope to Mr. Behrens, who opened it.[21] The note inside stated:

"Chas. Magee.

If you can wait O.K. with us. You people shot a lot of curves trying to get somebody killed then the copper's think will be heroes but Eddie will be the martyr. The copper's think that great but Eddie don't. We're done taking the draws and you can go fuck yourself now. From now on you make the contact. Better not try it till you make pull off every copper, newspaper, and radio station. From now on you get the silent treatment until you reach us someway yourself. Better not wait too long."

The following day, Mr. John Miller received a phone call shortly after 6:00 p.m. He was told he could find a Hills Brothers coffee can on his front porch. But when he arrived home, his wife had already found it, along with the note inside addressed to Chas. Magee or Adolph Bremer, instructing them to deliver $200,000 that night. In addition to the note, there was a baggage check tag. The note instructed Magee to take the tag to the Jefferson Lines Bus Station. The baggage check tag was for the baggage checking locker in the bus station waiting room, where a handbag would be found with further instructions. The handbag wasn't to be opened until exactly 8:19 p.m. Magee followed the instructions to the letter, and retrieved a large black zipper bag containing a pillow and another note.

This new note instructed Magee to assume the name John B. Brakesham, and to board a bus from Saint Paul to Des Moines, Iowa. However, something went wrong and the kidnappers called off the drop. No further word came until about 7:30 p.m. on February 5, when Edward Bremer's secretary, Lillian L. Dickman, heard someone knock on her back door. When she went to see who it was, she met a man at the door. It was Volney Davis. He asked, *"Are you Lillian Dickman?"* She answered yes, and he handed her a note. He said, *"Please take care of this."* As he left, she saw that the note was in her boss's handwriting, instructing his father to follow the kidnappers' instructions to the letter. [22]

Those instructions would arrive from an unlikely source. About 4:30 p.m. on the following afternoon of Tuesday, February 6, Volney Davis paid a visit to Father John Deere, Rector of Saint Michael's in Prior Lake, Minnesota. Volney asked the man who answered the door *"Are you Father Deere?"* He replied that he was, and he then asked, *"Do you know a family by the name of Bremer?"* He replied, *"Why yes, I do."* Volney then asked, *"Can you get to Saint Paul by 6:00 p.m.?"* Father Deere once again replied in the affirmative, and Volney quickly shoved an envelope into Father Deere's hands, instructing him to deliver it to Adolph Bremer immediately. He then walked to a brown sedan with wire wheels, and drove away. [23]

Father Deere immediately drove to Adolph Bremer's home and handed him the envelope. Bremer then had him contact Special Agent in Charge Harold "Pop" Nathan to inform him of what had just taken place. Father Deere did as he was told, and was instructed to call Mr. Nathan at the Division of Investigation at once, which he did. Father Deere insisted that he didn't want any newspaper publicity in regards to the incident, fearful of any repercussions that might occur if his name were brought into the situation. He wanted nothing further to do with it.

Inside, the note inside was address to *"Chas. Magee or Honest Adolph"* and stated. *"The copper's jimmied the last payoff."* This note gave specific instructions on delivering the money. Magee was to take the two satchels in his Ford to 969 University Avenue, where he would find a Chevrolet with Standard Oil decals on the sides. He was to use this car to deliver the ransom, and would find the keys and further instructions inside the pocket in the driver's side door.

Fearing that he might be driving into a holdup, Magee parked his car behind his house, and took his wife's Ford instead. He arrived at the designated location at about 8:00 p.m., finding the Chevrolet exactly as the note stated. He loaded the money into the Chevy, located the keys, and the instructions telling him where to go from there. The note stated:[24]

" Go to Farmington, Minnesota. The Rochester bus will arrive there at 9:15 p.m., and leave at 9:25 p.m. Follow one hundred yard in back of this bus, when it leaves Farmington until you come to four red lights on the left and proceed at fifteen miles per hour until you see five flashes of light; then stop and deposit packages of money on the right hand side of the road. Leave the two notes, get in car and go straight ahead."

Magee followed these instructions to the letter. The bus

continued on from Farmington to Cannon Falls, then on through Zumbrota. About five miles past Zumbrota, just over the crest of a hill, he saw the red lights along the left side of the road, at a gravel road that turned off to the left. He turned left, and about a half-mile down the road, a car came up from behind him and flashed its headlights five times. He quickly pulled over, walked around to the passenger's side, removed the two satchels and laid them on the right hand side of the road as instructed. He then got back into the Chevrolet and drove away. Once Magee was out of sight, Zeigler and Fred picked up the satchels and headed back to Bensenville. Once at the hideout they opened the satchels and counted the money. Inside one, the found a note Adolph Bremer had written, stating:

"To the parties holding Edward: I've done my part and kept my word 100 per cent just as I said I would. This money is not marked and is the full amount asked for. And now boys, I am counting on your honor. Be sports and do the square thing by turning Edward loose at once. - Adolph Bremer".[25]

The money, however, was indeed marked. The serial number of each and every bill had been written down, and the list sent out to every bank in the country. Alvin and Fred had a hunch that the money had been marked, so they made plans to find someone who could launder it. It had taken twenty long, grueling days to get the payoff. For Alvin and Fred, it had been twenty days of Hell, listening to Bremer's constant whining. Now that they had the money, they could be rid of him at last.

During his twenty days of confinement, Bremer had lost quite a bit of weight and could barely stand. However, during the times that his blindfold was removed and he was made to sit facing the wall of his room, he had memorized the design of the wallpaper. He had also listened to any noises that might help him determine where he was being held. He knew that there were two dogs near the house that barked quite a bit, and there were also children upstairs. One he believed was about a year old, and another sounded to be about four years old. He also heard the sound of trains nearby that ran mostly in the mornings and afternoons.

Finally, Alvin told Bremer he was going home. They waited until dark, blindfolded him, and hurried him out to a small coupe. After riding a short distance, he was transferred to a sedan. Once inside the sedan, he was made to sit in the floor with his back against the driver's seat. Two of his captors sat in the front seat, and one sat with him in the back seat. At his left he could feel what seemed to be a five-gallon gasoline can, upon which he could comfortably rest his left arm. Eventually, he heard the car leave the paved road onto a gravel road, and about fifteen minutes later, the car stopped. The men took a couple of gas cans out of the back seat and filled the gas tank, and let Bremer out to walk around a bit, then once that was done, they were off again. A few hours later, Alvin told Bremer, *"We're close to Rochester, Minnesota. and we'll put you off there on a dark street."* Once they reached town, Alvin turned off the main road and stopped the car to let him out. [26]

"Alright, Bremer, beat it! Get out of the car and face the direction we are in but which is not the direction you are to walk. Count to fifteen slowly before you remove your bandages. Then turn about face and walk into Rochester. Be sure not to let anyone recognize you. Go to the bus depot. Take the 9:40 bus to Saint Paul. In Saint Paul, don't go to the bus depot. Get off before you get there. Get a cab, and go home. But don't let anybody see you." [27]

Bremer did as he was told, and counted slowly to fifteen. But he hesitated momentarily when he heard the car stop. When he heard it take off again, he removed the bandages from his eyes, and got a glimpse of the back tail lights as the car vanished into the darkness. Edward G. Bremer was now a free man. His legs were still wobbly so he walked around in circles for a while until he regained his composure, and walked in Rochester. He walked and walked but couldn't find the bus station. Finally, he asked a man where the bus station was, but he told him there wasn't a bus to Saint Paul that night.

After finally arriving at the bus station, a lady there called a taxi to take him to the train station, where he bought a ticket to Owatonna. At Owatonna, he took a cab to the bus station, and bought a ticket back to Saint Paul. Finally back in familiar surroundings, he asked the bus driver to let him off after crossing the Wabasha Street bridge, then took a cab home.

A couple of days later, the gang met up to divide the ransom money. $25,000 for each of them in fives and tens. The remaining $25,000 was split between Harry Sawyer and Charles Fitzgerald, who was still in bad shape from being wounded during the South Saint Paul robbery. The question now was how to go about laundering the money. They decided to put Doc on an airplane to Reno to launder it there as they had the Hamm ransom, but the Reno guys wouldn't touch it. They knew it was hot. They did, however, give Doc $7,000 to split between them. They had all of this money but couldn't spend any of it. Then things got worse. Someone in Saint Paul had leaked information to the feds – and to the newspapers – that Fred Barker and Alvin Karpis had been spotted in town, and might be involved. Harry Campbell's name was brought up as well. Werner Hanni contacted Tulsa authorities to get Campbell's mugshot and fingerprint cards. They also sent for the records on Alvin and Fred.

Back in Saint Paul, Walter Magee retraced his route with Hanni and Nathan, who found the red-lensed flashlights, which they soon traced back to the store where Alvin had bought them. When they showed the sales clerk his photo, she immediately recognized him as the man who had bought them. Meanwhile, a farmer in Portage, Wisconsin had found several discarded gas cans on the side of the road and contacted the county sheriff. The cans were then turned over federal agents, who shipped them to their lab in Washington D.C., where they found some latent fingerprints. They proved to be those of Doc Barker. Alvin had specifically told everyone to not take off their gloves on the way to release Bremer. But Doc had spilled gasoline and had taken off a glove to wipe it off, and had inadvertently picked up a gas can with his bare hand and left his prints. Now, Alvin, Fred, Doc and Harry Campbell were named as suspects in the kidnapping. [28]

It was late February or early March when the boys contacted a quack doctor, Dr. Joseph P. Moran, to have their fingerprints removed. Moran had flown for the U.S. Signal Corps during the Great War, then graduated from Tufts Medical School in Boston. When he returned to Illinois, he operated a successful practice in LaSalle, but soon, his drinking nearly drove him out of business. For additional money, he turned to performing illegal abortions, for which he was prosecuted in 1928 when one of his patients died. He served two years of a ten year sentence at the Illinois State Penitentiary in Joliet. While there, he became head surgeon and so impressed the warden that he helped Moran get paroled, and also helped him get his medical license reinstated. But within just a short time, Moran was again prosecuted for illegal abortions and returned to prison for another 11 months for violating his parole. [29]

Dr. Joseph P. Moran

Thanks to his gangster connections, especially with a jewel thief named Oliver "Jew" Berg, he was able to set up a practice in Chicago, where he became the official physician of the Chicago Teamsters, Chauffeurs, Warehousemen and Helpers Union. In 1934, he got word out that he could remove fingerprints and do plastic surgery to change a person's appearance. Alvin and Fred didn't want to be connected with any further crimes, so they contacted Moran to remove their fingerprints. His fee was $1,250.

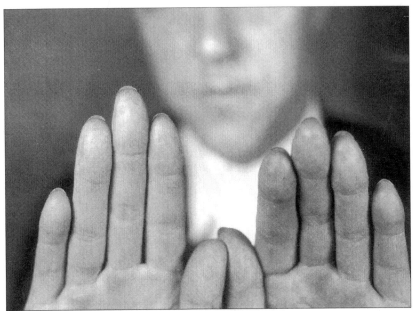

Moran's operation was a success removing Alvin's fingerprints, but not so for Fred Barker (FBI Photo)

Moran operated on Alvin's and Fred's fingers by first taking rubber bands to reduce the blood flow in their fingertips. Then, he injected cocaine into each fingertip to dull the pain. Once this was done, he used a scalpel to peel the layers of skin off to remove the fingerprints. Once he was finished, he bandaged their fingers. Once the cocaine wore off, the pain was excruciating, and nearly drove Fred insane. The surgery worked for Alvin but not for Fred. What was worse, they couldn't feed themselves, shave themselves, etc. until their fingers healed. [30]

On the evening of March 20, 1934, George Zeigler was standing in front of the Minerva Tavern at 4811-13 W. Cermak, in Cicero, Illinois. As he lit a cigarette a car drove up onto the sidewalk and someone inside yelled, *"Hey George!"* As he turned around, he was hit by four shotgun blasts. One of the slugs nearly blew his face away, making it all but impossible to identify him. However, he had several club membership cards in the name of "J. George Zeigler" and a $1,000 bill was in his wallet. The cops were certain they had a big-time gangster on their hands, as his killing was very similar to the hit carried out on Gus Winkeler, and was probably done by the same people. The police took his fingerprints and then called the feds. [31]

It took some time for the police to identify the body. At first, he was identified as John A. Rhodes, wanted for stealing checks in New York. But papers found on him led the police to an apartment at 7827 South Shore Drive, where lived a couple using the names George B. and Irene Seibert. When the police got there, Mrs. Seibert had disappeared, and the landlady let them into the apartment. Evidence of another apartment at 2141 Gunderson in Berwyn was discovered. They were eventually led to a gas station that he had been using as a contact location. Then came the big surprise. The fingerprints of George Ziegler, aka "George Seibert", aka "B. J. Johnson", matched those of none other than Frederick Samuel Goetz – a suspect they had been trying to catch since the mid-1920's in connection with over a dozen gangland murders; including the Saint Valentine's Day massacre on February 14, 1929. [32]

After Zeigler was killed, Alvin feared it would be only a matter of time before the feds caught up with them. Alvin and Dolores got out of Chicago and moved initially to Toledo, Ohio. Fred followed them with Paula the drunk in tow, and rented an apartment at 4419 W. 171st Street in Cleveland as "Mr. and Mrs. Earl Matterson"[33]. Harry and Gladys Sawyer fled to Las Vegas to lie low hoping things would cool off after a while. William Weaver and Myrtle Eaton moved to a cottage in Grand Forest Beach, Ohio using the names "Mr. and Mrs. J. A. Orhee". In the days the Bremer kidnapping, Weaver and Eaton had moved to Aurora, Illinois near Volney Davis and Edna Murray, and rented an apartment at 50 South 4th Street. From there, they moved to another apartment at 411 Claim Street in Aurora, which they shared with Doc Barker, who used the alias "Mr. Morley". Volney Davis and Edna Murray moved to a cottage on Lake Erie near Weaver and Eaton. Harry Campbell and Wynona Burdett also moved to Grand Forest Lake, renting a place under the names "Mr. and Mrs. George Wolcott, but they later moved to Cleveland, with Doc Barker staying with them. Willie Harrison and Doc Moran also moved to the area. [34]

Things were getting tough and everyone was frustrated. They had the Bremer cash but couldn't spend it. In addition, Paula the drunk was making life a living hell with her constant bickering. Volney Davis and William Weaver were fed up with the gang and wanted their cut of the loot, so they were paid about $20,000 each to shut them up. Volney then headed to Buffalo, New York to exchange his cut of the money for unmarked bills, and when he returned, he bought a Ford and moved to Glasgow, Montana, where Edna later joined him. They wanted to get as far away from the gang as they could, and life in the Wild West appealed to them. Volney and Corey Bates leased some land near Fort Peck Dam, where they built a saloon and gambling hall near Wheeler, which they called the "Hollywood Inn"[35]. Life was good until they were tipped off that the feds were snooping around Glasgow. Spooked, he and Edna fled to Kansas City. Weaver and Eaton took their cut of the loot and bought a chicken farm in Florida.[36]

Doc Barker was sent back to Chicago where he was able to unload about $25,000 through several stores, which was easy since it was in fives and tens. He was also able to peddle another $10,000 to John J. "Boss" McLaughlin, a local Democrat big wig, for ten percent. Mclaughlin, however, made some serious missteps and on April 26, his bookie, Edward Vidler, was arrested for passing some of the Bremer loot. McLaughlin was arrested on April 28. They were charged for dealing in unlawful currency, and on May 4, a Federal grand jury in Saint Paul indicted them, John J. McLaughlin Sr., John J. McLaughlin Jr., Alvin Karpis, Doc Barker, Phillip J. Delaney, Frankie Wright, William Edward Vidler and three other unknown suspects for the kidnapping of Edward G. Bremer. [37]

Eddie Green was shot in the back and mortally-wounded by Federal agents firing from the windows of his former hideout. He was unarmed. His wife Bessie was waiting in the car and taken into custody. He died nine days later. (FBI photos).

Other bad news reached the gang when they learned that on April 3, their former gang member, Eddie Green, had been mortally wounded by federal agents who were lying in wait for him at his former hideout at 778 Rondo Avenue in Saint Paul. The maids he hired to clean the house were startled to find federal agents inside going through his belongings. The maids told the agents that the man who hired them was using the name D. A. Stevens, and said he would be there to pick up a suitcase that morning. A few hours later, a green Hudson Terraplane pulled up and parked across the street. The driver got out and knocked on the kitchen door. She handed him his suitcase, but hurriedly shut the door in his face before he could hand her a ten dollar bill for her services. He turned and walked back towards the car, but as he reached the curb, the agents shot him in the back through the windows. His wife Bessie had been waiting in the car, listening to the radio, when he was shot dead before her very eyes. After searching him, the agents found that he was unarmed. Still alive, he was rushed to Ancker Hospital. Bessie was taken into custody. He had participated in the Fairbury robbery in Nebraska, and afterwards had joined the Dillinger gang shortly thereafter. Now, delirious and fading in and out of consciousness, he began spilling the beans about his associates, with his wife Bessie giving additional information, probably in hopes of cutting a deal to keep herself out of trouble. Bessie was no stranger to the underworld, having run the Green Lantern for Harry Sawyer for a while. Green told them that Alvin, Fred and Doc were traveling with an older woman posing as their mother. Using this information, they obtained the boys' prison records and fingerprint cards, which they then used to identify the fingerprint found on the gas can used in the Bremer kidnapping. It was Doc's. Eddie lingered on until dying on April 12. Up to this time, the feds had no idea that the Barker-Karpis gang even existed. This was the break they needed. [38]

A couple of weeks after Eddie was killed, Harry Sawyer's pal William "Pat" Reilly told John Dillinger about a place in Wisconsin where he and his gang could hide out for a while until things cooled down. It was a resort in Manitowish Waters, Wisconsin known as Little Bohemia Lodge, owned by Emil and Nan Wanatka. Reilly assisted the Dillinger gang on occasion, one reason being that his sister-in-law, Jean (Delaney) Crompton, was gang member Tommy Carroll's girlfriend. The arrangements were made and Dillinger and his gang arrived at Little Bohemia on April 20. The entourage included Dillinger, Tommy Carroll and Jean Crompton, John "Red" Hamilton, Homer Van Meter and his girlfriend Marie Comforti, and Lester

"Baby-face Nelson" Gillis and his wife Helen Gillis. Lester and Helen stayed in one of the nearby cabins while the rest of the gang had rooms upstairs in the Lodge. [39]

Lester "Baby-face Nelson" Gillis, John "Red" Hamilton (seated in car), John Herbert Dillinger, Tommy Carroll and Homer Van Meter arrive at Little Bohemia Lodge, April 20, 1934 (Author's illustration. Original in private collection)

Mrs. Wanatka soon began to feel t uneasy about these people, especially since they wore gun holsters under their jackets, which they rarely took off. The one they called "Jimmy" watched every move they made. He seemed friendly and courteous enough. Their son, however, thought "Jimmy" was a bully because whenever he played catch with him, he'd throw the ball too hard and it hurt his hand. Emil was getting suspicious as well, and began looking for photos of the Dillinger gang. Sure enough, he was certain it was them. "Jimmy" was actually Lester Gillis. Emil and Nan devised a plan to notify the authorities. Using a birthday party for one of her son's friends as a cover, she left and had her brother-in-law Henry Voss contact the feds, who in turn contacted Melvin Purvis in Chicago.

When Purvis was notified that the Dillinger gang was holed up at Little Bohemia he quickly put together a force of 17 agents and chartered a Northwestern Airlines flight to Rhinelander, Wisconsin. Another group of agents moved in to join them from Duluth. From the very beginning, thing were off to a bad start. Two of the cars they rented after reaching Rhinelander broke down just 30 miles from the lodge, forcing the eight agents from those cars to stand on the running boards of the remaining three cars, and endure the frigid Spring air the rest of the way. Once they neared the lodge about 7:15 p.m., they turned their headlights off and parked along highway 51. Once they pulled off the road, they walked carefully through the woods towards the lodge. As they drew closer, the Wanatkas' Collies heard them and began barking. But no one paid any attention to them.

Three other men were at the lodge playing cards. One of them, John Hoffman, was a salesman from nearby Mercer, and the other two, John Morris and Eugene Boisneau, were Civilian Conservation Corps workers. It was getting late, so they paid their bills and left together in a Chevrolet Coupe. As Hoffman started the car, he turned on the radio. Agents stepped out, identified themselves as Federal agents, and ordered the men to stop. However, the men never noticed them. They couldn't hear anything outside because the radio was too loud. Nor did they see the agents, since it was dark and it had begun to snow. Fearing it was Dillinger trying to escape, the agents began shooting at the car. Boisneau was killed. Morris was hit by four bullets, fell out of the passenger's side door, and managed to make his way back inside to the kitchen. Hoffman had also been wounded and crawled into the woods to take cover. The gunfire alerted Dillinger and his gang. They grabbed their weapons and began firing from their bedroom windows into the darkness. The agents returned fire, shooting up the lodge, but not hitting anyone inside. The gang quickly made their escape out of an upstairs window, onto the roof, and then to the ground, where they quickly disappeared into the woods. [40]

Lester Gillis had also heard the commotion, pulled out a machine gun and began firing. After commandeering a car, he was met by agent Carter Baum in another vehicle. In Baum's car was a local constable. Nelson shot them both, killing Baum, seriously wounding the constable, and driving away.

Jean (Delaney) Crompton,
Helen Gillis, Marie Comforti
(FBI photo)

The only members of the gang left inside were Helen Gillis, Jean (Delaney) Crompton, and Marie Comforti. They were quickly taken into custody but the rest of the gang escaped. The raid was a complete and total failure for the Division of Investigation. Dillinger had escaped once again. Further down the road from the lodge, he, Van Meter and Hamilton had commandeered a 1930 Ford Model A from Ray Johnson and made their escape. Tommy Carroll made his way on foot into Manitowish Waters, where he was able to steal a Packard and get away.[41]

When stories about the fiasco at Little Bohemia hit the papers, the public was outraged, and were calling for Hoover to be fired and the Division of Investigation disbanded. He was furious. The botched raid had been a complete and utter disaster, and a huge embarrassment for the Division of Investigation. Not only had a federal agent and a civilian been killed, two other civilians and a constable had been seriously wounded. Dillinger, Van Meter, Hamilton, Carroll and Gillis had gotten away unscathed. [42]

After driving all night, Dillinger, Hamilton and Van Meter were getting exhausted and could barely keep their eyes open. They had to find somewhere to sleep, so they pulled off down a small country road near Hastings, Minnesota, parked, and dozed off. But their respite would be short. They were soon thereafter awakened by the sound of gunfire. Suddenly, there was a loud "pop!" as Hamilton jerked violently and screamed, "I'm hit!" before falling forward. Dillinger looked behind them. On the crest of the hill was a police car. Three cops were firing at them with high-powered rifles. One of their rounds had found it's mark. It had penetrated the rumble seat of the Model A, bored through the seat and into Hamilton. The bullet made a hole in his lower back the size of a half-dollar, bored through his small intestine, and lodged in his liver. The seat was soaked in blood. Dillinger and Van Meter bailed out, stood on the running boards and returned fire. The cops got into their car and sped off in the opposite direction. [43]

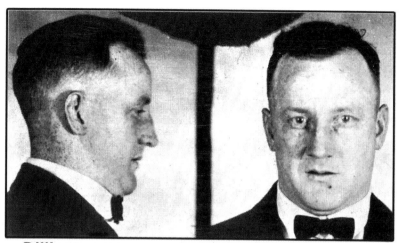

Dillinger gang member John "Red" Hamilton

Not wanting to stick around for the cops to return with reinforcements, they took off. As they sped down the road, a Maroon 1934 Ford V8 Deluxe Sedan approached. Realizing this was their chance to ditch the Model A, Van Meter quickly jumped out and forced the driver, Roy Francis, to stop. Francis was out for a drive that day with his wife Sybil, and their infant son. As they were herded out of the car, they were told to turn around and look away, since they didn't want them to see them load Hamilton into the back seat. Mrs. Francis was fearful that they would harm her baby, and began to cry, but Dillinger smiled and reassured her, *"Don't worry lady! We like kids!"* Finally, they drove off in the Sedan, leaving Roy, Sybil and their baby with the Model A. [44]

They had to get Hamilton to a doctor and drove to Chicago to contact Dr. Joseph P. Moran. But Moran refused to help, claiming they were "too hot". In frustration, Dillinger contacted his friends Bobby and Joey O'Brien at the Hi Ho Club, saying that Hamilton had been shot badly and needed help. They told him to meet them at Seafood Inn on North Avenue in Elmhurst. The

O'Brien's called Elmer Farmer, who then called Volney Davis, and asked him to meet them at the Inn. When Volney and his girlfriend, Edna Murray, arrived, they saw the O'Brien's, John Dillinger and Homer Van Meter. Doc Barker joined them as well.

When Dillinger explained what had happened, The O'Brien's responded by saying much the same thing Moran had said; Dillinger's gang was "too hot", and the Syndicate couldn't afford any more heat from the feds. Dillinger asked Volney if he could help. He agreed, and he helped load the dying man into the back seat of his car. They headed back to his apartment at 415 Fox Street in Aurora, Illinois, with Dillinger and Van Meter following closely behind.

Hamilton's wound had become badly infected with gangrene and it was now just a matter of time. No underworld doctor dared take a chance to help. There was nothing they could do except keep him as comfortable as possible. The end came quickly. He died on April 30, 1934 – just seven days after the shootout at Little Bohemia. The next day, Volney helped Dillinger and Van Meter bury their friend in a gravel pit he knew of about ten miles south of Aurora. They dug a shallow grave and covered the body with quick lime. Volney then placed a roll of rusty wire over the grave to mark it. After saying their final farewells, they drove away.[45]

Alvin was running out of money and needed to find some steady work, and spoke with some of his contacts in Toledo. They put him in touch with Arthur V. Hebebrand and James "Shimmy" Patton, owners of the Harvard Club, in Newburgh Heights, a suburb of Cleveland, who hired him to keep tabs on their opposition, who was harassing the hell out of them. They made him a nice offer, which he accepted.[46]

The Harvard Club was one of the largest illegal gambling joints in Ohio, if not in the Northeast. Karpis said, *"The club was located in an old walkathon hall, and it had enough room to accommodate every crap table in the entire city of Reno. There were slot machines, crap tables, roulette wheels, and on the first night I visited the place, there must have been a crowd of at least 1,500 people, all anxious to throw away their money. And they were doing it with the blessing of a few cops and politicians who drew their own share of the house take."* [47]

Alvin learned as much as he could about the Club's operations. He made sure everything was on the up and up, but also kept tabs on the opposition. He took down their names, and in addition to taking down their addresses, he drove to their houses taking detailed notes of each home, its surroundings, family members, and the habits of each person coming and going. He then had a courier deliver copies of his files to their boss, telling him that if he kept trying to shake down the Harvard Club, everyone in his files would be killed, and their houses would be burned to the ground. The tactic worked like a charm. [48]

Hebebrand and Patton were so impressed with his work that they cut him in for a percentage of the profits, plus they provided a nice bungalow for him and Dolores in Cleveland at 3977 W. 140th Street. The bungalow had a garage with a dirt floor, and Alvin buried the Bremer loot there for safekeeping. Dolores loved the place, especially since she found out that she was pregnant, and wanted to finally settle down. The rest of the gang arrived in Cleveland soon thereafter. [49]

Once they were settled in, Alvin had some business in Toledo, but also frequented Edith Barry's whorehouse at 524 Southard Street with William J. Harrison, Harry Campbell, Charlie Fitzgerald, Fred Barker, Jimmy Wilson, Doc Moran's nephew, and Doc Moran himself. Moran drank a lot and would play "The Last Roundup" five or six times in a row on the Victrola, much to the annoyance of everyone else. But Barry's place was a good hangout, and the gang especially enjoyed two of the girls there, Lou and Peaches. It was a good diversion from constantly looking over their shoulders. Harry and Gladys Sawyer joined them in June after he had sent a letter to Alvin via General Delivery, wanting his cut of the Bremer loot, and they moved in with Fred and Paula.

Then one day, tempers flared again. Doc Moran showed up at the Casino Club, over in Point Place, on Summit Street. Ted Angus rented the place from his mother-in-law, and it was another of the gang's favorite hangouts. Moran came in that afternoon, drunk as usual, and sat down at a table with Russell "Slim Gray" Gibson, Fred Barker and Doc Barker. Soon, they got into a drunken brawl, mainly because Moran was getting loud and running his mouth. They yelled for him to sit down and shut up, but he just kept getting louder. Finally, Moran boasted, *"I've got you guys in the palm of my hand!"* [50]

That night was the last time Dr. Joseph P. Moran was ever seen alive. Doc and Fred decided they wanted to do some "night fishing" using Ted Angus's motorboat which he kept at Bay View, near the Club. Once they got about a mile off shore, Doc Moran became the bait. They shot him, weighed his body down with some large rocks,, and pushed him overboard. A few weeks later, Fred said, *"Doc will do no more operating. The fishes probably have eat him up by now."*[51] It wasn't long until a badly decomposed body washed ashore. The man had been dead for so long it couldn't be immediately identified, but after dental records were checked, the remains were determined to be those of the missing Dr. Moran.

1934 was turning out to be a bad year for criminals all across the country. Bonnie Parker and Clyde Barrow had been hiding out in Bienville Parish, Louisiana with Henry Methvin's family. Methvin was facing the death penalty in Texas, and his father, Ivy Methvin, worked out a deal. If they would pardon Henry, he would help them get Bonnie and Clyde. In the early morning hours of May 23, Dallas County, Texas Sheriff's Deputy Bob

Alcorn, former Texas Rangers Frank Hamer, Ben "Manny" Gault, and Ted Hinton, Bienville Parish Sheriff Henderson Jordan, and his Deputy Prentiss Oakley, positioned themselves in the brush alongside the road leading South from Gibsland. Ivy Methvin had parked his log truck on the west side of the road so that the front faced east, and jacked up the back to make it appear that he had broken down. [52]

Shortly after 9:30 a.m., the posse spotted a 1934 Ford Fordor Model 40 Sedan coming towards them. As it came closer, the driver began slowing down. It was Clyde. He recognized Methvin's truck but didn't see him. Suddenly, Alcorn stood up and yelled "HALT!" Bonnie sees the men stand up with weapons drawn and screams. But before Clyde can reach for his weapon, all Hell breaks loose. The posse unleashes a torrent of lead that riddles the car and the two desperadoes inside. The car lurches forward, and comes to rest in a ditch. Then silence. The men carefully approach the car with their weapons still trained on the occupants. But as they draw nearer, they see that it's all over. Bonnie Parker and Clyde Barrow are dead. [53]

Former Dillinger gang member Tommy Carroll and his gorgeous girlfriend, Jean Delaney-Compton. She was the sister of Dolores Delaney, girlfriend of Alvin Karpis.

On June 7, in Waterloo, Iowa, Dillinger gang member Tommy

Carroll and his girlfriend Jean (Delaney) Crompton stopped to get gas. As the attendant checked the battery, he noticed a pile of license plates in the car. He called the police as soon as the couple drove away, and a search for their car began. As luck would have it, Tommy decided to stop at a bar in the 600 block of Lafayette Street called Jack's Welcome Inn. Unbeknownst to him, the police station was directly across the street. An officer walked up to him and said, *"You're under arrest!"* Carroll said, *"Like Hell I am!"* and as he went for his gun, the officer slugged him in the jaw. Tommy jumped up and ran down an alley as more officers closed in and began firing. Tommy fell to the fusillade of lead, and was transported to Saint Francis Hospital where he died. Jean was taken into custody and was later charged with harboring a fugitive.[54]

July 22, 1934. John Dillinger was gunned down outside the Biograph Theater in Chicago by federal agents led by Melvin Purvis. Illustration on left by author. Right: Dillinger's body in ambulance. Photographer unknown.

Then in Chicago on July 22, the Indiana bad man, John Herbert Dillinger, decided he wanted to see a movie. He was accompanied by two women, Hungarian-born Madam, Anna Sage and Polly Hamilton-Keele. Sage faced deportation over running a house of prostitution. She wanted to cut a deal to stay in the country. Discovering who Dillinger really was, she contacted Melvin Purvis' office to set him up for an ambush. In exchange for helping the feds, she expected to be spared from being sent back to Hungary. She would wear a bright orange skirt as a signal for them to move in on him. Polly was completely oblivious to the trap, and had no clue that her guy, "Jimmy Lawrence", was actually Public Enemy Number One himself. As they left the Biograph, Purvis and his men moved in. Suddenly realizing he was in danger, Dillinger bolted, but before he could get away, he was gunned down in an alley just a few doors down from the theater. In the end, the infamous "lady in red", as she became known, was double-crossed and shipped off to Hungary anyway. [55]

Dillinger gang member Homer Van Meter was cornered by police in Saint Paul and shot to pieces on August 23, 1934.

Slowly but surely, the steady decimation of the big time gangsters continued. In Saint Paul on August 23, Dillinger gang member Homer Van Meter was shot and killed in an alley at Marion Street and University Avenue as he fled police. As he turned to fire his .45 he was cut down in a hail of machinegun bullets.[56]

Alvin and Fred saw the handwriting on the wall. They would

have to get rid of the rest of the Bremer loot, and quickly. When they went to dig it up they found that the leather satchel they'd buried it in had leaked, and the money was soaking wet. Alvin sent Dolores out to buy some small electric fans, and they laid the money out on the floor and used the fans to dry the money out as best they could. Finally, they contacted a rich hoodlum in Gross Point, Michigan; Cassius "Cash" McDonald. He said he could launder the money in Cuba for fifteen percent. He also guaranteed it wouldn't turn up in Havana, but in other places like Mexico City and Caracas. Harry Sawyer and William J. Harrison were the ones delegated to head to Miami to make arrangements with McDonald, and on September 1, 1934 they checked into the El Commodoro Hotel. On September 5, McDonald flew to Havana using the name "O'Brien". Once there, he contacted a brokerage firm, saying he wanted to exchange some American currency for Cuban gold. He was able to exchange $18,000 for $14,000 in gold, which he then exchanged the following day at the National City Bank in Havana for fourteen $1,000 bills. On September 10, McDonald contacted the brokerage firm again, this time to exchange $72,000 in small bills into larger bills, which he was able to do with no difficulties.[57]

Meanwhile, on September 5, Campbell's girlfriend Wynona Burdette, Harry Sawyer's wife Gladys, and Paula the drunk went drinking at Cleveland Hotel bar, where they soon got plastered, and completely out of control. The bartender called the police, and after a violent scuffle with the officers, they were carted off to jail and charged with being drunk and disorderly. Had they not had Gladys' five year old daughter Francine with them, they might have been released. However, she innocently told the cops who her mother and the other ladies really were. As a result, the feds were called and the ladies were transported to the Division of Investigation's Chicago office, where they gave a detailed account of the gang's activities. The women were then were released. Gladys returned to Saint Paul, Wynona returned to her sister's home in Hominy, Oklahoma, and Paula was so rattled over the ordeal mentally that she wound up in the state insane asylum in Texas. The feds were as a happy as possums in a persimmon tree. This was the big break they needed. The hunt for the fugitives was on! [58]

Late that night, Fred, Doc and Campbell banged on Alvin's door and told him what had happened with the girls. He contacted Hebebrand and Patton at the Harvard Club, who advised them to leave Cleveland as quickly as possible. No one had to tell him twice. They were already packing. The first thing they did was to scout out Fred's apartment. When the coast was clear, they went in and retrieved their machineguns and other weapons. Next, they went to Campbell's apartment. After scouting it out, they suddenly saw a light come on inside, and saw the shadows of several men standing outside. [59]

They quickly left the area and contacted a friend of theirs, a guy named Josh. Alvin told him the situation, and said he needed to check things out a bit more. So they cooked up an idea to get Josh inside. Harry gave Josh a check signed with the alias he had used to rent the apartment, and told him to tell the guys that the tenant had written him a bum check and he wanted his money. The ploy worked like a charm. When Josh knocked on the door, some burly guys answered, grabbed him and roughed him up a bit. They were armed to the teeth. He showed them the check and said all he wanted was to collect the money he was owed. They bought the story, and allowed him to leave. He told the boys, *"Goddamn! They've got shotguns, pistols, and everything in there! They grabbed me and roughed me up a bit, but those guys aren't local cops. They're feds!"* [60]

When they scouted out Freddie's apartment, they saw five or six cars parked out front, with about five men per car. They had gotten their guns out just in the nick of time. Alvin rushed to his bungalow. He packed a Thompson, plenty of ammo, and a couple of bullet-proof vests. Dolores was packed and ready to go, so they all headed to Toledo, and then on to Chicago. After dropping in to see Ma Barker for a while, Alvin decided that now might be a good time to get out of the country, and take a trip to Cuba until things died down. So they headed for Miami and checked into the El Commodoro Hotel, Hotel Located at 33 SW 2nd Avenue. This was one of the nicest, and newest, hotels in Miami and had been built only 9 years before in 1926. It stood 14 stories high and had 250 rooms. Once they got into their room, he called his friend Joe Adams, who owned the Biscayne Kennel Club. Joe told Alvin he could store his car and guns there while he was in Cuba, so the following day they drove to Key West and boarded the S.S. Cuba for Havana.

Fred meanwhile, wanted to find a quiet place to live. He was tired of all the noise, hustle and bustle of the big city, and just wanted to get away to someplace quiet. He asked Joe Adams if he knew of any such place. Adams told him a friend of his, Carson Bradford, had a cottage near Ocala, and said he would look into it. [61]

Once Alvin and Dolores reached Cuba, they found a nice beach house near Veradero, just up the coast from Havana. One of his friends, Joe "Nate" Heller, had the inside dope on what was going on with all the gangsters hiding in Cuba, and he kept Alvin up to date on everything. One day, they visited the American Bar in Havana. The bartender's wife was reading a copy of *Famous Detective Magazine*, when she turned a page and saw a photo of him. She laughed and said, *"If I didn't know better, I'd swear that was you!"* Alvin smiled sheepishly as he glanced at the photo and answered, *"Yeah, image that! I suppose there is a bit of a resemblance!"* [62]

Alvin and Dolores kept up with goings on back home, and listened every afternoon to Lowell Thomas on the radio. One afternoon, Mr. Thomas reported that former Dillinger gang members Harry Pierpont and Charlie Makley had been shot during an attempt to break out of the Ohio State Penitentiary in Columbus, Ohio. On October 12, 1933, they sprung John Dillinger from the Allen County jail in Lima, Ohio, killing Sheriff Jeff Sarber in the process. After the Dillinger gang was arrested in Tucson, Makley and Pierpont were extradited to Ohio to be tried for Sarber's murder, and were sentenced to death. While sitting in the Death House, Makley came up with the idea to use fake guns to break out of prison just as Dillinger had done at the Lake County Jail in Crown Point, Indiana the year before. So, he had some soapstone sent to him and Pierpont, which they used to carve the fake pistols. On September 22, the two pulled the phony guns on the guards. The guards didn't buy it. They opened fire on them, killing Makley and seriously wounding Pierpont, who survived long enough to be executed in the electric chair on October 17. [63]

Then in late October, Thomas announced that "Pretty Boy" Floyd had been killed. On October 22, Floyd had been cornered at a farm outside East Liverpool, Ohio by Federal agents led by Melvin Purvis. As Floyd fled across the farmer's field, agents opened fire and shot him dead. Adam Richetti had been caught a short time earlier after a brief gun battle. He was eventually extradited to Kansas City, Missouri to stand trial for his alleged role in the infamous Union Station massacre. He was found guilty and executed in Missouri State Penitentiary's new gas chamber on October 7, 1938. [64]

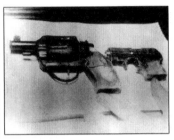

On September 22, 1934, Dillinger gang members Charles Makley (left) and Harry Pierpont attempted to escape from death row at the Ohio State Penitentiary with guns carved from soapstone and blackened with shoe polish. The guards didn't buy it, shooting Makley dead, and wounding Pierpont - who survived only to be executed on October 17, 1934 for the murder of Allen County, Ohio Sheriff Jess Sarber.

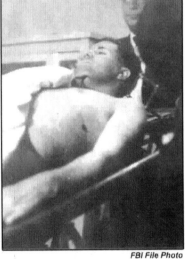

FBI File Photo

Charles Arthur "Pretty-boy" Floyd
Killed by federal agents led by Special Agent in Charge Melvin Purvis near Liverpool, Ohio on October 22, 1934

Again, in late November, Thomas announced that yet another

member of the Dillinger gang, Lester Joseph Gillis, a.k.a. George 'baby-face' Nelson, had been killed following a shootout in Barrington Illinois on November 27. Gillis had been mortally wounded during the shootout, but he killed two Federal agents, Herman Hollis and Samuel P. Cowley, and then stole their Hudson. He died shortly after midnight and his body was left at a cemetery near Niles Center. After Floyd's death, "Baby-face" had been named Public Enemy Number One. Now that he was dead, Alvin Karpis was moved to the top of the list. [65]

 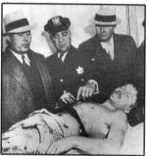

Lester Joseph Gillis a.k.a. "George 'baby-face' Nelson. On November 27, 1934 in Barrington, Illinois , he killed two federal agents in in a gunfight and stole their car. He, however, was mortally-wounded and died a few hours later.

Alvin and Dolores were having the times of their lives, and hung out in some of Havana's finest clubs, such as Sloppy Joe's and The American Bar, and the Hotel Nacional de Cuba. One day, he was standing in the lobby of the Parkview Hotel in Havana when he spotted a tall, stocky fellow – obviously an American – who walked up to the desk and registered. When the clerk asked him for his name, Alvin overheard him say *"L. E. Kingman"*, and that he lived in Jacksonville, Florida. Right away, Alvin grew suspicious of this new visitor and later that evening during dinner, Heller told him that a federal agent had arrived and had shown him Alvin's photo. Alvin asked, *"What's the agent's name?"* He replied, *"Kingman"*. [66]

That wasn't the only thing that struck a nerve. He went to cash a $1,000 bill at the Royal Bank of Canada, located at the Prado in Havana. He asked for $750 in tens and $250 in fives. When he checked the money, he noticed that some of the bills were discolored. Once he got to the hotel, he checked them over much closer and realized they were the same bills he had buried in the garage at his bungalow in Cleveland! Cassius McDonald, who had promised none of the Bremer money would show up in Cuba had lied. Kingman's presence in Havana could mean only one thing. The feds had traced the money to Cuba. It was time to leave.

When they got back to Miami, he called Joe Adams. He found a house for them at 1121 N. E. 85th Street, being rented by a Mrs. Grace Thomas. He also hooked Alvin up with a brand new 1935 Buick Special Sedan. Duke Randall bought for him, under the name LeRoy Morrison, from the Unger Buick dealership. Once they were all settled in, Alvin learned that Fred and Ma had rented a cottage up near Ocala, along Lake Weir, and decided to drive up with Harry and Wynona to visit with them for a while. Dolores was tired of traveling, so she stayed behind to rest.

Alvin was pretty impressed with the cottage. The place was right off Highway 41, and it was quiet. It was good to see Fred and Ma again, and they spent a lot of time fishing and hunting deer. Harry also spent a lot of time drinking, and one day, he got lit and nearly got them all caught. Late one evening while drunk, he was driving near Ocklawaha when a young couple ran a stop sign in front of him. He couldn't stop in time, and collided with their car. The couple was killed. Miraculously, their baby was uninjured. When the Sheriff arrived, he saw that Harry was drunk and hauled him to jail. He just knew the cops would take his fingerprints, but for some reason, they didn't. He was shaking in his boots, terrified that the Sheriff would start asking the wrong questions, and talking to the wrong people.

Suddenly, he had an idea. Harry told the Sheriff that he needed a new car, and hinted that he would be willing to buy one from a dealer right there in his town if he could work out a deal for him. Surprisingly, the Sheriff said that as a matter of fact, one of his best friends ran the Ford agency. So the Sheriff took Harry over to pick out a car. He bought a brand new Ford Sedan and donated $250 towards the care of the couple's baby. Satisfied with the deal, the Sheriff shook his hand, thanked him, and let him go. No questions asked. [67]

Finally, their "vacation" was over, and it was time to head back to Miami. As they were leaving, Ma was unusually chipper, and said something that completely shocked him. Ma didn't much care for the boys' women, but she had taken a liking to Dolores, and told Alvin to let her know when the baby was born and she'd come down to help out. They said their goodbyes, and he left with Harry and Wynona for the drive back home.

CHAPTER 8:
GATOR JOE

Gunfight between Fred Barker and Federal Agents at Lake Weir, Florida. January 16, 1935 (Author's illustration)

In November 1934, Joe Adams called his friend Carson Bradford, a successful automobile salesman. He said he had spoken with a well-to-do elderly lady, Mrs. Blackburn and her sons, who were interested in renting his vacation cottage up at Lake Weir, just on the outskirts of Ocklawaha in Marion County. She had cash and would pay up front. He knew Marien, his wife, wouldn't be too happy about him renting it out, but he could use the extra cash. Without ever meeting his prospective tenants, he agreed to rent it out, and Marien reluctantly sent Adams the keys. So Adams contacted Mrs. Blackburn. She was thrilled. When she came to pick up the keys and get directions, she plopped down a wad a cash large enough to choke a horse.[1]

Bradford had built the cottage in 1930. It was right on the

north side of Lake Weir, at 13250 East Highway C-25, (Highway 41 in 1935) just about 30 miles Southeast of Ocala. The Bradfords had also built a boat house and pier just a short distance from the cottage. It was beautiful and peaceful, a far cry from the noise and traffic in Miami. Furthermore, the neighbors were friendly and watched out for each other. The Bradfords would come here often and spend time fishing, swimming, and just kicking back to relax.[2]

Cottage looking northeast (Photo courtesy George Albright III)

"Mrs. Blackburn" was really Arrie Barker. When she and Fred arrived at the cottage, she immediately fell in love with it. Ma was happy as could be. The little cottage was like Heaven to her. She was thrilled. It was a two story building with four bedrooms upstairs. Two of them faced south with a clear view of the lake. The screened front porch extended across the front of the house, with a spacious kitchen and dining room.

Photo of cottage taken from boat ramp, looking North (Courtesy George Alright III)

North side of cottage looking towards Lake Weir (Photo courtesy George Albright III)

The Bradford's boat house (Photo courtesy George Albright III)

The feds where hot in Chicago, and they had found out where Doc, Byron Bolton, and Russell "Slim Gray" Gibson and his wife were holed up. The tip came from a doctor in Toledo, Ohio who stated that a young woman patient, Mildred Kuhlman, had recently married to a man named "Esser", and that they were living in an apartment building in Chicago practically right under their noses. They knew that Kuhlman was Doc Barker's girlfriend, and were positive that this "Mr. Esser" was most likely Doc. The Chicago Bureau soon learned that Mildred was a frequent visitor to an apartment occupied by Barbara and Patricia Lonquist, at 439 Arlington Place. Barbara was a confidential informant, and the Chicago office found it advisable to place a tap on her phone. However, the only other suitable location to place the other end of the tap was at an apartment at 425 Arlington Place occupied by Dr. William R. Cubbins, his wife Cora, and his sister-in-law Alma Brindley. [3]

One day in mid-December, Dr. Cubbins left his office at 104

South Michigan Avenue to go to the nearby University Club. While he was there, a page boy announced he had a visitor. The young man identified himself as agent with the Justice Department, and stated; *"The federal government wants your aid. In short, I wish to quarter a group of my men in your home. We will desire to make necessary wire connections. I believe there is a woman living at 439 Arlington Place, through whom we can make the desired contacts. We have considered using quarters at Nos. 2450 and 2440 Lake View Avenue, but we have concluded that 425 Arlington Place – your home – will be the ideal location."* [4]

Dr. Cubbins was speechless, and realized that phone taps could mean only one thing. There were dangerous men in the neighborhood. But having served honorably as an Army Major during the War who had led men in combat, and being an honorable man, he replied, *"Sir, our facilities are at your full disposal!"* Once the Agent had left, Dr. Cubbins hurried home to inform his wife and sister-in-law to expect important visitors. He swore them all to secrecy. [5]

Once the phone tap was set up, the agents kept a constant vigil listening in on every call made to and from the apartment at 439 Arlington Place. Another group of agents had established an apartment across the street at 442. They watched everyone who came in and left, but it was Mildred Kuhlman herself that they watched most intently. They had tried to follow her on one occasion, but had gotten stuck in traffic and lost her. Finally, during the first week of January 1935, they watched as Mildred left wearing a fur coat, walked down the street past Dr. Cubbins' apartment building, and caught a cab. They quickly followed her and observed her entering the apartments at 432 Surf Avenue. This location was immediately placed under surveillance.

Meanwhile, as the feds continued their relentless decimation of gangsters large and small across the country, tensions arose between several of the Barker-Karpis gang members. William J. Harrison had become especially troublesome. Harrison was too talkative, and Fred was afraid he would rat them out to the feds over the Bremer kidnapping to save his own neck. He contacted Doc and said it needed to be dealt with. A few days later, Fred received a letter from Doc: *"I took care of that business for you boys. It was done just as well as if you had did it yourself. I am just Standard Oil – always at your service. Ha-ha!"* [6]

On January 5, Doc had lured Harrison to Ontarioville, in DuPage County north of Chicago, claiming he needed him to help retrieve some of the Bremer money that had been buried in a barn. When Harrison showed up, Doc blew him away with his Tommygun. He then chopped off his head and limbs, doused the remains and the barn with paraffin, and burned it to the ground. DuPage authorities found the roasted torso in the ashes the next day. The head and limbs were never found. The remains were subsequently identified as Harrison's.[7]

Earl J. Connelley was the Special Agent in Charge of the operation at the apartments where members of the gang were living, having been appointed to replace Special Agent in Charge Sam Cowley who had been killed in Barrington, Illinois on November 27, 1934 by "Baby-face" Nelson. He assigned twelve agents to keep the place under surveillance. The Surf Lane Apartments were located at 432 West Surf Avenue, and "Mr. Esser" resided at Apartment G-1. [8]

The waiting paid off. About a week later on January 8, they saw none other than Arthur "Doc" Barker himself strutting up the sidewalk arm in arm with Mildred. The agents quickly rushed the couple. Doc tried to run but slipped on the ice and fell. He was unarmed. All he could do was look up and smile sheepishly at one of the agents, a new guy who had just recently joined the Division of Investigation, Walter Walsh, asked him,

"Where's your heater Doc?" He answered, *"It's up in the apartment."* Then Walsh replied, *"You're lucky Doc. Ain't that a hell of a place for it?"* For a tough guy, Doc didn't put up much of a fight this time. They loaded him and Mildred into a car and drove them off to jail. Doc knew this was the end of the road for him. He was tired of running.[9]

Arthur "Doc" Barker   **Mildred Kuhlman**

Connelley quickly dispatched another group of twenty agents to the Pine Grove Apartments at 3920 Pine Grove Avenue. The raid on Bolton's apartment was a comedy of errors from the beginning, as the feds tear-gassed the wrong apartment, throwing the tenants into a panic. The local police were called. They came very close to opening fire on the feds, thinking they were the bad guys. It turned into a Mexican standoff until finally the cops realized they were federal agents. Once that drama was over, the agents called for the occupants in the apartment to come out. Russell "Slim Gray" Gibson's wife Clara Gibson was the first to come out, gagging from the tear gas, and holding her Chow in her arms. Next was Byron Bolton, who initially claimed his name was "William Harrison". Another female in the apartment, Ruth Heidt, came out as well. She was William J. Harrison's ex-wife. [10]

RUSSELL GIBSON
a.k.a. "SLIM GRAY"

MRS. CLARA GIBSON

JANUARY 8, 1935
Mrs. Clara Gibson, wife of Russell Gibson, and Byron Bolton were caught in a raid by Federal agents at 3920 Pine Grove Ave. Chicago. Bolton orignally gave his name as "Willie Harrison". Russell Gibson was killed in a gun fight with agents as he tried to escape down a fire escape.

BYRON BOLTON

Russell Gibson, however, tried to take advantage of the confusion. He quickly donned a bulletproof vest, grabbed a

Browning Automatic Rifle and a .32 Colt automatic pistol, and bolted out of the window and down the fire escape. He didn't have a chance. Agents were down below and at the end of the alley. He opened up on them with the BAR, but missed, and then his weapon jammed. They immediately returned fire and He fell to the ground, hit with a round from a .351 rifle that penetrated the front edge of his vest, went through his chest, and flattened against the vest's rear panel. It had proven useless. Gibson was taken to a nearby hospital, but died shortly thereafter. His last words to the agents were, *"I'll tell you nothing!"* [11]

Post Office where Ma Barker mailed her fateful letter to Doc Barker, telling him about Gator Joe. (Photo by Tony E. Stewart)

Meanwhile, back at Doc's apartment, the agents hit pay dirt. As they searched through his belongings, they found lots of weapons and ammunition. Among the weapons they found was a Thompson submachine gun. When the serial number was traced, it was proven to have been the Thompson stolen from Officer Yeoman's patrol car during the South Saint Paul, Minnesota robbery that left Officer Leo Pavlak dead. The agents also found a map of Florida with a red circle drawn around Ocala, and the area around Lake Weir. Also found was a letter from Ma Barker. "Ma" had never been the sharpest crayon in the box, and in her letter she had told Doc all about the alligator the locals alternatively called "Big Joe", "Gator Joe" or "Old Joe". Fred had gone out trying to bag this monster. Gator Joe was estimated to be about sixteen feet in length, and was said to be one of the oldest alligators in that area. He had been seen for years. The agents all read the letter, looked at each other and smiled. They too, would go hunting for Old Joe. Unbeknownst to Ma Barker, she had just sealed their fate.[12]

The task at hand now was to keep Doc's capture under wraps. Hoover knew that if the Chicago papers got wind of it, the chances of catching up to Fred and Alvin Karpis would be gone. The fact that Doc Barker was in custody had to be kept a closely guarded secret. The Chicago police department was mad as Hell over the raid, and the Chicago Tribune raked Hoover over the coals. In frustration, he shot back, *"There has to be a reason why criminals flock to Chicago!"*

Byron Bolton, who also used the alias "Monty Carter", seemed very willing to cooperate, and he took a particular liking to special agent Brown, since Brown had treated him with some measure of courtesy. He told Brown that he and William Harrison had taken a trip to Miami but hadn't contacted any of the Barkers there, so he didn't know their exact location at the time. However, he said that he and Harrison later met Doc Barker and Russell Gibson about thirty of fifty miles south of Macon Georgia. Doc told Bolton that Ma and Fred had rented a place about six to eight hours south of Macon, on a fresh water lake near Ocala, with good deer hunting and fishing, and that the lake had a motor boat. Then, they told Bolton about the alligator, Gator Joe. The same alligator Ma had mentioned in her letter. [13]

From Bolton's description, the area where Fred and the other gang members were hiding was along Highway 41, which matched other information they had received. Bolton had also given them a lineup of everyone involved in the kidnapping of Edward Bremer. The hideout in Bensenville had been secured by Both Bolton and George Zeigler through Elmer Farmer. The others involved were Volney Davis, Harry Campbell, Doc and Fred Barker, and Alvin Karpis. [14]

Hoover quickly sent Special Agent in Charge Connelley to Florida with his men to find Fred Barker and the rest of his gang. Time was of the essence. Gator Joe was the clue they needed to locate Fred Barker, and hopefully Karpis and the rest of the gang. The agents arrived in Jacksonville, then drove down to Ocklawaha, where they checked into the Ocklawaha Inn. The next morning, they got busy checking every fresh water lake within the area Doc had circled on the map to see if any of the locals knew of such an alligator. [15]

Fred was having a ball. Like his mother, he loved living on the lake. It sure beat the freezing temperatures, ice and snow further north. Compared to Chicago, Florida was like Heaven. One of the few pleasures he had in life was fishing, and while they were here for the winter, he intended to do as much fishing as he possibly could. He went on frequent fishing trips with some of the neighbors. When they told him all about Old Joe, he lit up like a Christmas Tree and asked them all about him. He wanted to be the one to bag the beast so one day, he bought a small hog from a local farmer, killed it, then towed the hog behind his boat as bait as he circled the lake. He hoped Gator Joe would come after it so he could shoot him with his Thompson. [16]

234

On January 14, a jailer in Jacksonville advised Connelley to contact a former Deputy Sheriff named Milton Dunning. Upon doing so, Dunning informed the agents that an alligator matching the description of Old Joe had lived in Lake Warburg, but that it had disappeared about 1925. They kept looking. Agents Campbell and Jones checked Lake Bryant, and Connelley and Brown checked Lake Bowers and Lake Weir. The next day, Connelley dropped in to visit the Postmaster at Ocklawaha, J. T. Greenlee, who was shown photos of the gang members they were searching for. He didn't recognize any of them, but he said that individuals under the names Blackburn and Summers had rented a cottage from Carson Bradford, and had been receiving mail along with newspapers. Mr. Greenlee suggested they contact Frank Barber, who just happened to live on the lane leading to the Bradford cottage. Barber, it turned out, had been a former employee of the Federal Penitentiary in Leavenworth, Kansas. Connelley dropped in discreetly to speak with Barber, and made arrangements to pay him for any assistance he could render. Also, Barber kept an eye on the cottage for the Bradfords. When Joe Adams arranged for the 'Blackburns" to rent it, Mrs. Bradford left him a note about letting them have the keys to look over the place.[17]

When shown the photos, he immediately recognized the photo of Ma and Fred as the people using the name Blackburn, and that they had a Buick Coupe. Harry Campbell was the man using the name Summers. He said "Summers" had left with a woman a few days earlier but "Blackburn" had told Barber that they were expected back that very night. The woman was no doubt Harry's girlfriend, Wynona Burdette.[18]

Close-up view of the southwest corner of the cottage. Arrow points to the room where Fred and Arrie Barker were found dead (FBI photo)

Alvin Karpis had been to the cabin only a short time before and had returned to Miami with Harry and Wynona, but the agents had missed them by mere days. That afternoon, Connelley and Agent Brown took up a discreet position near the cottage, and saw Arrie Barker and Fred Barker in the yard. They quietly left and made preparations to raid the place. It was hoped that Harry Campbell would return with Ms. Burdette. Connelley drew up a map of the property and surrounding area, and assigned them their positions around the house. [19]

Early the next morning, January 16, 1935, around 5:30 a.m., fourteen Federal agents quietly took up positions around the cottage. Agent J. T. McLaughlin set up west of the cottage on Highway 41 to divert traffic away coming from that direction, and Agent T.G. Melvin did likewise east of the cottage. The County Sheriff's Department also assisted in directing traffic. Along Highway 41 at the north side of the cottage were positioned Agents C. B. Winstead, G. C. Woltz, Charles G. Campbell, and D. P. Sullivan. In order to prevent any escape attempt to the north or east of the house, Connelley positioned Agents Brown and McKee were positioned along the lane leading to and from the house. The lane itself was blocked by a car parked across it. Along the west side of the cottage were positioned Agents "Doc" White, R. L. Jones, A. A. Muzzey, J. L. Madala, Thomas McDade, and Special Agent in charge E. L. Connelly. Everyone was in position by 6:00 a.m.[20]

Connelley was the first to approach the house and shouted, *"We are Federal agents of the Division of Investigation, United States Department of Justice! Come out with your hands up and you will not be harmed, provided you do as instructed. Otherwise, we will use gas to drive you out!"*. No response. They waited about ten minutes, and Connelley shouted once more, this time saying, *"Fred Barker, come out with your hands up!"* After this, Connelley had agents McDade and Muzzey fire tear gas canisters through a window. Immediately, they heard a woman scream. But then everything went quiet once again.

Connelley called out one last time for them to come out of the house. This time, he distinctly heard a woman's voice ask someone in the house, *"What are you going to do?"* and then *"All right, go ahead!"* Thinking the people in the house intended to come out and surrender, Connelley stated for Fred to come out first. But instead suddenly, the muzzle of a Thompson machinegun appeared from the upstairs southwest bedroom window. Fred fired about 50 rounds at Connelley, who took cover behind a tree. Agent White returned fire. Fred then rushed downstairs and fired from the front door with a rifle. White, armed with a .351 Winchester semiautomatic rifle, returned fire. Connelly then fired into the house with his 30-06 Springfield rifle. Again, machinegun fire rained down from the window, then sporadically from different windows throughout the upstairs.[21]

Bullet-riddled tree in front of cottage. Boathouse in background. (Photo by Tony E. Stewart)

Close-up of the bullet-riddled tree trunk (Photo by Tony E. Stewart)

Fred then turned his attention to Agents Jones and Muzzey who were positioned on the west side of the house near a grove of orange trees. They returned fire, and Fred then began firing from the rear of the house towards the agents positioned along the highway. Fire was also directed from the opposite side of the house, as bullets from a .33 Winchester rifle had been fired through the home of Mrs. A. T. Westbury, who lived on the east side of the Bradford property near the lake. He had positioned firearms near the windows and entrances all over the house, and was running frantically firing at the agents, who thought the whole gang was there shooting back at them.

The townspeople soon realized that something big was happening, and several curious onlookers arrived but the officers kept them at a distance as best as they could. One of them, George Albright, drove up but saw that the road was blocked. He parked in the middle of the road and walked down to the edge of the property. He stood beside an oak tree but Fred saw him and fired. As the bullets hit the oak tree, Albright quickly ducked for cover, ripping the seat of his pants. Undaunted, he made his way to the local hardware store, bought a new pair of pants, and returned to his perch behind the oak tree to watch all of the excitement. [22]

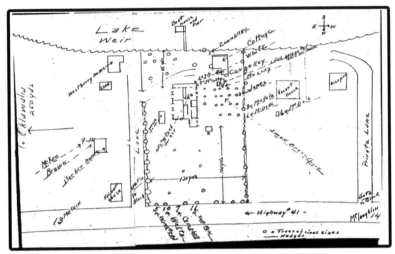

Map showing the positions of Federal agents at the Bradford cottage on January 16, 1935 (FBI photo)

The battle continued on for about three more hours, with Fred firing sporadically as if to conserve ammunition. The agents concentrated the majority of their fire towards the upstairs southwest bedroom where most of the shots had come from. Finally, about 11:30 the firing had ceased. After a considerable amount of time elapsed, Connelley asked the cottage's caretaker, a black gentleman named Willie Woodberry, to attempt to gain entry and see what the situation was inside. He had been hired by Ma as a caretaker and cook, and lived with his wife in a small outbuilding on the property. He didn't like the idea, but they jokingly bribed him with $20.00 if he'd go in to check on them. Chances are that since they knew him, he wouldn't be in any danger anyway, so reluctantly he agreed.[23]

Curious locals watching the gun battle between Federal agents and Fred Barker at the Bradford Cottage, January 16, 1935 (photo courtesy George Albright III)

Finding the door locked, he cut a hole in the screen door, reached in and unlocked it. He eased into the house, and called out, *"Hey it's me, Willie! Don't shoot! Are y'all ok? Is there anything I can do?"* Silence. The tear gas still lingered in the air, so he covered his nose and mouth with a handkerchief. He slowly and quietly walked through the house, but didn't see anyone. He noticed, however, that a cot had been positioned in the front room facing the main entrance. This was most likely where Fred had been lying when he fired out the front door. He then walked up the staircase, and called out again. *"Are you alright? Do you need help?"* Again, no answer. [24]

The first place Willie checked was the southeast bedroom, which was Ma's bedroom. No one was there, but there was a trail of blood on the floor leading to the other bedroom. He followed it to the southwest bedroom. It was shot all to Hell, as was most of the house. But it was obvious this room had caught the brunt of the fighting. What he saw next sent shivers down his spine. He couldn't open the door all the way, as something was behind it blocking it. He peeped around the door to see what it was. It was Ma Barker. She was lying in a fetal position, barefooted, on her left side just inside with her back against the closet door. Her hands were under her face. She had caught three bullets in the chest, and one had gone through her heart. Fred was lying face down in the middle of the room at the foot of one of the two beds in the room. His right arm was extended, and just beyond his right hand lay a Thompson machinegun. The agents had caught him with a volley that sent ten rounds across his left shoulder and chest, and another shot from a 30-06 had hit him in the right temple. He had been hit with so many bullets they had ripped his shirt into tatters. Blood was everywhere.

Willie made his way through the debris littering the floor towards the window. He yelled down to the agents, *"They are both up here! They are both dead!"* Connelley and his men rushed upstairs. From the position of the bodies, it was ascertained that the fatal shots were most likely fired by agents J. C. White, A. A. Muzzey, and R. L. Jones, who had taken up positions near the southwest corner of the house. Connelley made arrangements for the county coroner and local law enforcement officers to come view the crime scene. Marion County Judge L. S. Futch served as the coroner, and he was joined by County Attorney Wallace E. Sturgis, District Attorney A. P. Buie, and Prosecuting Attorney A. P. Meadows. Sheriff S. C. Thomas, who had been directing traffic away from the area, arrived at the scene. Once the agents finished examining the crime scene and taking photos, he and Mr. Futch then arranged for a Coroner's jury to view the bodies. Harold Martin and his assistant F. L. McGehee, then transported the bodies to a mortuary operated by Samuel R. Pyles at 1322 East Fort King Avenue, in Ocala.[25]

Barker hideout immediately after the gun battle
(FBI photo)

Word spread quickly that Federal agents had killed the last of the Barker gang, and crowds of people poured in to get a glimpse of the bodies. Many were appalled that an old woman had been killed, so Hoover had to come up with something quickly. He explained to the Press that "Ma" Barker had also been firing at his men while resisting arrest, and she had died clutching a machine gun in her hands. It was a bold-faced lie, but most everyone bought it.[26]

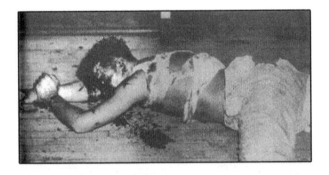

Fred and Arrie Barker dead in the upstairs southwest bedroom of the Carson Bradford cottage as found by caretaker Willie Woodberry after the agents sent him to check on the Barkers after the shootout (FBI Archives)

The End
Hearse carrying the bodies of Fred Barker and his mother Arizona (Clark) "Ma" Barker leaving the Carson Bradford cottage on the way to the morgue in Ocala. January 16, 1935.

FBI file photo

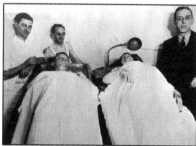

The End:
Fred Barker and his mother, Arizona Donnie (Clark) Barker at Pyle's Mortuary, January 1935.

They would remain there for almost nine months before their remains were finally claimed for burial by George E. Barker.

They were interred at Williams-Timberhill Cemetery in Welch, Oklahoma next to Herman Barker, who had been killed in a police shootout in Wichita, KS in 1927.

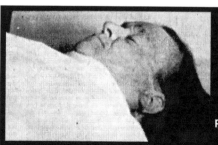

Ma Barker in death at Pyles' Mortuary in Ocala, Florida.

Photographer unknown

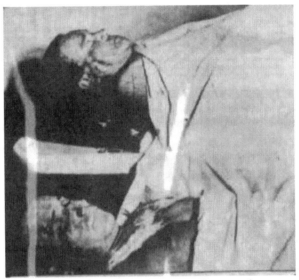

Another photo of Fred and Ma Barker at the morgue.

In late January, George E. Barker was represented in a lawsuit by Joplin attorney Claude Kenney against the government for the return of the money found on his wife Arrie, and son Fred, which federal agents had taken following the gun battle. Agents had found a large arsenal of weapons and ammunition along with $14,293 in cash, in addition to their Buick. Kenney argued that the government couldn't prove the money came from criminal activity so therefore, it rightfully belonged to him as their next of kin. The Court agreed, and after all the fees and other payments, he eventually received about $1,200 total.[27]

Mr. Kenney helped George make the necessary arrangements to have Arrie and Fred returned home for burial, and on September 25, 1935, their bodies were transported to Haines-Woodard Funeral Home in Webb City, Missouri.

BODIES OF GANGSTERS TAKEN THROUGH HERE
"John Woodard, a member of the Haines-Woodard

Undertaking Company of Webb City, MO., stopped at the Ancell Brothers Service Station Friday morning with the bodies of Fred Barker and his mother Kate (Ma) Barker, who were shot to death by federal agents at Ocklawaha, Fla., eight months ago. Woodard, who left Florida with the bodies Wednesday, expected to reach Webb City in time for a scheduled burial service Saturday morning in Timber Hill cemetery, an isolated graveyard three miles west of Miami, Okla. The bodies, in expensive caskets, were to be placed beside that of Fred's brother, Herman Barker, who killed himself rather than surrender to officers at Wichita, Kan. Arrangement for the burial were made by Claude Kenney, a Joplin attorney who has been trying to secure for George Barker, husband and father of the slain persons, $16,000 in money and valuables left by the two."[28]

SMALL GROUP ATTENDS LAST RITES FOR PAIR SLAIN IN FLORIDA

"Freddie Barker and his mother, Kate Barker, who were slain eight months ago in Florida by government agents after a prolonged battle, were buried together Tuesday afternoon in a cemetery west of Miami, by the side of Herman Barker, another son of the widely known "Ma" Barker, who died with a machine gun in her hands. Approximately 50 persons, a few of them relatives and including George Barker, father and husband of the two, attended the brief service."[29]

Once the services were over, and folks began leaving the cemetery, George stood with some of his kinfolk by the graves of his wife and his two sons. After a long silence, with tears pouring down his haggard face, he told them about how Arrie would drag the boys to church most every Sunday, then said, *"I don't know why, because every time I'd try to straighten them up she would fly into me. She never would let me do with them what I wanted to!"*[26] He truly had wanted to raise his boys to be hardworking, honest men but when he tried to discipline them,

Arrie fought him tooth and nail. She refused to correct them during their formative years when they needed it most, nor would she allow anyone else to lift hand to them. Then, when they began getting into trouble, she lashed out at their victims as "liars", and claimed the police and the courts were "persecuting" them. Lloyd was in Leavenworth, Doc was in Alcatraz, and now she, Fred and Herman were dead. The proverbial buzzards had come home to roost.

Fred Barker's weapons cache after the raid (FBI Archives)

The weapons found after the raid were listed in a report written by Special Agent R. A. Alt on January 22, 1935, and were as follow: [30]

GUNS, PISTOLS, CARTRIDGES and EMPTY SHELLS
TAKEN AT THE BARKER HOUSE IN OKLAWAHA FLORIDA,
ON JANUARY 16, 1935

One Thompson machine gun – 1921 model – number

illegible.

One Thompson machine gun – 1921 model - number illegible.

One 50-cartridge drum for Thompson Machine gun – did contain 50 loaded shells.

One 50-cartridge drum for Thompson Machine gun – empty

One 100-cartridge drum for Thompson Machine gun – did contain 70 loaded shells.

One stock for Thompson Machine gun – Number 13578

One 45 Calibre Colts Automatic Pistol Number C-160657 – damaged by bullet hitting handle

One 45 Calibre Colts Automatic Pistol Number C-161841

Nine 45 automatic pistol clips

One 380 Automatic Colt Pistol – number illegible

Five 380 automatic pistol clips

One Browning 12 gauge Automatic Shotgun – Number 92870

One Remington 12 gauge pump shotgun – Number 272907

One Winchester 33 calibre lever-action rifle – Number illegible

The above were shipped to the Division, Washington D. C., on January 22, 1935 via Railway Express Agency. A 1934 Buick Straight 8 Coupe, engine number 2884746, with 1934 Illinois license tag number 750-974, was found in the garage. The Barker's personal possessions were loaded into the car, and it was transported to Jacksonville until family members could claim them later.

Front Room (Photo courtesy of George Albright III)

Dining room showing the fireplace in the front room (photo courtesy George Albright III)

Other side of Dining Room showing front entrance (Photo courtesy George Albright III)

Upstairs Southeast bedroom. (photo courtesy George Albright III)

The other side of the same bedroom. The caption written on the footboard seems to say "The bed $10,000 was found in." (Photo courtesy George Albright III)

Entry door of Southeast bedroom, (Photo courtesy George Albright III)

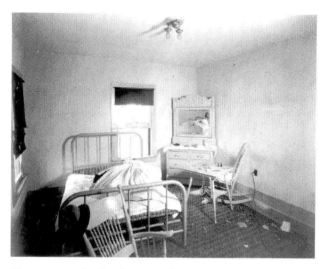

Rear upstairs bedroom. (Photo courtesy George Albright III)

Ma Barker's body was lying in front of the closet door on the right. (Photo courtesy George Albright III)

The other side of the same room, taken from entrance. (Photo courtesy George Albright III)

West side of Southwest bedroom (Photo courtesy George Albright III)

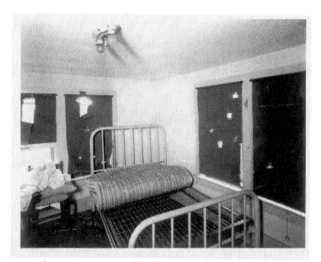

Another upstairs bedroom (Photo courtesy George Albright III)

East side of the Bradford Cottage. (Photo courtesy George Albright III)

Barker graves at Williams-Timberhill Cemetery, Welch, Craig County, Oklahoma. (Photo by Autumn LeMasters, June 25, 2016)

Arizona (Clark) Barker's funeral home marker at Williams-Timberhill Cemetery. She is buried between her sons Herman and Fred.
Photo by Autumn LeMasters, June 25, 2016

256

Fred Barker's funeral home marker at
Williams-Timberhill Cemetery.
Photo by Autumn LeMasters, June 25, 2016

UPDATE - OCTOBER 2016:

George Albright III and Tony E. Stewart in
front of the Carson Bradford cottage.
Photo by Tony E. Stewart.

The Barker Death House has been transported by barge across Lake Weir to a new lot owned by the Marion County, Florida parks department, where it will be turned into a museum!

Recently, Marion County, Florida Tax Assessor George Albright III was able to acquire the Bradford cottage, where Fred and Ma Barker were killed, in order to preserve it as a museum. As of this writing (October 2016) it has been moved by barge three miles across the lake to the Carney Island Recreation and Conservation Area, where it will be preserved as a museum.

Crime author Tony E. Stewart was at the Bradford cottage in October 2016, to take photos of the house as it was being prepared for the move. Much thanks to Tony for sharing these to the author for inclusion into this book! Also, much thanks goes to Mr. George Albright III for his help with the photos and other details for use in this chapter.

Tony E. Stewart at the Lake Weir Post Office window where Ma Barker mailed her letters. (Courtesy Tony E. Stewart)

Just down the beach a short distance from the Bradford cottage is a bar named after – you guessed it – none other than Lake Weir's most famous resident, Gator Joe himself. When the alligator was finally killed in 1956, he measured at 16.5 feet. The bar has one of Gator Joe's paws on display. Several businesses in Ocklawaha have done well from the notoriety surrounding the Barker shootout. Another such establishment, appropriately named "Ma Barker's Hideaway Bar, is located on Highway 25, just up from Gator Joe's.

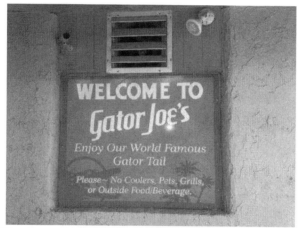

The famous Gator Joe's in Ocklawaha, Florida
(Photo by Tony E. Stewart)

Gator Joe's - Located just down the beach from the Bradford cottage, and named for Lake Weir's most famous resident. Photo by Tony E. Stewart

Another view of Gator Joe's (Photo by Tony E. Stewart)

Tony E. Stewart on the walkway to the Bradford Cottage boathouse. (Photo courtesy Tony E. Stewart)

Tony E. Stewart with his Tommygun
(Photo by George Albright III)

Bradford Cottage ready to be moved onto barge
(Photo courtesy George Albright III, via Tony E. Stewart)

House on the barge and on the way to its new home
(Photo by George Albright III, via Tony E. Stewart)

Much thanks to Louis LaCava for the use of this amazing photo! It is the perfect image for the end of this chapter!

CHAPTER 9:
MANHUNT: THE SEARCH FOR ALVIN KARPIS

Danmore Hotel in Atlantic City about 1930
(Photographer unknown)

Once they were back in Miami, Harry left Wynona to stay with Dolores while he and Alvin went fishing in the Gulf Stream and then near Everglades City to fish for mackerel. Luckily for them all, Harry decided to stay one more day, and they went out fishing again and didn't get home until almost dark. As he approached his place, he saw a car parked about a block away. Dolores and Wynona were sitting in the front seat visibly shaken, and crying. Something was wrong. He pulled over and stopped as Dolores ran over to his car. She was crying hysterically. [1]

"Alvin, You should have come home sooner!" He told her to take it easy, and asked her what the problem was. She had trouble speaking, but finally, through her sobs, she said, *"The feds shot up Freddie and Ma's place! Freddie's dead! Ma's dead too!"* He, Harry and Wynona realized that if they had left the day Harry had originally planned to return to Lake Weir, they would probably have been killed as well. Harry's decision to stay one more day to fish saved their lives. Shortly before they got back from their fishing trip, Dolores had received an anonymous call from one of their underworld friends in Cleveland, telling her that they needed to get out of town by nightfall. Then a short time later, while listening to the radio, she heard about Fred and Ma being killed. Alvin rushed over to Joe Adam's place where he picked up the $1,000 Adams had been holding for him. Duke Randall also handed Dolores a note he had written to William Morley, who owned the Danmore Hotel in Atlantic City, asking him to take good care of her. Alvin put them on a train to Atlantic City and said he and Harry would meet them there later with the Buick. [2]

On the same day Fred and Ma were killed in Florida, the feds arrested Elmer Farmer in Bensenville, Illinois in connection with the Bremer kidnapping. He admitted everything. The following day, Harold Alderton, the former owner of the house at 180 May Street, where Bremer had been held, was arrested in Marion, Indiana. The feds contacted the Bremer family in Saint Paul, and Edward arrived at the house in Bensenville on January 19. As he walked through the house, he closed his eyes and listened to every sound. The trains in the distance. The children playing outside. The dogs. Everything. It was just as he remembered it. When he walked into the bedroom, he knew for a fact that this had indeed been the place. He remembered the wallpaper in the minutest detail, and here it was again. This was it. The wheels of Justice would begin to move faster now. Kidnapping George Edward Bremer would prove to be the worst mistake the Barker-Karpis gang ever made. [3]

Dolores and Wynona arrived in Atlantic City about 2:00 p.m. on Friday, January 18, and took a cab from the train station to the Danmore Hotel, at 123 South Kentucky Avenue. They registered as Mrs. A. B. Graham and sister of Macon, Georgia, and were assigned to a room on the 4th floor, room 400. Once they got settled in, Dolores called the desk. Daniel Young, Morley's partner, answered the phone. She asked if he were Mr. Morley, and Young said, "No, he's across the street at the cigar store. Would you like for me to have him come over?" Dolores told him that wouldn't be necessary, and ended the call. A few minutes later, she came down to the lobby, then crossed the street to the cigar store, where she met Mr. Morley and his wife, and handed him the note that Duke Randall had written for her. It asked Morley to take care of his friend Mrs. Graham, and to see to it that she got a good doctor.[4]

Alvin and Harry arrived at the hotel early the next morning at about 1:00 a.m., and were checked into room 500 as R. S. Carson and G. C. Cameron, from Rock Harbor, Florida. After learning that the girls were on the 4th floor, Alvin asked for another room near theirs, and were moved to room 403. Alvin stayed in 400 with Dolores, and Wynona stayed with Harry in 403. Alvin then asked if there was a garage where they could park their car, Young recommended the Coast Garage, just down the street, so Alvin called the garage attendant, James Smoot, to park the car for him.[5]

The following morning about 8:45, Alvin came downstairs to the lobby and took a short walk up the street to stretch his legs, and when he returned, he saw the bellboy, Grady Boney, in the lobby. Handing Boney a twenty, he asked him if he'd go get him some shaving cream, Listerine, and some other personal items. James V. Hewitt's Pharmacy was just down the street at 105 S.

Kentucky Avenue, so Boney hurried down there to pick up the items Alvin asked for. While Boney was out, Mr. Morley arrived and saw Alvin's note to call him. Alvin wanted to find a doctor for Dolores, and Morley recommended Dr. Carl Surran, whom he knew very well, as Surran had delivered one of their children in 1932. So he called for the doctor, who arrived around 11:00 and took Dolores into one of the vacant rooms to examine her. [6]

Meanwhile, Alvin invited Morley up to his room. He was interested in renting a furnished apartment, and asked Morley if he knew where he might find one for about $75.00 per month. Not knowing of anything himself, he woke Young up and asked him to come into the room and join the discussion. Alvin told them he had a kennel of racing greyhounds in Miami that he intended to move to California, and that Duke Randall was making good money working at Joe Adams' dog track in Biscayne Bay, Florida. The conversation then moved from apartments and dog tracks to clothes. They all needed some warm clothing since all they had was what they were wearing in Florida, and he asked for their recommendations. Morley referred him to Sloteroff's on the corner of Arctic and Virginia Avenues, and had his handyman, William Haiges, take Alvin and Harry to Sloteroff's in his car. [7]

While there, Alvin bought a dark oxford grey overcoat and two suits. The suits would have to be altered, and the tailor said he would have them finished by 5:00 that afternoon. Alvin handed him a $50 to pay the tab, and put the overcoat on as he headed back to the car. Haiges had another errand to run for himself before heading back to the garage. One of his dogs had died, and he dropped in on his veterinarian, Dr. Goldberg, on Virginia Avenue to check on the results of the post mortem he had ordered for the dog. From there, Haiges drove back to the garage and parked Morley's car. Alvin then drove his Buick to a service station to have the oil changed, and had the attendant install a Hades heater. Then it was off to have it washed and waxed so he'd have it ready to go by Sunday.[8]

Meanwhile, Dolores and Wynona were out doing what women do best – shop. They needed some warmer clothing also, and took a cab to Learner's Dress Shop at 1326 Atlantic Avenue, where they bought and coats totaling about $50, then returned later that afternoon to buy some slips and nightgowns. From there, they went to Elger S. Hill's haberdashery at 133 Atlantic Avenue. Finally, they headed back to the hotel with two huge shopping bags with rope handles, which the poor bellboy had to lug up to their rooms. Unbeknownst to them, however, their stay in Atlantic City would be shorter than expected.[9]

At 2:30 a.m., Sunday, January 20th, the Police Department in Atlantic City received a broadcast teletype from Jacksonville, Florida, which stated:

"GB454 1-20-35 POLICE INFORMATION WANTED BY JACKSONVILLE, FLORIDA POLICE ON A SERIOUS CRIMINAL CHARGE. WHITE MAN FIVE FOOT TEN DARK COMPLEXION DARK HAIR DARK EYES VERY SLENDER BUILD ACCOMPANIED BY WOMAN WHO WILL BECOME MOTHER IN FEW DAYS. DRIVING NINETEEN THIRTY FIVE BUICK SEDAN NINETEEN THIRTY FIVE FLORIDA LICENSE D5306 MOTOR 4949155. HE IS ARMED WITH .45 CALIBER AUTOMATIC AND RIFLE. REPORTED TO BE DANGEROUS. USE EXTREME CAUTION IN APPREHENSION. LEFT MIAMI JANUARY 16 NINETEEN THIRTY FIVE HEADED NORTH. WANTED BY JACKSONVILLE FLORIDA POLICE ON A CRIMINAL CHARGE. CONTACT ABOVE POLICE FOR CHARGES IF APPREHENDED. RADIO WEST HARRISBURG PENNSYLVANIA 2:30 A.M."[10]

The information was given to each patrolman as they called into the station from their boxes. Officer Elias Saab called in at 3:25 a.m. from his box at the corner of Kentucky Avenue and the Boardwalk. He decided to check some of the garages, and since he was closest to the Coast Garage, he decided to start there and see if any of the cars matched the description in the bulletin. To his surprise, he found it. He immediately called Captain Yates, who then dispatched Detectives Mulhern, Brennen, and Witham. After questioning James Smoot, he told the detectives that the occupants of the car were staying at the Danmore Hotel. A patrolman was assigned to guard the car, and three other officers hurried over to the Danmore to find out who the men were. Roberts, the bellboy, told them that a party had arrived from Florida. He called Mr. Morley to come downstairs to speak with the officers. But Morley wanted to avoid trouble in his hotel, and told them he felt it simply involved a young unmarried couple who were expecting a child, who were wanted on state charges in Florida. Furthermore, he said he didn't know who was registered, since his partner, Daniel Young, handled booking, and had the room cards locked up in the safe. [11]

All of the noise and ruckus had awakened Mrs. Morley, who dressed and came downstairs to see what was going on. The officers explained the situation, and she said the persons in question were probably the two guests in room 403. Not wanting any disturbance, she went to the room and softly knocked on the door. Alvin answered and she asked him to come outside, saying she needed to speak with him. They went into the next room, 404, and she told him, "The law is downstairs looking for someone from Florida who had gotten a girl in trouble." He was horrified, and wanted to hide under the bed, but Mrs. Morley would have none of that, and began pushing him towards the door. As she did so, three officers came up to the 4th floor with their guns drawn. Two stood on either side of room 403, while the other officer, seeing the door to 404 ajar, entered and was face to face with Alvin. The officer stuck his gun in Alvin's face, demanding to know who he was.[12] Alvin played dumb, and demanded, *"What is all this? Don't point that gun at me. I haven't done anything!"* [13]

Another of the officers banged on the door, *"Come out of there. Come out with your hands up!"*

Alvin said, *"He's probably a little hung-over. We had a party last night and he drank too much. Is that why you're here? Did we make too much noise?"*

Alvin continued playing dumb, and the detectives were beginning to buy the act. Then he said, *"Look, I'll go in there and get the guy out. He's probably still drunk. He doesn't realize that you guys are policemen. I'll get him."*

Finally, the officer said, *"All right. Go in and bring him out, but remember, we have these guns on you every minute!"* [14]

Alvin opened the door, then jumped back against the wall. Harry opened up with his .45, firing wildly. While he didn't hit anyone outside in the hall, one slug blasted through the opposite wall into the Alvin's room, and hit Dolores in the calf of her right leg. The bullet went completely through her calf and hit the wall on the far side of the room. Wynona quickly bandaged the wound, and when the coast was clear, they joined Alvin and Harry in the hallway. [15]

The officers began to retreat down the stairs. Finding that the rear stairwell was unguarded, Alvin and Harry made their way downstairs with the girls in tow, and with Dolores limping badly. They made their way out of a rear entrance that exited out onto Westminster Avenue. Alvin told the girls to hide under the fire escape stairwell while he and Harry went to get the car. As the boys approached the Coast Garage, they saw several officers standing around the front of the hotel. The attendant, Smoot, saw them, and yelled to the cops, *"Hey! Here they are! Down here!"* While Harry opened fire on the cops, Alvin rushed in to get the Buick. He couldn't find it. As luck would have it, he found a pea green 1934 Pontiac Special with the keys in the ignition and a full tank of gas. They piled into the Pontiac and went to retrieve the girls. But he made a wrong turn into a blind alley. It was a dead end street. He turned around and headed back out. The cops were at the end waiting, but suddenly, he saw an alley and turned. Then after several more turns, he finally found the place where the girls were supposed to be. They weren't there. Knowing that they'd be caught soon if they didn't leave, they said their goodbyes to the girls, and drove away. [16]

1934 Pontiac Special stolen by Alvin Karpis in which he and Harry Campbell escaped Atlantic City (FBI archives)

Dolores and Wynona were shivering in the frigid New Jersey air, and decided to go back to their rooms. They had been standing outside in their bare feet and their nightclothes, and Dolores was growing weak from the loss of blood. Mrs. Morley saw them as they came back inside, and was horrified at seeing the blood gushing from Dolores' leg. She immediately called Dr. Surran who had her transported to Atlantic City Hospital.

Wynona was placed under arrest, and taken to the police station for questioning. [17]

Harry Campbell's girlfriend, Wynona Burdette

Alvin and Harry got out of town as fast as they could, and hit the back roads out of New Jersey. Once they knew they were home free, they found a secluded place to pull off the road and get some rest. Deciding to drive at night, they waited until the sun began to disappear over the horizon and headed towards Camden, New Jersey, where they got gas and a road map. Once they got across the Delaware River, they knew they'd have to switch cars. As luck would have it, as they neared Allentown, Pennsylvania, they came up behind a 1934 Plymouth with a doctor's emblem on the rear bumper. It was perfect. No one would pull over a doctor's car. They hurriedly pulled alongside and yelled at the driver. *"State Police! We want to talk to you!"*

The driver pulled over. Harry quickly jumped in and commandeered the car, and made the driver move over into the passenger's seat. He followed behind the Pontiac until they came to a side road. Alvin parked and left the Pontiac running and jumped into the Plymouth. They then drove away. When the cops found the Pontiac, they would think Alvin and Harry ran out of gas and were on foot. They would be wasting time searching for them around Allentown when they were already miles away.[18]

Dr. Horace Hunsicker turned out to be a pleasant fellow who told them he had been visiting his parents and was returning to the Allentown hospital. He said if he were gone for a few hours, no one would miss him. He seemed to actually be intrigued with this sudden adventure, and the three got along as though they were old buddies. The doctor's emblems on the bumpers worked like a charm. The boys ran into a police roadblock on the way towards Altoona, but when the cops saw the doctor's emblems, they waved them on through. Finally, they reached Ohio. They stopped at the Grange Hall in Wadsworth, where they took Dr. Hunsicker into the basement and tied him up near the furnace where he would stay warm. By this time, he realized who they were, and was afraid they were going to kill him. But they told him not to worry, and stuck a $50 dollar bill in his breast pocket so that he had money to return home on. They then headed towards Toledo in the Doctor's Plymouth. It would be a long, tiresome ride across northern Ohio, but they decided to ditch the car in Michigan. They left it at a tourist camp near Monroe Michigan, a little town situated just southeast of Detroit, then made their way back to Toledo, and Edith Barry's whorehouse, where Alvin had spent a lot of time the year before. Alvin shacked up with Edith, while Harry shacked up with one of her girls, Lillian Merea, who also went by the name Lou Poole.[19]

For the next ten days, Alvin and Harry laid low. They listened intently to the radio and read the newspapers to keep up with the latest news. They learned that Dolores and Wynona had been charged with harboring fugitives. Dolores had been transferred from Atlantic City Hospital to Hahnemann's Hospital for Women in Philadelphia under heavy guard, and on February 6, she gave birth to Alvin's son, whom she named Raymond Alvin Karpis. Alvin's father pleaded with authorities for custody of the baby, and offered to take in Dolores as well, if at all possible. He was given custody of little Raymond, and took him to Chicago. Finally, Dolores and Wynona were returned to Miami to be tried for harboring Federal criminals. They were found guilty and sentenced to five years in the Federal Women's Detention Farm in Milan, Michigan.[20]

Stolen Car Abandoned By Karpis, Pal

Police are shown examining the car which Alvin Karpis, abductor and public enemy number one, and his killer companion, Harry Campbell, abandoned near Monroe, Mich. The car was identified as that of Dr. Horace Hunsicker of Allentown, Pa., whom the desperadoes abducted near Quakertown, Pa., and released at Wadsworth, O. Police of Ohio and other states kept a sharp lookout.

Dr. Horace Hutsinger's 1934 Plymouth found at a tourist camp in Monroe, Michigan after being left there by Karpis and Campbell.

Edith's whorehouse would be one of the gang's primary hangouts in Ohio for the next few months as they tried to regain some traction. Their opportunities were dwindling quickly. All of the big time gangsters were now either dead or in prison, and all the up and coming hoodlums were more interested in robbing gas stations and Mom and Pop stores than banks. Volney Davis was still in play, but his days were numbered as well.

On January 30, Volney Davis, Jess Doyle, and John Langan robbed the Montgomery County Treasurer's Office in Independence, Kansas of $1,938. This was chicken-scratch compared to the jobs he pulled with Alvin and Fred. But the feds had been tailing him from Glasgow, Montana, where he had been running a saloon with Corey Bates. They caught up with him in Saint Louis, Missouri, and arrested him as he was picking up his Pontiac at a garage where he had it stashed. [21]

The two agents, Garrity and Trainor, who had Davis in custody, decided to charter a plane from Saint Louis to Chicago in order to expedite him as quickly as possible. But bad weather and low fuel forced the pilot to land in a field owned by William Matlock outside Yorkville, Illinois. Apparently thinking the pilot had experienced mechanical problems, Matlock's neighbor, William "Bill" Ford, jumped in his car and drove out to the see if everyone was alright, and to render whatever assistance was needed. The agents were no doubt pleased to see Ford, but not wanting him to know they were transporting a prisoner, Garrity removed Davis' handcuffs and leg shackles before getting into Ford's car. He drove them to the Nading Hotel and dropped them off. [22]

The agents entered the hotel lobby with Davis, and went to the bar. Trainor then went to the phone to call in while Garrity bought a beer for himself and one for Davis. But Davis picked up the mug and knocked Garrity off his stool, then bolted towards a window. As Garrity scrambled to his feet he got off three shots at Davis, but missed. Davis then smashed headlong through the window, got to his feet and ran as fast as he could. As luck would have it, he found a Ford with the keys in the ignition and a full tank of gas, and off he went. [23]

It would be just short of four months before federal agents caught up with him. By this time, the Division of Investigation had a new name. On March 22, it officially became the Federal

Bureau of Investigation (FBI). On June 1, 1935, Volney Davis was recaptured on a street corner in Chicago, and flown to Minneapolis, then taken to Saint Paul to face charges in the Bremer kidnapping. He subsequently pled guilty and was sentenced to life in prison on June 7.[24]

On the same day Davis escaped in Yorkville, Illinois, Jess Doyle and Edna Murray were arrested in Pittsburgh, Kansas. Edna had been indicted in Saint Paul on January 22, in connection to the Bremer kidnapping, but was found not guilty. However, she was returned to the Missouri State Prison for Women in Jefferson City to finish serving her 25 year sentence for robbery.[25]

Alvin wanted to put a new gang together, and got in touch with some of his old contacts at the Harvard Club, in Cleveland. There, he met John F. "Sharkey" Gorman and Fred Hunter, who were working there. He and Harry also took a trip down to Tulsa to see their old pal from the Central Park gang, George "Burhead' Keady, who put them in contact with a local hoodlum named John Brock, who had served time in the Oklahoma State penitentiary at McAlester with Doc Barker, Volney Davis and William Weaver. They wanted Brock to join them in some jobs, and on March 23, Brock arrived in Toledo, where he registered at the Lorraine Hotel as "T. F. Evans." He met the gang at Barry's place, and they all began planning their next robbery.[26]

Through Freddie Hunter, they learned that a large payroll was coming in through the post office in Warren, Ohio for the Youngstown Sheet and Tube Plant. The plan was for Alvin, Harry and one of Freddie Hunter's pals, Joe Rich, to hijack the mail truck as it left the post office on the way to the factory. Brock was a stand-by in case they needed an extra hand.

Alvin knew that the truck would stop at a railroad crossing at a particular time, so he made sure he got his truck in front of the mail truck before it got there. Alvin watched the truck in his rearview mirror, and after crossing the tracks, he slammed on his brakes and cut across the road, forcing the driver of the mail truck to stop. Harry and Joe jumped out with their weapons. They ran back to commandeer the mail truck. The driver, Burl Villers, had already pulled out his own pistol, but instead of firing a shot, he held it out the window and dropped it to the ground. They forced him to drive out of town behind Alvin's truck to an abandoned garage. Once there, they tied Villers up, and made off with the mail bags. The take was $72,000 in cash, and $53,000 in registered bonds. This job made Alvin nervous, mainly because Fred Barker wasn't there to help, but it went off without a hitch, and Brock returned to Tulsa.[27]

The authorities found the bags in a nearby creek a short time later. Only the cash and one $1,000 bond was missing. The rest of the bonds were left behind. Alvin, Harry and Joe split $60,000 between themselves, plus gave $5,000 to Freddie Hunter for suggesting the job, and the rest they used to cover expenses. Postal Inspectors interviewed Villers, who said one of the robbers had a Tommygun, and was wearing a white shirt, grey trousers, and horn-rimmed glasses. Another of the robbers he described as having curly hair. Two days later, two local hoodlums, George Sergeant and Tony Labrizzetta, said to be members of the Licavolie mob, were arrested for the crime. Villers identified them as the bandits, and they were convicted and sentenced to 20 years in prison. [29]

Alvin knew it wasn't safe to hang around Toledo for too long after the Warren job, so he and Harry drove down to Oklahoma, where Harry very nearly fell into a Fed trap. When he dropped in to visit Wynona's sister in Hominy, she handed him a telegraph, presumably from Wynona, sent from Saint Paul asking for $100 for attorney's fees. Alvin told him it smelled like a trap, and to ignore it. For one, Wynona and Dolores had been sent to prison in Milan, Michigan – not Minnesota – to serve their sentences for harboring fugitives. But Harry wouldn't listen. He handed the money to Wynona's sister, and said to send it to her. He said he'd call back in a few days. But after he left, the rusty wheels in the back of his mind slowly began to turn, and he thought that just maybe Alvin was right after all. He never returned. It actually had been a trap. The feds in Saint Paul knew Wynona's relatives were dirt-poor, and if anyone sent her money, it would have to come from Harry. When the money arrived in Saint Paul, the feds descended upon Hominy, Oklahoma in droves, waiting for him to show back up so they could cuff him.[30]

Soon thereafter, Alvin learned that Harry Sawyer and his wife Gladys had been arrested in a small town on the Gulf Coast between Gulfport and Biloxi, Mississippi, called Pass Christian. After leaving Cleveland, they had set up a gambling hall for colored people under an assumed name. This didn't sit well at all with the white business owners, who grew suspicious of them and contacted authorities. They were soon placed under surveillance once Harry was recognized from wanted posters. The feds moved in and arrested them both on May 3, 1935.[31]

Then on August 28, acting on information from Volney Davis and Edna Murray, federal agents descended upon a gravel pit near Oswego, Illinois, just a few miles south of Aurora. They began digging, and soon found a badly decomposed body that had been covered with quick lime. According to Davis and Murray, the body was that of John "Red" Hamilton, whom they had helped John Dillinger and Homer Van Meter bury after he died in their apartment in Aurora in April 1934. [32]

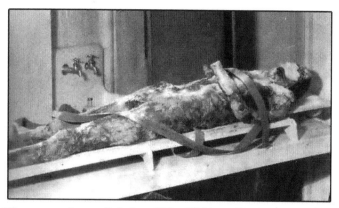

The remains of John "Red" Hamilton found in a gravel pit near Oswego, Illinois (FBI Photo)

Two days later, on September 1, federal agents surrounded a small chicken farm in Allendale, Florida and quickly arrested Phoenix Donald, a.k.a. "William Weaver" and his girlfriend Myrtle Eaton. They nabbed Weaver as he came out of the house to pick up his newspaper, then rushed into the house to arrest Eaton. After moving to Allendale, Florida, and buying the chicken farm, they lived under the aliases of Mr. and Mrs. J. W. Osborne. When the agents arrested them, they found a young boy they had adopted who was known to the neighbors as Bobbie Osborne. The child was left in the care of local authorities, and on September 3, Weaver and Eaton were flown back to Saint Paul, and held in the Ramsey County jail.[33]

Phoenix Donald a.k.a. "William Weaver'
and his girlfriend, Myrtle Eaton

In September 1935, Alvin Karpis began putting together plans for a robbery that would prove to be his very last. The plan was to rob a train, and it would be the last great train robbery in American history, in true Wild West fashion that would have made the likes of Frank and Jesse James proud. He had learned that the afternoon "Steel King", eastbound from Cleveland to Warren, Ohio would make a stop at the depot in Garrettsville, in Portage County, carrying the Republic Steel Corporation payroll for the workers at the Mahoning Valley steel mills. Alvin would take especially great pains with this job. He didn't want anything left to chance. He called in his gang from the Warren mail robbery, plus some additional people, including Milton Lett and an older man named Benson Groves, who used the alias "Ben Grayson". On September 5, Keady drove up to McAlester to pick up Sam Coker, who had just been paroled, thanks to Karpis paying off a politician who got him released. He arrived in Toledo a couple of weeks later, and Alvin got him settled in. [34]

On October 25, Milton Lett purchased a car for the gang to use. It was a gray 1935 Plymouth PJ four door Sedan with a trunk. Alvin then contacted one of his pals, Joe Roscoe, who arranged a meeting with a former bootlegger pilot named Joe Zetzer. During Prohibition, Zetzer had made decent money flying bootleg whiskey out of Canada. The only problem was that Zetzer no longer had an airplane. So Alvin arranged to give him $1,700 to buy one. He knew a man in Toledo, Adelbert Gross, who owned Gross Automatic Services, Incorporated. He had a black Stinson Reliant single engine monoplane, License Number NC12180, which he had been trying to sell for several months. He contacted Gross and purchased the plane on November 7, flying it to the airport in Port Clinton. [35]

Alvin needed one more man for the job because at the last moment, Sam Coker came down with a bad case of Gonorrhea, which put him out of commission. After he got out of McAlester, he had hit every whorehouse in Tulsa, and had gotten infected. Then, he got the dumb idea to treat himself by filling a syringe with diluted iodine and injecting himself. He nearly died and wound up in Mercy Hospital in Toledo for the next twenty-four days. To replace Coker, Alvin sent Freddie back to Tulsa to get Brock. They returned to Cleveland about November 4, and early on the morning of November 6, he and "Sam" joined Alvin, Harry, Freddie, and Benson Groves, at the home of Edward McGraw, at 3011 ½ Adams Street in Toledo to go over the plans for the heist. From there, they drove out to Clyde Rochet's farm outside Leavittsburg, Ohio to make arrangements for Brock, Harry and Groves to spend the night there. The next day, Rochet drove the men to a place called Four Corners, where they were met by Alvin and Freddie Hunter in the Plymouth. Groves had found a fake mustache which drooped down below the corners of his mouth, and rubbed rouge on his cheeks. He looked like a first class movie villain, and Alvin said, *"For Chrissakes Ben. Don't move too close to the people on the platform. You'll scare the hell out of them!"* They quickly piled into the Plymouth and off to Garrettsville they went.[36]

As Alvin approached the depot, he pulled over about a block

away to let Groves, Campbell and Brock out. They proceeded towards the depot on foot. Alvin continued on to the depot parking lot. He assigned Hunter the job of making sure no one on the platform escaped to their car to go warn the authorities. Hunter got out and casually walked to the depot. Under his coat he had a Thompson hidden with a 20 round clip. Alvin stayed in the car so he could observe the surroundings and watch for any potential problems, such as the two telephone repairmen at the top of a pole nearby. But suddenly, one of the repairman looked down and began laughing hysterically. He poked his partner and pointed down towards the depot. Now both of them were laughing. Alvin looked to see what they were pointing at, and saw Groves. They were laughing at his ridiculous disguise![37]

Erie Depot at Garrettsville, Ohio in the 1930's

While they were enjoying themselves at Groves' expense, Alvin heard the train's whistle blow. Erie Train 626 was right on time. It was 2:15 p.m. As soon as the train rolled to a stop, Alvin looked back to see Groves climbing into the engine to take control of the engineer and fireman. Brock was on the platform, getting ready to round up everyone. Earl Davis, a news agent from the local newspaper, was at the depot picking up a copy of the afternoon edition of the Cleveland Press, and Mrs. W. L. Scott was there mailing a letter, as Brock came in with his Thompson. Brock stuck his machine gun in their backs and forced them and about ten other people out to the platform, ordering them to put their hands on their heads. [38]

Campbell was collaring a flagman, and Hunter was taking care of the parking lot. Alvin rushed the mail car and pulled out his Thompson. He pointed it at the heads of the mail clerks. But to his amazement, instead of them throwing up their hands, they ran to the back of the car and hid! Just then, he heard a car start, and looked out to see Freddie chasing two old hoboes while a man and a woman jumped in their car. Alvin rushed to the car yelling at them to get out. He grabbed the car keys and flung them as far as he could. Freddie returned and Alvin yelled at him, *"Do NOT leave the lot!"*[39]

Alvin rushed back to the mail car, and the clerks were still hiding. He pulled a stick of dynamite out of his pocket and flung it to the back of the mail car, *yelling "I'm going to heave another stick in there, and it'll be burning! You got five seconds, and I'm counting now. One...Two....Three.... "* They came out. Two white men and a huge black guy, who yelled back, *"You can't do this man. Get off with that gun!"* Alvin cocked the Thompson, aimed it above their heads and pulled the trigger. All that happened was a "click" as it failed to fire. But that did the trick. They were scared to death and quickly reached towards the ceiling.[40]

The car was filled with over a hundred mail bags, and Alvin asked the chief mail clerk which one had the payroll. He gave no answer. Alvin told him, *'Buddy, you know and I know that there's another train coming down the line in a few minutes. If you don't tell me what I want to know in a hurry, that train is going to run right into this one, and there'll be a lot of dead people. I don't care about that, but you might."* [41]

The clerk pointed out a heavy bag with a big padlock on it. He said it was the Warren payroll. Alvin then asked for the Youngstown payroll. The clerk responded, *"It's not here."* Alvin threatened to shoot him, but the clerk pleaded. *"It went through yesterday."* He pulled out the ledger and showed it to Alvin to prove he wasn't lying. The clerks hauled the Warren bag and three bags of registered mail out to the front of the mail car, and joined the others on the platform.[42]

By this time, Earl Davis's arms were growing tired from holding his hands on his head, so he crossed his arms. Seeing him, Hunter poked him in the back with his Thompson and ordered him to load the bags in their car. He also ordered one of the mail clerks – the same black guy who had mouthed off in the mail car - to help, but he said, *"I'm not helping you rob the train!"* Before he could finish his sentence, Hunter kicked him in the ass and told him to get moving. He quickly obliged. Once the bags were loaded, they piled back into the Plymouth and sped out of town West towards Ravenna. The route back to Port Clinton was deliberately planned with a series of twists and turns to prevent anyone following them.[43]

Alvin had made arrangements with Zetzer to stay at his house that night, and fly out the next morning. When they got to his place, they quickly unloaded the bags and took them inside. After opening the bags, he was in for an unpleasant surprise. He had expected a payroll of over $180,000. What he found was only $34,000 in cash and $12,450 in bonds and securities. It was divided up between them, and the bags were burned in a furnace there in Zetzer's garage. Then Alvin handed him another $500 to get rid of the car. Zetzer scooped the ashes from the stove, bagged them up, and then loaded them in the Plymouth; which he then drove off a bluff into Lake Erie.[44] Early the next morning, Zetzer drove Alvin and Freddie out to the airport. After giving the Stinson a thorough pre-flight check, they boarded the plane. The engine roared to life, and soon they were taxiing down the runway, and then off into the clouds. Alvin thought of how he had pulled off a train robbery in true Jesse James fashion, and now instead of getting away on a fast horse, he was making his escape in an airplane! It would be the last great American train robbery. Unbeknownst to him, it would also be the very last robbery of his career.

After the Garrettsville, Ohio train robbery, Alvin Karpis and Fred Hunter made their escape in a Stinson Reliant airplane to Arkansas. He committed the last great American train robbery, and became the first bandit to make his escape in an airplane.

Illustration by W. D. Smith

Brock returned to Toledo then left for Tulsa, as Alvin and Freddie got ready for their flight. Before taking off, Alvin had made arrangements with Grace Goldstein, another Madam he knew in Hot Springs, Arkansas, to meet him when they landed. Grace, like Edith Barry, operated several brothels and she wielded a lot of influence with the local authorities and political big wigs in and around Hot Springs. Once they arrived, Alvin contacted Goldstein, to come pick them up. It had not been an easy trip. While over Indiana, Zetzer had to land the plane in a field near Evansville, then walk to town to have forty gallons of fuel delivered. They slept in the plane that night, and continued on the next morning. The same thing happened over Tennessee, near Memphis. Finally, on November 10, they landed in Hot Springs. They were met at the airport by Goldstein and Freddie Hunter's girlfriend, Connie Morris.[45]

Grace Goldstein

Grace's real name was Jewel Laverne Grayson, a pretty peroxide blonde from poverty-stricken Blossom, Texas. She lived at 123 Palm Street, near downtown, which was another of her brothels. Alvin shacked up with her, while Freddie Hunter stayed with Connie, whose real name was Ruth (Hamm) Robison. Hot Springs, like Saint Paul, was well-known as a gangster haven for hoodlums of one shade or another, from the likes of big league gangsters such as Al Capone, Owen "Mad Dog' Madden, and Lucky Luciano, to lesser-known thugs and gangster wannabes.

Hot Springs had some of the largest illegal gambling casinos in the country. The hotels were, for the most part, classy joints that catered to the rich and powerful, and offered many amenities, including women. Grace Goldstein ran a brothel in two upstairs floors of the Hatterie Hotel, above the haberdashery she ran downstairs. It was located on the north side of the Arlington Hotel, and across the street from Mike Jacobs' gambling joint, the Southern Grill. Goldstein was said to run the finest brothel in Hot Springs, and her clientele included corrupt Mayor Leo P. McLaughlin, and three corrupt members of the Hot Springs Police Department; Chief of Police, Joseph Wakelin, Chief of Detectives Herbert "Dutch" Akers, and Police Detective Cecil Brock.[46]

Joseph Wakelin was a native of Hot Springs, and was born there May 21, 1876. He attended school through the 8th grade, and became involved in police work beginning in his early adult years, working his way up to become Chief of Police in April 1927 – a position he held until January 1, 1937.[47]

Herbert "Dutch" Akers was the Chief of Detectives in Hot Springs, and was known by underworld figures throughout the country that he was willing to harbor fugitives for a price. It was later revealed that he and Wakelin were involved in a major car theft ring with various underworld figures. He was widely known as one of the most corrupt police officers in the United States, and involved in stealing from prisoners in his custody, bribery, confidence rackets, and other serious offenses.[48]

Cecil Brock was born in Nashville, Tennessee January 16, 1904. His family moved to Paris, Texas and then to Hot Springs, Arkansas in 1922, where he soon afterwards was employed with the Hot Springs Police Department, where he was promoted to Lieutenant by 1935. He was fired from the police department in 1937, and afterwards worked as a private detective. In December 1936, a prisoner named John Dickson was beaten to death. His death was ruled as "natural causes" but upon further investigation, it was proven that Brock was one of three officers who had brutally beaten Dickson, causing his death. He was fired January 2, 1937. [49]

On January 14, 1936, Alvin and Grace went to the airport and hired a pilot there, John Stover, to fly them to Canton, Ohio for a few days. Once they returned, Grace wanted to visit her brother in Texas, so she and Alvin took off in Grace's car to a small town near Paris. At the same time, Freddie and Connie went to San Antonio to visit his sister. The trip to Texas appealed to Alvin because in Paris, Texas, there wouldn't be any heat from the law. In fact, there wasn't much of anything there, especially the FBI. There were plenty of dried up fields, sage brush, rattlesnakes and misery, but no feds. Seeing the abject poverty in that part of Texas made Alvin glad he was a crook. At least he had money. Even if he didn't come by it honestly. [50]

Central Avenue, looking north. Bathhouse Row is on the right. The large white building at top is the Arlington Hotel. The Hatterie Hotel was immediately next door. Published circa 1924. (Public Domain image)

After the road trip was over, Alvin and Grace headed back to

Hot Springs. Freddie and Connie weren't far behind. Alvin knew that he and Freddie would have to keep moving around a lot to avoid being captured. The FBI was all over the country looking for him. They were especially keeping a close eye on Alvin's parent's home in Chicago, hoping he would try to sneak in to see his infant son. But as much as he wanted to, he knew he couldn't risk it. About a month after arriving in Hot Springs, Alvin and Freddie rented a small cabin From Mrs. Al C. Dyer , and her caretaker Morris Loftis at a place known as Dyer's landing, at Lake Catherine. Alvin loved the place, and had begun talking to Dyer about buying it until Freddie brought two unwelcomed visitors; Sam Coker and Keady. Keady was a lot like the "old bastard" Arthur Dunlop and Doc Moran. He drank too much, and when he drank, he got mouthy. Fearing that Coker and Keady might squeal to the feds, he spoke with Grace the next day about finding a new place. His fears weren't unfounded. [51]

As it turned out, police in Tulsa had initiated a series of raids on illegal gambling joints. One of these joints was run by a local hood named George Hurford. While searching his place, the police found a bag containing about $3,200 mostly in twenties, issued from the Federal Reserve Bank in Cleveland, Ohio. Hurford said the money belonged to Burrhead Keady. The police and Postal Inspectors then contacted Keady, who claimed he had gotten it from John Brock. To divert attention away from himself, Keady agreed to be an informant for the inspectors and made arrangements to come to their office. They handed him $5.00 for gas, plus a note with an agent's name and phone number on it. [52]

Accused With Karpis

Bespectacled John Brock, pictured as he was booked in Cleveland, was charged with Alvin Karpis and three others with the $46,000 machinegun robbery of an Erie railroad mail train at Garrettsville, O., last November. (Associated Press Photo)

John Brock (Associated Press Photo)

But Keady wound up getting delayed, and when he didn't show up at the agreed to time, the inspectors picked him up and hauled him in. Once at their office, he told them about Brock, but denied any involvement with the Garrettsville robbery. They didn't buy his story, and flew him incognito up to Ohio for a lineup at the police station. Witnesses from Garrettsville positively identified him as the man using the name "Sam". Connelley's agents had also been watching him, but despite this, the Postal Inspectors were able to spirit him away out from under their noses. They didn't find out about it until late February, when a newspaper in Cleveland reported on it. They were furious, and demanded to know if it were true. The inspectors denied it, and stopped sharing information with the FBI. They knew Hoover was a would-be glory hound, wanting to take credit for capturing the robbers.[53]

Keady fingered John Brock for the robbery, and almost as soon as the Postal Inspectors nabbed him, he began to sing like a canary. Brock confessed to having taken part in the Garrettsville train robbery, and identified the others as Alvin Karpis, Harry Campbell, Freddie Hunter, and Benson Groves, a.k.a. "Ben Grayson". When asked about where Karpis and Hunter had gone, he said they had flown to Hot Springs and were shacked up with a woman, Grace Goldstein, who ran a whorehouse there.[54]

Soon, Hot Springs was crawling with postal inspectors and FBI agents alike, engaged in their own separate investigations. A rivalry ensued between the two because Special Agent in Charge Connelley dismissed the leads the inspectors had relayed to him. He told Hoover *"I don't believe they have half as much as they would have you believe."* A week or so later, postal inspector Sylvester Hettrick called the FBI office in Cleveland to set up a meeting in Youngstown. When the agent arrived, they informed him that they had picked up a man named Clayton Hall in connection with the Garrettsville robbery, threatening to throw the book at him if he didn't tell them what they wanted to know. He spilled his guts, even giving up the location of the Malvern Road house where Karpis and Hunter were living.[55]

Things were quickly put in motion for a raid on the Woodcock house, which took place on March 30, 1936. They full well expected a drawn out gun battle like the one in Ocklawaha, when Fred and Ma Barker were killed. Connelley brought in twelve agents, armed to the teeth. Hall had drawn them a detailed map of the property. Believing they would wind up in another drawn out gun battle like the one in Ocklawaha, Florida, Special Agent Earl J. Connelley and over twenty law enforcement officers and postal shot the Hell out of the place. Several flares were fired through the windows, and one of them landed on a bed catching it on fire. When the agents rushed in to put the fire out, they found it abandoned. Karpis and Hunter were long gone. They had missed them by only four days. The raid was just one more embarrassment to Hoover, and he would soon be called on the carpet for it. Woodcock, the owner of the house, was mad as Hell. A close friend of Arkansas' Democrat Senator Joseph Taylor Robinson, he told the Senator about the G-men shooting up his property, and wanted something done about it.[56]

The postal inspectors in Kansas suspected Karpis was responsible for several robberies there, and the Garrettsville heist brought in the postal inspectors from Ohio. These forces were looking for both Karpis and Hunter just as the , and one of their informants was a Kansas State Patrolman named Joe Anderson. Anderson knew a cab driver, Ercell Brock, who was infatuated with Freddie Hunter's girlfriend Connie Morris. Anderson asked Brock to find out what he could about Hunter, and gave him $5.00 to go make a date with her at the Hatterie. But while there talking with her, he got drunk and accidentally let it slip that the postal authorities were looking for her boyfriend. After he left, Morris tipped off Alvin and Freddie. Connie was terrified. She went to see Grace, and told her what had happened, and that she was afraid she might go to prison. But Grace told her not to worry, and got her a ride to Arkadelphia so she could lay low for a while until things blew over. After a few days, she returned to Grace's place on Palm Street. [57]

Alvin and Freddie got out of Hot Springs, and took a trip into Mississippi to case more places to rob. One of his plans was to rob the mail train when it arrived at the Southern depot in Iuka, Mississippi, located in the northeast corner of the state, in Tishomingo County. When they returned, they spirited Grace and Connie out from under the noses of both the FBI and the Postal Inspectors, and went to New Orleans. While there, Grace found some doctors she knew who could treat Connie for Syphilis. Alvin and Freddie also got in to doing some serious fishing in the Gulf, before finally sneaking Grace back into Hot Springs. Alvin, Freddie and Connie then returned to New Orleans. [58]

Both the FBI and the Postal Inspectors were convinced that Grace knew where Karpis was, so one day as she returned to the Hatterie, she was detained and taken in for questioning. She continued to deny knowing anything, until they threatened to have her mother arrested and charged with harboring fugitives just as they had done to the mothers of Bonnie Parker and Clyde Barrow. Grace broke down, and told them that she didn't know where Karpis was, but she did know where Freddie Hunter and Connie Morris were staying. She was taken to New Orleans where she pointed to Freddie's apartment, and then was taken home. Freddie had rented Apartment 3 at 3343 Canal Street under the name Edward O'Hara. He had also bought a new black 1936 Plymouth Coupe under the same name.[59]

In April 1936, Director J. Edgar Hoover went before Congress, but he was soon drawn into a near shouting match with Tennessee powerful senator, Kenneth D. McKellar; the same senator he had insulted three years earlier. McKellar had slashed the FBI's budget, claiming that Hoover was being irresponsible with government money. He wanted answers. McKellar hadn't forgotten the snub and he took this opportunity to get even. After several biting questions that unnerved the Director, McKellar asked whether or not he had employed professional writers. He lied and said he hadn't.[60]

However, Hoover had a favorite ghost writer, Courtney Rylie Cooper, who he paid a great deal of money to spruce up the FBI's public image. In fact, it had Cooper who helped Hoover and Tolson concoct the story about Ma Barker being the brains of the Barker-Karpis gang, and they used Cooper to promote it. Hoover and Tolson lived together, ate together, and were always seen together, so much that many referred to them as the "Gold Dust twins', after the characters on Fairbank's Gold

Dust brand washing powder. They seemed to be the modern equivalent to Tweedledee and Tweedledum, which raised eyebrows and spawned hushed rumors about their sexuality for many years.

The Gold Dust Twins
(Image Source: Pinterest)

McKellar then grilled Hoover about how much money he spent to pay stool pigeons. The confrontation continued to escalate when Senator McKellar stated bluntly, *"It seems to me that your department is running wild, Mr. Hoover."* The Director shot back, *'Will you let me make a statement?"* McKellar shot back, *"I think that IS the statement!"* [61]

Hoover became defensive, and said that eight desperadoes and four federal agents had been killed since the FBI was allowed to use firearms. McKellar, unimpressed, replied *"In other words, the net effect of turning guns over to your department has been the killing of eight desperadoes and four G-men."* Hoover insisted that his agents were under orders to arrest, rather than kill, suspects if at all possible. But Senator McKellar continued; *"I doubt very much whether you ought to have a law that permits you to go around the country armed as an army would and shoot down all the people you suspect of being criminals, or such as you suspect of having guns, and having your own men shot down."* [62]

Hoover was boiling mad, and said his men had the right to use firearms in their own defense; a point which McKellar conceded, but then the Senator struck a nerve. He asked, *"Have you ever made an arrest?"* He replied that he had, but McKellar then asked, *"How many arrests have you made and who were they? Did you make the arrests?"* [63]

The Director was flabbergasted. *"No, the arrests were made by officers under my supervision."* Angrily, McKellar looked him square in the eye, raised his voice, and asked, *"I'm talking about actual arrests. You never arrested them actually?"* Hoover conceded that he, himself, in the nearly twelve years that he had served as Director, had never personally made any arrests. Senator McKellar sat back in his chair and glared down at Hoover, gloating. He had extracted his revenge. He had made the powerful Director of the FBI look like a coward. [64]

Hoover's face was red as a lobster as he left the hearing. He had been embarrassed before the entire country. He was boiling mad when he returned to his office, and fired off a memo to all of his field offices across the country. He demanded that he be notified immediately the moment any information turned up concerning Alvin Karpis and where he was hiding. Senator McKellar had called Hoover a *"swivel chair detective who left it to his men to make arrests and risk their lives"*. He told Connelley he wanted to arrest Karpis personally. He didn't have long to wait.

Early on the morning of April 30, the Director was informed that Alvin Karpis, Fred Hunter and a woman were in New Orleans renting an apartment at 3343 Canal Street, near the intersection with Jefferson Davis Parkway, per information forced out of Grace Goldstein. Actually, Karpis' apartment was at 3300 St. Charles, but he spent much of his time at Freddie's place. The Director and Clyde Tolson chartered a flight aboard a Trans World Airlines DC-3 to Louisiana, arriving in New Orleans that evening. They checked into the Roosevelt Hotel and contacted Connelley to let him know they'd arrived.[65]

Early on May 1. A new agent, Ray Tollett, had found a nice hiding spot in an empty house near Hunter's apartment, and a few minutes before 10:00 a.m. he spotted a maroon 1936 Terraplane drive up and park in front. A man got out of the car and went inside. A few minutes later, he came back out with another man. Tollet zoomed in with his binoculars to get a good look at them. It was Karpis and Hunter! Karpis got back onto his Terraplane, and Hunter got into his Plymouth coupe and drove off.

Alvin was on his way to the United Motors Garage to drop his Terraplane off to be serviced, but before they got there, they pulled off on a side road near Lake Pontchartrain, where Alvin transferred his guns and ammunition to the trunk of Freddie's Plymouth, then drove on the garage. The service station attendant told him he'd have the car ready about 5:00 p.m., so Alvin and Freddie drove around a while then headed back to the apartment.[66]

3343 Canal Street Apt 3, New Orleans, Louisiana.
Where Karpis and Hunter were arrested. (FBI photo)

Tollett's heart was pounding as he rushed to get to a telephone. He found one at a drugstore around the corner and called in. Connelley answered the call, and immediately notified the Director and gathered his men. He had amassed fourteen men to take Karpis down, and two of them were expert marksmen. He drew a picture on a chalkboard of the area at the intersection of Canal Street and Jefferson Davis Parkway, and explained how the raid was to be conducted. Once everyone knew his assignment they left to take their positions.

Connelley joined Tollet in the empty house, and waited. Inside the apartment, Connie Morris asked the boys to run to the grocery store for her and buy some strawberries. After cautiously looking around a bit, the two got into the Plymouth and drove off. One of the agents followed a short distance behind them, trying to stay out of sight. Karpis stayed in the car while Hunter was in the store. As they made their way back to the apartment, the agent followed. A short while later, Karpis left on foot and walked down to the drugstore to buy some cigarettes and a magazine, then returned a few minutes later. Finally, at about 4:45 p.m., Alvin got ready to go pick up his car. It was a hot, humid day – almost 90 degrees. So Alvin decided not to wear a jacket or vest. He put on a light colored shirt, light tan pants, and his favorite hat – a straw boater. Since he couldn't carry his .45 without his jacket, he hid it under a cushion on the sofa.[67]

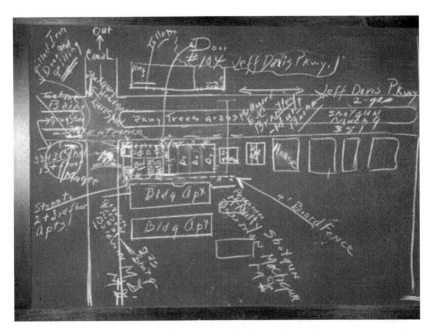

The FBI's chalkboard diagram of the raid on Karpis' hideout (FBI photo)

As he and Freddie headed out the door, Alvin asked for the car keys. He unlocked the driver's side door and slid in behind the steering wheel, then reached over to unlock the passengers' side door for Freddie. The heat inside the car was unbearable, so Alvin quickly cranked down the window. He pushed the key into the switch and as he began to start the engine, a car roared across his path, cutting him off. As soon as it stopped, five big guys piled out. [68]

It was then that he heard someone to his left say, *"Alright Karpis! Just keep your hands on that steering wheel!"* As he turned towards the sound of the voice, he felt the muzzle of a gun against his head. Then, looking straight ahead at the car in front of him, he saw two men leaning over the hood. They had Thompson machine guns pointed straight at him. Everyone was so focused on Karpis that no one noticed Hunter slowly exiting the car and walking away. They were also distracted momentarily as a little boy on his bicycle came rolling down the sidewalk as Freddie walked on. As soon as the kid got past the cars, he heard the guy with the gun say, *"Okay, Karpis. Get out of the car and be damn careful where you put your hands."* As he exited the car, he heard another agent yell, *"Stop that guy on the sidewalk! He's getting away!"* They quickly nabbed Freddie and brought him back.[69]

"Keep your hands up!" One agent with a Thompson pointed at his face demanded. He asked, *"Do you have a gun on you?"* "No", Alvin answered.

"Alright, Karpis, I'm putting the safety on this gun. There's no need for anybody to get hurt here!" Alvin replied, *"Please tell that guy behind me with the rifle to put his safety on. He's liable to kill me and you both!"*

The agent holding the rifle was obviously nervous, but the quip angered him. He told Alvin, *"Wait till we get you downtown, Karpis! I'll show you who's running things!"*[70]

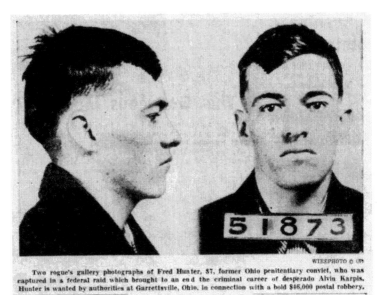

Two rogue's gallery photographs of Fred Hunter, 37, former Ohio penitentiary convict, who was captured in a federal raid which brought to an end the criminal career of desperado Alvin Karpis. Hunter is wanted by authorities at Garrettsville, Ohio, in connection with a bold $46,000 postal robbery.

Freddie Hunter. Associated Press photo

Suddenly, he saw the other agents waving their arms and looking off towards the side of a building. One of them shouted, *"We've got him, Chief! It's all clear!"* From the corner of his eye, Alvin saw two men approach who had been waiting in the wings out of sight. He looked up as they drew closer, and recognized them immediately. To his surprise, it was the "Gold Dust twins" themselves: J. Edgar Hoover and Clyde Tolson.

Still butt-hurt from the scolding he had received from Senator McKellar, Hoover wasted no time making sure there were plenty of photographers on the scene to record him "personally" capturing Karpis. He intended for all the glory and accolades to go to him. His days of being called a "swivel chair detective" were over. He refused to allow himself to be embarrassed again.[71]

J. Edgar Hoover in foreground with Alvin Karpis
(FBI Photo)

Soon, a car pulled up and someone yelled, *"Handcuffs! Someone cuff Karpis!"* The agents looked at each other and shrugged, realizing that no one had even bothered to bring any. Finally, agent William J. "Buck" Buchanan took off his necktie and tied Alvin's wrists together. It was then that FBI photographers showed up for his photo-op. One photo showed the Director in the foreground with Alvin and an agent walking behind him. The photo made front page headlines all over the country. Next, he was led to the car and placed in the front seat. Three other people piled in the seat behind him; Hoover, Connie Morris, and Tolson. Agents had entered the apartment and arrested her. Hoover sat on her right, and Tolson on her left. Agent Clarence Hurt climbed in behind the steering wheel. No one said a word until Hurt took off. He wasn't at all familiar with New Orleans, and asked "Does anyone know where the Post Office building is?" [72]

Alvin replied, *"I do!"* Tolson asked him how he knew where

it was, and jokingly, Alvin answered, *"We were thinking of robbing it."* No one was amused. The next day, Hoover, Tolson, Alvin and some other agents boarded a Trans World Airlines DC-3 bound for Saint Paul, where Alvin would be indicted for the Hamm and Bremer kidnappings. It was the end of the road for Public Enemy Number One. Only one more loose end remained – Harry Campbell. [73]

Alvin Karpis being led into custody by agents (FBI Photo)

Fred Hunter's 1936 Plymouth Coupe (FBI Photo)

Rear of Hunter's Plymouth (FBI Photo)

Trunk open showing weapons cache (FBI Photo)

On May 7, just six days after Karpis, Hunter and Morris were arrested in New Orleans, J. Edgar Hoover and his agents landed in Toledo. Informants had led them to Campbell's apartment at 2132 Monroe Street, which he shared with his bride of less than a year, Gertrude Billiter, he had married on May 29, 1935 in Bowling Green, Wood County, Ohio, using the name Robert "Bob" Miller. Gertrude had no idea who her husband really was, only that he was good to her. He was employed as a bartender at 2130 Goulet Grill, just next door to their apartment.

Hoover never notified the Toledo Police Department about the raid. His reason for this was simple; he was afraid corrupt officials in the police department would tip Campbell off. The FBI quickly surrounded Campbell's apartment and took him into custody without incident. A few hours later, they also arrested Sam Coker, who lived just a few blocks away.

Toledo Police Chief Ray Allen protested vehemently over Hoover's refusal to inform his department about the raid, but the Director replied, *"I won't cooperate with corrupt, inefficient or publicity-mad forces."* Campbell was flown back to Saint Paul, by way of Cleveland, to stand trial for his part in the kidnapping of Edward G. Bremer. Campbell's arrest marked the extinction of the infamous Barker-Karpis gang.[74]

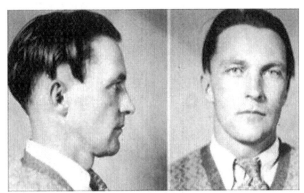

Harry Campbell (FBI photo)

A little more than a month after Alvin was arrested in New Orleans, his old pal Lawrence "Larry" DeVol was put out of commission permanently. Devol's mind had begun to deteriorate while sitting in the Minnesota State Penitentiary. The guards watched him closely. He refused to eat and claimed someone was trying to poison him. Soon, he began to attack other prisoners and guards, and acted so erratically that he was committed to the Saint Peter Hospital for the Criminally Insane, in Saint Peter, Minnesota. On June 6, 1936, DeVol led a gang of fifteen inmates who overpowered the guards and escaped from the hospital. Two were captured soon after the break, but DeVol and fourteen others remained at large for several months more.

On the night of July 8, 1936, DeVol walked into the German Village Beer Parlor at the corner of Broadway and Grand Avenue in Enid, Garfield County, Oklahoma. As he and two women sat in a booth, the manager, Jim O'Neal, thought he recognized him from some wanted posters. O'Neal had already been tipped off that someone was planning to rob the bar, so he was keeping close tabs on everyone who came in and left. O'Neal was a former Enid police officer, and he called the police and asked them to come check him out.

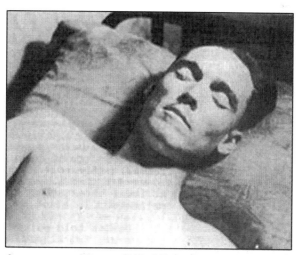

Lawrence "Larry" DeVol after being shot and killed by police in Enid, Oklahoma

DeVol was recognized as one of the men who had robbed the bank in Oklahoma City a day or two previously. When Officer Cal Palmer and his partner, Ralph Knarr, walked into the bar, they spoke with O'Neal for a moment, then approached the man at the booth. They said, *"Come go with us."* The man asked to finish his beer, and said, *"I think I know what you want me for."* As he sat the beer mug down with one hand, he quickly pulled a gun with the other and started shooting.

Palmer was killed instantly with a bullet through the heart, and Knarr was shot four times. The gunman ran out of a side door into an alley, and was quickly pursued by five police officers. At the end of the alley, he spotted a car occupied by two men, and ordered them to take off. Instead, they ducked down, opened the car doors and bailed out of the car.

DeVol was left alone in the back seat, and when the officers opened fire on the car, he jumped out. As he began to return fire, he was shot in the head and killed instantly. For Lawrence James "Larry" DeVol. His days of "robbin' banks and killin' cops" were over. His accomplice Donald Reeder was captured a short time later.[75]

AFTERMATH – The Hamm and Bremer Trials. Acquittals and Convictions[76]

1935

Arthur "Doc" Barker – Convicted in the Bremer kidnapping, and sentenced to life in prison at Alcatraz. Killed during an escape attempt in 1939.

Doc Barker on his way to trail in St. Paul 1935

Doc Barker and his jailer, William Gates in St. Paul 1935

Dolores Delaney – Convicted in Miami, Florida of harboring a Federal criminal on February 17, 1935. Sentenced to five years in the Federal Women's Detention Farm in Milan, Michigan.

Wynona Burdette – Convicted in Miami, Florida of harboring a Federal criminal on February 17, 1935. Sentenced to five years in the Federal Women's Detention Farm in Milan, Michigan.

Harry Clinton Stanley – Convicted March 10, 1935 of harboring criminals (Jess Doyle and his sister, Edna (Stanley) Murray, a.k.a. "the Kissing Bandit"). Sentenced to 6 months in the Sedgewick County jail in Wichita, Kansas, plus $1,000 fine.

Sybil Mary Stanley, wife of Harry C. Stanley - Sentenced to five years (suspended) for harboring Jess Doyle and Edna Murray.

Oliver A. Berg – Convicted May 17, 1935 in connection with the Bremer kidnapping. Sentenced to life, but had already been sentenced to life on a murder charge, and was incarcerated at the Illinois State Penitentiary in Joliet.

Phillip J. Delaney – Acquitted May 17, 1935.

William Vidler – Acquitted May 17, 1935.

Harry Campbell – Convicted May 12, 1935 for conspiracy to transport a kidnapped person. Sentenced to life in prison at Alcatraz.

Jean (Delaney) Crompton, sister of Dolores Delaney – sentenced for harboring a Federal criminal (Tommy Carroll) to one year in the Alderson Federal Correction Facility, Milan, Michigan. Received June 11, 1934. Paroled May 31, 1935.

Volney Davis – Pled guilty to kidnapping Edward G. Bremer June 7, 1936, and sentenced to life in prison at Alcatraz.

Harold Alderton – Convicted June 14, 1935 for conspiracy to transport a kidnapped person in interstate commerce in connection with the Bremer kidnapping case. He had owned the house in Bensenville, Illinois where Edward G. Bremer had been held. Sentenced to 20 years, and sent to Alcatraz.

Elmer Farmer – Convicted in the Bremer kidnapping case on June 7, 1935 for conspiracy to transport a kidnapped person in interstate commerce. Sentenced to 20 years at Leavenworth, Kansas.

James J. "Jimmy" Wilson – Convicted in the Bremer kidnapping case on August 11, 1935 for Conspiracy to transport a kidnapped person in interstate commerce. Sentenced to five years in the U.S. Northeaster Penitentiary, Lewisburg, Pennsylvania.

1936

John J. "Boss" McLaughlin – Died January 4, 1936 at the Federal Penitentiary in Leavenworth, Kansas, where he had been sentenced in 1934 for his part in laundering part of the Edward Bremer ransom money.

Harry Sandlovich (a.k.a. Harry Sawyer) – Convicted February 7, 1936 for kidnapping in the Bremer kidnapping case. Sentenced to life at Leavenworth, Kansas.

Cassius McDonald – Convicted February 7, 1936 for conspiracy in connection with the Bremer kidnapping. Sentenced to 15 years at Leavenworth, Kansas.

Fred Hunter – Convicted May 27, 1936 of harboring a Federal criminal and sentenced to two years.

Myrtle Eaton – Convicted June 10, 1935 for harboring a Federal criminal and sentenced to six months in prison, and fined $1,000.

Alvin Francis Karpis – confessed to his involvement in the William Hamm kidnapping on July 14, 1936, and was sentenced to life in prison at Alcatraz. The unprecedented heat wave in the summer of 1936 was so oppressive that Karpis chose to confess rather than *"spend another day in that hot courtroom."* On the day he confessed, the temperature in the Twin Cities of Minneapolis – Saint Paul had topped 108 degrees, and 51 people in Saint Paul fell dead from heat stroke. Karpis would serve the longest sentence at Alcatraz than any other prisoner – 25 years. When Alcatraz was shut down in 1962, he was transferred to McNeil Island Penitentiary in Washington State until he was paroled in 1969 and deported to Canada. While at McNeil Island, he met a young con known as "Little Charlie", whom he taught how to play a guitar. The young man became very proficient with the instrument and wanted to join a rock and roll band when he was released. One thing Karpis picked up on about the young man was his uncanny ability to manipulate people. But a musical career was not to be for "Little Charlie". In August 1969, Charles "Little Charlie" Manson and his "family" of misfits were arrested and later charged with the murders actress Sharon Tate, her unborn child, coffee heiress Abigail Folger, hairstylist Jay Sebring, Leno and Rosemary LaBianca and two other people.

Karpis would go on to write two books. "The Alvin Karpis Story" in 1970 and 25 Years on the Rock, released by co-author Robert Livesey in 1980. In 1973, Karpis moved from Canada to Torremolinos, Spain, where he died on August 26, 1979.

Phoenix Donald, a.k.a. "William Weaver" – Convicted July 31, 1936 for his role in the Bremer kidnapping case. Sentenced to life. Transferred to Alcatraz, where he died of a heart attack in 1944.

John "Jack" Peifer – Sentenced to 30 years in connection to the William Hamm kidnapping case. He committed suicide in his cell at the St. Paul jail two hours later by chewing gum laced with cyanide.

Jack Peifer

Edna (Stanley) Murray – Acquitted July 31, 1936 in connection with the Bremer kidnapping case, but returned to Missouri

State Penitentiary for Women in Jefferson, Missouri, to complete her 25 year sentence for robbery. She was paroled December 20, 1940.

Freed of Kidnaping Charges

MRS. EDNA MURRAY and JESS DOYLE.
CHARGES connecting them with the kidnaping of Edward G. Bremer Sr., banker of St. Paul, have been dismissed. Mrs. Edna Murray, however, will be returned to the Missouri State Prison from which she escaped. Doyle is wanted in Minneapolis for bank robbery.

Associated Press photo July 31, 1936

Jess Doyle – Acquitted July 31, 1936 in connection to the Bremer kidnapping case, but pled guilty to bank robbery in Minneapolis, MN.

Charles J. Fitzgerald – Convicted July 31, 1936 for his role in the William Hamm kidnapping, and sentenced to life in prison.

Edmund C. Bartholmey – Former Postmaster in Bensenville, Illinois. Convicted for his role in the Hamm kidnapping, and sentenced to six years.

Byron Bolton – Convicted for his role in both the Hamm and Bremer kidnappings. Sentenced August 25, 1936 to three years each, with sentences to run concurrently.

1937

Arthur W. Hebebrand – Convicted June 30, 1937 of harboring a Federal criminal (Alvin Karpis), and sentenced to two years, and fined $1,000.

John Francis Gorman – Convicted June 30, 1937 of harboring a Federal criminal (Alvin Karpis), and sentenced to three years in prison, and fined $1,000.

1938

In the late Spring of 1938, the proverbial buzzards came home to roost for the corrupt officials in Hot Springs, Arkansas who had aided and abetted criminals from all across the country, and who had harbored Alvin Karpis.

On May 19, 1938, Grace Goldstein was arraigned before a U.S. Commissioner, waived removal, and her bond was set at $10,000. On May 23, she was ordered to be sent to Little Rock, in the Eastern District of Arkansas, where she arrived on June 4, and placed under bond of $10,000 for conspiracy to harbor Alvin Karpis. She was also placed under additional bond of $5,000 for violation of the White Slave Traffic Act. She made bond and was released on June 13.

On May 31, Joseph Wakelin, Herbert "Dutch" Akers, Cecil Brock, John Stover, Morris Loftis, and Mrs. Al C. Dyer were arraigned at the United States District Court in Little Rock, where they pled not guilty to conspiracy. Ruth (Hamm) Robison, a.k.a. "Connie Morris", pled guilty in U.S. District Court, and was sentenced to 1 year and 1 day in a Federal penitentiary.

The defendants were tried in U. S. District Court in Little Rock on October 18, 1938. On October 26, Mrs. Al C. Dyer, Morris Loftis, and John Stover were found not guilty. On October 29, Joseph Wakelin, Herbert "Dutch" Akers, Cecil Brock, and Grace Goldstein were found guilty. Their bonds were then revoked, and they were placed in the Pulaski County jail in Little Rock.

Ruth (Hamm) Robison, a.k.a. "Connie Morris" – Pled guilty June 23, 1938 and sentenced to 1 year and 1 day.

Herbert "Dutch" Akers – Convicted October 29, 1938 for harboring a Federal criminal (Alvin Karpis), and sentenced to two years.

Joseph Wakelin – Convicted October 29, 1938 for harboring a Federal criminal (Alvin Karpis) and sentenced to two years.

Cecil Brock – Convicted October 29, 1938 for harboring a Federal criminal (Alvin Karpis) and sentenced to two years.

Jewell Laverne Grayson, a.k.a. 'Grace Goldstein" – Convicted October 29, 1938 for harboring a Federal criminal (Alvin Karpis), and sentenced to two years.

CHAPTER 10:
THE SAD LIFE OF LLOYD WILLIAM BARKER

Lloyd William Barker, the second oldest son of George and Arrie Barker, was born March 16, 1897 in Aurora, Lawrence County, Missouri. He tagged along with his brothers in the days when they were members of the Central Park Gang in Tulsa, but by and large, he escaped any real trouble until 1921. The Tulsa City Directories listed him in 1916 and in 1919. He worked as a driver for the Crystal Springs Water Company, where his father also worked.[1]

In 1918, Lloyd entered the U.S. Army in the waning months of the First World War, serving with the 162nd Depot Brigade, 87th Division, as a cook. The 162nd had been authorized by Secretary of War Newton Baker, and appointed Major General Samuel Sturgis to organize it as an element of the 87th Army Division. It's base of operations was Camp Pike, near Little Rock, in Pulaski County, Arkansas. Its purpose was to train replacements for the American Expeditionary Forces fighting in France, and to act as a receiving unit for men inducted into the Army by their local draft boards. Lloyd was honorably discharged in February 1919 with the rank of Sergeant.[2]

Early mugshot of Lloyd Barker. Possibly Tulsa

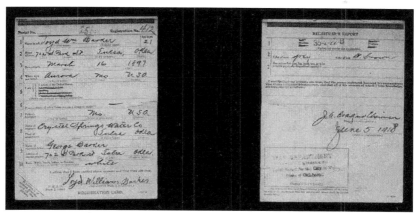

Lloyd William Barker's draft card, Tulsa, 1918

Camp Pike, Arkansas 1918

After returning home, Lloyd went back to work briefly at the Crystal Springs Water Company, but in 1920 was arrested for vagrancy by Tulsa Police. He soon fell back in with the wrong crowd, using the aliases of Lloyd Anderson and Frank Anderson.

At 3:40 a.m., on the early morning of June 17, 1921, Guy Shields, a 26 year old mail messenger, picked up five bags of mail from the Oklahoma Meteor, Frisco Train 111. As he loaded the bags into his vehicle to head to the postal office in Baxter Springs, a car pulled up behind him and four men got out. They held him up, transferred the bags to their car, and forced Shields to get into the car with them. A few miles out of town, they let him out along the side of the road and drove off. He quickly made his way back to town and reported the robbery. Later that morning, several pieces of mail were found floating in the water in Spring River, and the mail pouches were recovered in a field soon thereafter. They had been cut open and rifled. Shields had reported that as far as he knew, the pouches contained no money.[3]

On July 6, Miami, Oklahoma policeman Harry Wilbur was involved in a shootout with a member of the Central Park Gang, William Green, who was wounded and taken to Miami Baptist hospital. As he lay on a cot at the hospital, Julius Payne, a U.S. Deputy Marshall, arrived and charged Green with being involved with the mail robbery at Baxter Springs. Meanwhile, Lloyd Barker and Gregory O'Connell had been arrested in Oswego, Kansas. Jess Brown and Fred O'Connell had been arrested in Tulsa. All of them were charged with the Baxter Springs robbery.[4]

Lloyd was tried and convicted for his role in the Baxter Springs robbery, and sentenced to 25 years. On January 16, 1922, he, Will Green, and Gregory O'Connell were received at the Federal Penitentiary in Leavenworth, Kansas. Lloyd became prisoner number 17243. This was the end of his criminal career. He would complete his entire sentence and not be released until the latter part of 1938.[5]

Lloyd Barker's prison photo, Leavenworth, Kansas

Lloyd was first assigned to working in the prison shoe factory, but he eventually was sent to work as cook, and then as an orderly in the prison hospital's tubercular ward. He never caused any problems, and from all indications, he was a model prisoner. In 1932, he was eligible for parole, and it was granted, but then quickly rescinded. He was probably right in thinking the reason was because of his brothers' crime spree, and the authorities were afraid he would join them. Again, this probably saved his life. On October 29, 1938, Lloyd was finally released from prison. By this time, his mother, Herman, Fred, and most of their gang had been killed or were in prison. Doc was still at Alcatraz, and his father was living in Webb City. Lloyd lived briefly in Kansas City, but in 1940 he and George were living with Ronnie Farmer in Webb City, where Lloyd was working as an electrician.[6]

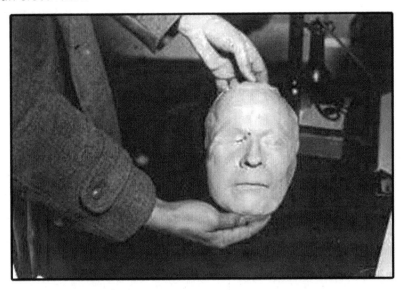

Arthur "Doc" Barker's death mask (FBI Photo)

In December 1938, Doc Barker, Henri Young and Rufus McCain began organizing a plot to escape from Alcatraz. They attempted to execute their plan on the night of January 13, 1939. One of them had smuggled saw blades from the prison work shop. They sawed through the bars of their cells, and crawled out. The men managed to make it outside without detection and then down to the shoreline on the west side of the island. Doc worked feverishly attempting to tie a makeshift raft together. But an alert guard had discovered that the men in Cell Block D were missing, and sounded the alarm. The island launch, *The McDowell,* soon arrived and flooded the shoreline with its spotlight. It didn't take long for the crew to spot the escapees and began shooting at them. One man was shot in the legs. Doc caught a bullet in the left thigh and another in the head behind his right ear. This shot exited out of his right eye. The prisoners were quickly subdued, and the wounded were taken to the infirmary. Doc was heard to say, *"I'm shot all to Hell. I was a fool to try it."* He died about an hour later. He did finally succeed in making it to the mainland. But not in the way he wanted. He arrived in a pine box. [7]

Arthur Raymond "Doc" Barker was buried at Olivet Memorial Park, at 1601 Hillside Boulevard, in Colma, San Mateo County, California. His grave is marked only by a stone with his prison number on it. Years later, a funeral home marker was placed at Williams-Timberhill Cemetery for him near his family, giving rise to rumors that his body was exhumed and reburied with his family in October 1939. However, his remains are still interred at Olivet Memorial Park. [8]

On February 8, 1941, George Elias Barker died at his home at 1201 East Seventh Street in Webb City, Missouri of arteriosclerosis and chronic myocarditis. He would be the only member of the family to die of natural causes. Lloyd was the informant on his father's death certificate. He stated that he was a resident of Denver, Colorado, so he had moved there sometime during the previous year. Out of his entire immediate family, he was truly the last man standing. [9]

On December 7, 1941, the Japanese bombed the U.S. Naval fleet at Pearl Harbor, Hawaii. America found itself at war once again. In 1942, despite having been a felon, Lloyd was allowed to rejoin the Army. He was stationed at Camp Custer, near Augusta, Michigan. Ironically, he served at the Prisoner-Of-War camp as a cook. Lloyd received the Army Good Conduct medal, and again was honorably discharged once the war ended. [10]

Panoramic view of Camp Custer, Michigan, about 1943

Last known photo of Lloyd Barker alive, about 1938

After leaving the Army, Lloyd moved back to Denver and got a job as a bartender at Denargo Grill, at 515-516 Denargo Market street, off Broadway and 29th Avenue near the railroad. Sometime about late 1947, Lloyd met a young divorcée named Jennie Wynne, and the two hit it off very well. Jennie was from New York, and was born Jennie Virginia Farrell on February 20, 1912. She married William J. Wynne in Brooklyn on July 3, 1937. The couple had two children; Ronald, born about 1935, and Virginia, born about 1938. They moved to Denver by 1945, but were divorced about two years later. Jennie moved in with Lloyd by the early part of 1948.[11]

According to the 1948 Denver City Directory, they were living at 535 West 46th Avenue, Apartment 1. Things seemed to be fine between them, and they had two additional children together. Eileen Barker was born in 1947, and Michael Barker was born about May 1948. Lloyd was doing very well at Denargo Grill, located at 215 Denargo Market, and his boss, Charlie Klein, promoted him to Assistant Manager. Life was good. In late 1948, they moved into a house of their own at 3426 W. 73rd Avenue in Westminster, a suburb of Denver. Then in February of 1949 they were married in Brighton, another suburb of Denver. He had gone straight. He had served his time, had outlived his criminal brothers, and now things were looking up.[12]

Very few people in Denver knew who Lloyd really was. Jennie, of course, knew. He had told her that the infamous Ma Barker was his mother, and that he was the only one of his brothers left living. She was no doubt shocked at first, but she never let on to Lloyd that it bothered her. However, this may have been one of the things that plagued her troubled mind. Michael was only 9 months old, and she may have been suffering from post-partum depression. No one really knows. But it was clear that she had mental problems. Maybe this was why she and her first husband had divorced. Whatever the reason, during the morning hours of March 18th, 1949, Jennie paced nervously back and forth through the house. She seemed to be afraid of something. Terrified, in fact.

She told Lloyd she wasn't feeling well. When Lloyd got to the Grill, he told Charlie he had to go home to get someone to watch after the kids, because Jennie was ill. While he was gone, Jennie woke Ronald up and asked him to load her .20 gauge shotgun, claiming she'd heard noises that frightened her coming from the laundry room. He loaded it for her and went back to sleep. Virginia had been awakened by Jennie's pacing during the night, and she saw her pass down the hallway towards the kitchen carrying the shotgun.

She took the weapon to the laundry room and waited. Lloyd returned home about 7:00 a.m. that. He walked up the sidewalk from the garage to the back door. Jennie pointed the shotgun towards the door. As Lloyd was unlocking the door to come inside, she leaned against the washing machine, closed her eyes and pulled the trigger. He never knew what hit him.

The blast blew the glass out of the back door, and struck him in the left side of his neck, blowing his head almost completely off. He was dead before he hit the ground. The noise woke Ronald up, who ran to the utility room where he saw his mother standing with the shotgun, and glared in horror at Lloyd lying dead in a puddle of blood on the back steps. The neighbors also heard the shot and called the police. Jennie quickly retreated into the house and called the police herself. She said, *"I have shot my husband!"* [13]

Jennie Virginia (Farrell) Wynne-Barker, wife of Lloyd William Barker

The children. Ronald Wynne, Virginia Wynne with Michael Barker and Eileen Barker. Michael and Eileen were Ma Barker's only grandchildren.

When the police arrived, Jennie was clearly out of her head, claiming she was afraid Lloyd was going to kill her and the children. She said, "Lloyd didn't like any of the children except Eileen". They took her to the Adams County jail in Brighton for questioning. Her son Ronald told George Fischer, who was the Assistant District Attorney, that Jennie had him load the shotgun for her. The children were placed in state custody until they could be placed with next of kin, if any could be found. The following day, it was decided that Jennie would be transferred to the State Psychiatric Hospital for evaluation. While Sheriff Homer Mayberry was transporting her to the hospital that evening, Jennie tried to jump out of his car, but was finally subdued. Witnesses who saw the car swerving back and forth along the road called the police, as they thought someone had been kidnapped. But once the patrolmen identified the Sheriff's license plates, they realized there was no cause for alarm.[14]

Lloyd William Barker after his wife went crazy and blew his head off with a .20 gauge shotgun at the back entrance of their home on March 18, 1949.

On Monday, March 21st, Jennie was taken before Judge Harold Davies, Brighton District Court, and was charged with the murder of her husband. She at first pleaded "not guilty", and then "not guilty by reason of insanity." Judge Davies ordered her to be returned to the psychiatric hospital.[15]

After a lengthy evaluation, Jennie Barker was sentenced to life on April 9, 1949 in the Colorado State Insane Asylum in Pueblo. She died there on August 2, 1986, and was buried at Mountain View Cemetery near Pueblo in Plot: W Block 11, Lot 125 : 5. Her grave is unmarked.[16]

Once it was known who Lloyd really was, the news spread like wildfire all over the country. The Tulsa Tribune reported the last of "Tulsa's Spawn from Hell Wiped Out"[17](March 22, 1949). He had kept his secret well. His boss, Charlie Klein, stated, *"He never talked about his family. He was a good worker and never got mad."* Patrons of Denargo Grill were surprised as well. *"So he was one of Ma Barker's boys. Well I'll be danged."* Another one of Lloyd's friends confided that *"he was afraid he would meet the same kind of death his mother and brothers had."* [18]

Lloyd William Barker was buried at Elmwood Cemetery in Brighton, Colorado in Section 6, Block 40, Grave 2996. His grave is unmarked, although someone has placed a funeral home marker for him at Williams-Timberhill in Welch, Oklahoma, near his family. On the day of his funeral, Time Magazine reported that Klein closed the restaurant for the day, and 50 patrons paid their last respects to a man they had grown to love and respect. *"The only one of Ma's boys who ever did an honest day's work."* [19]

Funeral Home marker placed at Williams-Timberhill Cemetery in Welch, Oklahoma for Lloyd Barker. It is to the left of Herman Barker's gravestone.

Photo taken June 25, 2016 by Autumn LeMasters

CHAPTER 11:
IN MEMORIUM: END OF WATCH

The Barker crime spree cost the lives of almost a dozen Law Enforcement Officers between 1921 and 1935, the year Fred and his mother were killed. The purpose of this chapter is to honor the memory of these men. Our LEO's put their lives on the line for us each and every day. They deserve our honor and our respect, especially in the times we find ourselves in now. Above all else, they need our prayers and our support.   Rest In Peace, Gentlemen. Thank you for your servic and your sacrifice. You shall never be forgotten.

1. **Night Watchman Thomas Jefferson Sherrill**, was shot and killed August 25, 1921, by Arthur "Doc" Barker at   Saint John's Hospital, which was then still under construction in Tulsa, Oklahoma. While not technically a Law Enforcement Officer, he was serving as an armed Security Officer. He was born February 1868 in Cedar County, Missouri to Ephraim C. and Mary Elizabeth (Willet) Sherrill. Thomas moved to Indian Territory near Kingfisher by 1900. Thomas married Lulu Bell Kennel, the daughter of Abraham Deardorf and Rachel Elizabeth (Hamilton) Kennel, probably in Jasper County, Missouri about 1887. Mr. Sherrill was survived by his wife,

and their children Harry O., Clyde L., Clarence Ted, Glen Walter, Virgil, Irma, and Purl Vernon Sherrill. [1]

2. **Capt. Homer R. Spaulding,** Muskogee Police Department, Oklahoma. Capt. Spaulding was mortally wounded in a shootout with the Central Park Gang on January 9, 1922 near Muskogee, Oklahoma. He had been with the Police Department for nine years. Future Barker-Karpis gang member Volney Davis was involved in this incident, and was one of the suspects who managed to escape. He died ten days later on January 19, 1922. Homer R. Spaulding was born September 24, 1876 in Whitney, Hill County, Texas to James Alexander and Mary Ellen (Mallory) Spaulding. His family moved to Muskogee, Indian Territory, about 1898, and on Christmas Day of 1899, he married Edith Asbill, the daughter of Samuel C. and Sarah A. (Cook) Asbill. She was born April 16, 1881 in Indian Territory and died April 13, 1945 in Shelby County, Texas. They had one son, George Winston Spaulding (1900 – 1942).[2]

3. **Deputy Sheriff Arthur Emil Osborn**, Laramie County Sheriff's Department, Wyoming. Deputy Sheriff Osborn was shot and killed August 1, 1927 near Pine Bluffs, in an attempt to apprehend Herman Barker, who had cashed stolen travelers checks in Cheyenne, Wyoming earlier that day. Arthur Osborn was born June 22, 1882 in Furnas County, Nebraska to William Francis and Sarah Alice (Dinwiddie) Osborn. He married Beulah M. Bird in Cheyenne County, Nebraska in 1911. Deputy Osborn was preceded in death by a daughter, Maxine, who died in 1916. He was survived by his wife, and their other children, Arthur Raymond, Wayne Neville, and Maxwell Elroy Osborn. He, his wife, and Maxine are buried at Pine Bluffs Cemetery. Arthur Raymond Osborn (1917 –

1942) was killed in the Battle of Midway during World War Two.[3]

4. **Officer Joseph Earl Marshall**, Wichita, Kansas. Officer Marshall served as a motorcycle patrolman with the Wichita, Kansas Police Department. He was killed August 29, 1927 by Herman Barker. He had been with the police department two years at the time of his death. Joseph was born June 23, 1899 near Hunnewell, Sumner County, Kansas to Joseph Phenix and Jessie May (Parks) Marshall. He married July 15, 1919 in Sumner County to Marie Fair, the daughter of Daniel Logan and Amanda (Koozer) Fair. Joseph's family and Marie's family were neighbors in 1910, in Grant County, Bluff Township, Kansas. He worked as a Grain Buyer in Sumner County, Kansas before moving to Wichita. He was buried at Wichita Park Cemetery.[4]

5. **Patrolman Elisha Lenore Hagler**, Monett, Barry County, Missouri. Officer Hagler was shot the night of September 21, 1931 by Fred Barker, while he and Alvin Karpis were stealing a car from the Chevrolet dealership in Monett. Others were later convicted for the crime, and it wasn't until 1971 when Alvin Karpis published his book, "The Alvin Karpis Story", that the real killer became known. Officer Hagler died a month later on October 21, 1931. He was born December 14, 1885 in Barry County, Missouri to John Addison and Dolly A. (Fly) Hagler. He married Blanche Odessa Combs about 1909 in Barry County. She was born March 27, 1891 and died February 16, 1921. He was survived by three daughters; Mildred, Edwina, and Mary Margaret Hagler.[5]

6. **Deputy Sheriff Albert Manley Jackson**, Randolph County Police Department, Pocahontas, Arkansas. Deputy Jackson was captured and disarmed by Fred Barker and Alvin Karpis

who saw him writing down their license tag numbers while they were trying to hotwire a car. They drove him to a gravel pit, where Fred Barker shot him in the back five times on November 8, 1931 with a Colt .45 semiauto. His body was discovered the next day. Again, the wrong people went to prison for this murder. Albert was born January 1, 1900 in Randolph County, Arkansas to William A. and Isora (Presley) Jackson. He married Rheta Price, the daughter of John W. and Maggie L. (Johnson) Price, July 7, 1922 in Pocahontas. He was survived by his wife and two young daughters, Albertine and Magalee Jackson. He was preceded in death by an infant son, John William Jackson, who died August 10, 1926. Rheta never remarried, and died in Los Angeles, California June 11, 1984. She was buried next to her husband at Masonic Cemetery in Pocahontas, Arkansas.[6]

7. **Sheriff Calvin Roy Kelly**, Howell County, Missouri. Murdered December 18, 1931 in West Plains, Howell County Missouri Davidson's Motor Company by Fred Barker and Alvin Karpis. Calvin Roy Kelly was born February 12, 1886 in Carter County, Missouri to Aaron and Mary (Bales) Kelly. His father died in 1895, and his mother remarried to Shadrach Chilton, by whom she had one son, Arvil Chilton. Roy married Lulu Victoria Jaco, the daughter of John Wesley and Eliza Jane (McSpadden) Jaco, about 1911. Lulu was born September 18, 1887 in Carter County, Missouri. She and Roy had no children. Sheriff Kelly was buried in Van Buren, Carter County, Missouri on December 21, 1931 at Masonic and Van Buren Cemetery. Lulu Victoria Kelly was appointed Sheriff to complete her husband's term. She remarried a few years later to James Calvin Oliver on October 18, 1944, who worked for a hotel in Fremont, Missouri. James died August 7, 1950 in West Plains, and was buried in Carter County, Missouri with his first wife,

Amanda (Ellis) Oliver, at Evaline Cemetery in Fremont. Lulu died October 23, 1972. She was buried in Poca Hollow Cemetery near her family, in Van Buren, Carter County, Missouri.[7]

8. **Officer Ira Leon Evans**. Minneapolis Police Department. Officer Evans was killed by the Barker-Karpis gang during the robbery of the Northwestern National Bank at Central and Hennepin Avenues, on December 16, 1932 He was survived by his wife, Lillian D. Evans. They had no children. He was buried at Fort Snelling National Cemetery.[8]

9. **Officer Leo Gorski,** Minneapolis Police Department. Officer Gorski was mortally wounded by the Barker-Karpis gang during the robbery of the Northwestern National Bank at Central and Hennepin Avenues, on December 16, 1932. He died two days later, leaving a wife and son.[9]

10. **Officer Leo Pavlak**, South Saint Paul Police Department, Minnesota. Officer Pavlak had joined the Police Department in April 1933. On the morning of August 30, 1933, two couriers from the Stockyards National Bank were robbed of $33,000 by the Barker-Karpis gang. Pavlak was killed by Arthur "Doc" Barker His partner, John Yeoman was shot several times, but survived his wounds. Officer Pavlak was survived by his wife Pauline (Wolanski) Pavlak and their two children, Eleanor and Robert. He was buried at Calvary Cemetery in South Saint Paul.[10]

11. **Officer Miles A. Cunningham**, Chicago Police Department. He was born in Cuskery, Northern Ireland about 1897, and immigrated to the United States aboard the Tuscania on June 21, 1915. This ship was torpedoed by the Germans on February 5, 1918, with a great loss of life to American

servicemen who were headed to England.[11] After arriving in Chicago, he lived with relatives and in 1920, worked as a printer. By 1930, he was working as a Patrolman with the Chicago Police Department. Miles married Margaret (maiden name unknown but possibly also Cunningham) about 1927, and by 1930, they had two children. Myles Cunningham Jr. was born about 1928, and Margaret Cunningham was born 1930. On the evening of September 22, 1933, he and three other officers were on foot patrol and witnessed an accident caused by another vehicle cutting off a Hudson while trying to pass. As he approached, one of the occupants in the Hudson, Byron Bolton, fired at him with a Thompson machinegun, killing him instantly. Bolton, Fred Barker, Doc Barker, William Weaver, and George Zeigler had just robbed the Chicago Federal Reserve Bank messengers. After shooting Cunningham, the five men hijacked a passing Buick and sped off. Officer Cunningham was buried at Saint Joseph Cemetery in Cook County, Illinois.[12]

CHAPTER 12:
CREATING A MONSTER: J. EDGAR HOOVER
AND THE MA BARKER MYTH

"Ma couldn't plan breakfast. When we'd sit down to plan a bank job, she'd go in the other room and listen to Amos and Andy or hillbilly music on the radio."
- Harvey Bailey

According to FBI Chief J. Edgar Hoover, Arizona "Ma" Barker was *"the most vicious, dangerous and resourceful criminal brain of the last decade"*.[1] But those who knew her in life, vehemently disagreed with the idea that she was anything more than an overindulgent, overprotective, mother, who's only mistake was her failure to discipline her sons when they desperately needed it most during their formative years. But since her death, Ma Barker has been portrayed as a ruthless, blood-thirsty monster in movies, plays, and literature. After the deaths of Dillinger, Baby-face Nelson, the Barker-Karpis gang, Hollywood wasted no time using them as their gangster cash cows, and they would milk it for all it was worth. Everyone likes a good shoot em up gangster movie, and Hollywood was ready, willing and able to quench the public's thirst for blood and gore with such films as:

1. **Queen of the Mob (1940).** "Ma Webster" was played by Blanche Yurka. The FBI specifically asked the title character's name be changed.
2. **White Heat (1949).** Starring James Cagney. Margaret Wycherly as "Ma Jarret".
3. **Guns Don't Argue (1957).** Ma Barker is portrayed by Jean Harvey.
4. **The Untouchables (1959 Television).** Season 3, Episode 2. Robert Stack as Elliot Ness, Claire Trevor as Ma Barker. (Ness worked for the Treasury Department, and not the FBI. Hoover was livid over Ness being portrayed as the leader of the Ocklawaha raid).
5. **Ma Barker's Killer Brood (1960).** Directed by Bill Karn. Starring Lurene Tuttle as Ma Barker.
6. **Batman and Robin (1966 Television).** Season 2, Episode 10. Adam West, Burt Ward. Character "Ma Parker" played by Shelly Winters.
7. **Bloody Mama (1970).** Directed by Roger Corman. Ma Barker played by Shelly Winters.
8. **The Goonies (1985).** Directed by Steven Spielberg. A Ma Barker-esque character, "Mama Fratelli", played by Anne Ramsey.
9. **Public Enemies (1996).** Lions Gate. Directed by Mark L. Lester. Theresa Russell as Ma Barker. Also starring Alyssa Milano.

As entertaining as these films were, they're based largely on pure myths created by none other than J. Edgar Hoover himself. Hoover claimed that Ma Barker was the "brains" of the entire Barker-Karpis mob, planned their robberies, and even ran a school for robbers out of her home in Tulsa.[2] But the facts paint an entirely different picture of her. First of all, there is no record of Arrie Barker ever having been arrested. Nor are there are no accounts of her ever firing a gun, or ever having shot anyone. Even Alvin Karpis and Harvey Bailey argued that Ma was in no way the leader of the Barker-Karpis gang. Had she been captured alive rather than killed, the only crime she could have been tried for would have been for harboring fugitives, just as the mothers of Clyde Barrow and Bonnie Parker had been.

So what was Hoover's rationale for telling these stories? He had to account for why an elderly woman was killed during a gunfight between his agents and a dangerous fugitive, namely Fred Barker. He was hell-bent upon preventing the sort of firestorm he had found himself in after the disastrous raid at Little Bohemia Lodge, Wisconsin had resulted in the shooting of three innocent men, and the death of one of his agents.

In January 1934, John Dillinger and members of his gang were captured by police in Tucson, Arizona. Dillinger was flown back to Chicago then held under heavy guard at the Lake County Jail in Crown Point, Indiana. On March 3, 1934 he broke out of jail using a wooden gun and made his way to the jailhouse garage, stealing Sheriff Lillian Holley's 1933 Ford Fordor Sedan.[3] He made a hasty escape to Chicago, thus violating the Dyer Act by transporting a stolen car across state lines. This gave Hoover's Division of Investigation the authority to track him down. harboring fugitives.

Little Bohemia Lodge, Manitowish Waters, Wisconsin

A little over a month later, on April 20, Dillinger and gang members Tommy Carroll, John "Red" Hamilton, Homer Van Meter, and Lester "Baby-face" Nelson' Gillis, arrived at the Little Bohemia Lodge in Manitowish Waters, Wisconsin, owned and operated by Emil and Frieda "Nan" Wanatka.[4]

Earlier that day, Homer Van Meter, his girlfriend Marie Conforti, Pat Cherrington, and Harry Sawyer's cohort in Saint Paul, Pat Reilly, arrived to make guess arrangements for the rest of the gang. Dillinger, Hamilton, Lester and Helen Gillis, Tommy Carroll, and Jean (Delaney) Crompton, arrived about 5:00 p.m. Jean was a sister of Alvin Karpis' girlfriend, Delores Delaney. The men were polite and well dressed, but during a card game, Wanatka noticed that the men had guns holstered under their jackets. The next day, Frieda Wanatka and their son went into town for a children's birthday party. She informed her brother-in-law that she believed the men at Little Bohemia were, in fact, John Dillinger and his gang. They immediately notified the Milwaukee Police Department, who then instructed them to call Special Agent Melvin Purvis in Chicago.[5]

Early Saturday morning, Pat Reilly and Ms. Cherrington left for Saint Paul to pick up $2,500 for an unnamed night club owner (in all likelihood this individual was either Harry Sawyer at the Green Lantern, or Jack Peifer at the Hollyhocks) who was holding $10,000 for Van Meter for safekeeping. Purvis was excited over the news, and quickly gathered up a team of agents and boarded a plane to Wisconsin. He notified the Minnesota Office, and another team rushed from Saint Paul to join them.[6]

They arrived at the lodge that Sunday evening, on April 22, just as the Sunday night dinner crowd were leaving, and took up positions in the woods around the front of the Lodge but failed to post men behind the building. One of the last to leave were two Civilian Conservation Corpsmen, Eugene Boisneau and John Morris, and a salesman, John Hoffman. They got into a 1933 Chevrolet Coupe and headed down the main drive towards home. The driver had the radio on, and the volume was so loud he didn't hear the men up ahead calling for him to stop. In fact, he never even noticed them. It had begun to snow and he could barely see the road. [7]

The agents got spooked. Thinking it must be Dillinger and his men trying to make a run for it, they opened fire. Two of the men were badly wounded, but Boisneau later died. Back at Little Bohemia, Dillinger and his men heard the gunshots and grabbed their weapons. They had no time to get to their cars, which were parked out front. The agents rushed towards the lodge and opened fire. A short gun battle ensued and then the gang retreated out of a two story window and escaped through the woods.[8]

Gillis and his wife Helen had taken a cabin close to the lodge, and when he heard the gunfire, he and Helen rushed to the lodge. Lester went looking for a fight. Helen stayed behind with Marie and Jean and took cover. Lester then ordered Wanatka to take off in his car, but it was too slow, so, he had him drive to a nearby residence where they stole another car. While leaving this residence, they met another car driven by agent Carter Baum. He was accompanied by agent Jay Newman and a local constable, Karl Christenson. When Gillis asked them who they were, they said they were Federal agents. Gillis picked up his modified M1911 machine pistol and shot them, killing Baum instantly and wounding the other two men.

The raid had been a total and complete failure, with Federal agents killing and wounding unarmed civilians, with one of their own agents killed and another seriously wounded. The Media went into a feeding frenzy. When the newspapers hit the streets, the public was furious. They demanded answers. More than that, they demanded Hoover's head on a silver platter, and wanted the Division of Investigation shut down.

After Ma Barker was killed in the crossfire at Ocklawaha, Hoover was hell-bent upon doing some major damage control. He didn't want to be embarrassed again as he had over the Little Bohemia raid. He knew that if the public got wind of an unarmed old woman being gunned down by federal agents, it could spell the end of his career and of the Division of Investigation. He had no intention of allowing that to happen.

Special Agent in Charge Earl J. Connelley left Ocklawaha with his men and returned to Jacksonville, Florida to write his report on the raid. It was written in such a way to make it seem that Ma was also involved in shooting at his agents. They had to put a gun in her hand, even if only on paper.[9]

He stated, *"Upon entering the house, it was ascertained that they had apparently fired from the downstairs through the window and front door with a [illegible] caliber Winchester rifle, and that they had fired from the windows in all four directions from all of the rooms on the second floor, there being four bedrooms in the house. Kate Barker and Fred Barker were found dead in the south-west corner bedroom. Fred Barker was lying in the middle of the room, face down, with a .45 caliber automatic under him and a machine gun with a 50 round drum beyond his left hand, and* **Kate Barker was found in the north-east corner of this same room, lying on her back, with a machine gun at her left hand with a 100 shot drum on same.** *There was also found a 50 shot drum in the bedroom by Kate Barker, which had evidentially been completely fired; a 50 shot drum in the gun apparently used by Fred Barker was completely empty, and a 100 shot drum from the gun found beside Kate Barker had approximately 30 or 40 shots fired from same."* [10]

Connelley's statement that Ma Barker was found *"lying on her back, with a machine gun near her left hand"*, was completely false. The crime scene photo of Ma's body at the scene clearly shows her lying on her left side in a fetal position in a corner of the room and not on her back. Also, the clutter lying in front of her obstructs any view of her right hand, and part of her head. The photograph completely contradicts Connelley's report. [11]

Ma Barker dead. Lying on her left side, not on her back per Connelly's report. (FBI photo)

The very idea of Ma being even remotely proficient with a

firearm was completely out of character for her, and to those who knew her. In fact, there is no known recollection by anyone that she had ever held a gun, let alone fired one. Ma's age and stature would have made it next to impossible for her to have fired a Thompson. The recoil would have likely knocked her to the floor before she squeezed off the first three rounds

The Little Bohemia disaster was a major embarrassment for Hoover, and no doubt contributed to his disdain for Melvin Purvis, who had been thrust into the limelight as the man who got John Dillinger the year before. He stole Hoover's thunder, and Hoover, being the narcissistic, paranoid, neurotic, egomaniac that he was, hated him for it. The feeling was mutual, since Purvis wasn't very fond of him either. Hoover had no intention of being embarrassed again, or sharing the limelight with anyone else.

The term *"History is written by the victors who have hung the heroes"* is attributed to Sir William Wallace, executed by the English in 1305. The FBI had emerged victorious over the Depression-era gangs and had just taken out Fred Barker. But now, an old woman had been killed alongside him, with three Fed bullets through her chest. Hoover had to come up with something fast to keep the Division of Investigation out of more hot water. He and his constant companion, Clyde Tolson, derisively called *"the Gold Dust twins',* would have to rewrite the narrative to cover their asses.

Ma would become his scapegoat. The victim would become the perpetrator. She would be cast as the mastermind, the guiding spirit, behind the Barker-Karpis gang. Before their bodies were even cold, Hoover and Clyde Tolson told the newspapers and anyone else that would listen that since Ma was found with a machine gun in her hands, her death was justifiable. The Press and the American public bought the story hook, line, and sinker. Hoover continued to perpetrate the myth of Ma Barker as the brains behind the Barker-Karpis gang.

Four years previously, Universal Pictures had brought Mary Shelley's classic novel, "Frankenstein", to the Big Screen, starring Boris Karloff. As Henry Frankenstein's monster comes to life, he screams maniacally, *"It's alive! It's alive!"*. Ma Barker would now be vilified in History as the cold-blooded, ruthless, trigger-happy leader of one of the worst outlaw gangs in American History. The Gold Dust twins had created a monster. It was alive, and they were ecstatic.

Whispers in the Dark....

Eerie white vortex near Herman Barker's grave at
Williams-Timberhill Cemetery
Photo by Shelley Mitchell

Another vortex-like figure
near Herman's grave.
Photographer unknown

The Gangster Era truly was a pivotal time in America's history, and like the Old West, it has provided us with many legends, tall tales, and especially stories of the supernatural. For years after their deaths, people have reported eerie encounters with what they believe were the ghosts of Bonnie and Clyde, Al Capone, John Dillinger, and the Barkers. Clyde Barrow and Bonnie Parker are said to haunt the lonely stretch of road in Bienville Parish, Louisiana where they met their end on May 23, 1934. Others have reported encountering the mournful spirit of John Dillinger in the alley where he died near the Biograph Theater in Chicago on July 22, 1934. Both Al Capone's and Doc Barker's ghosts have been seen and heard at the old Federal prison on Alcatraz Island.

Then there is Ma. Ma Barker is said to haunt the Bradford cottage where she and Fred were killed by Federal agents in 1935. According to a Bradford descendant, psychic Sybil Leek performed a séance at the cottage and Ma told her she wasn't going anywhere. That this was now *"her"* place. Not long after the family decided to sell the property, Ma scared off a potential buyer. As he walked around looking the property over, he saw a portly elderly lady facing away from him. When he spoke to her, she turned around to look at him. He could see right through a hole in her chest, and she immediately vanished! Needless to say, he didn't buy the place! She obviously grew weary of the gang being on the run for so long, and she just wanted to settle down and rest.

Herman Barker was killed in Wichita, Kansas in 1927, and his ghost may haunt Williams-Timberhill Cemetery outside Welch, Oklahoma, where his parents, and his brother Fred are buried. This ghost has been photographed on several occasions near his grave, and that part of the cemetery has an eerie, foreboding feel that makes a person's hair stand on end.

Whether or not these are real spirits or the product of overactive imaginations, Americans love a good ghost story; and these tales add some good chills and thrills while sitting around the campfire deep in the woods in the dead of night. Who knows? Maybe these folks, though long gone, visit us on occasion with whispers in the dark to let us know they're still around, reminding us of an age long past. Such is the ever fascinating folklore and legend that is all part and parcel of the field of historical research we like to call *"Gangsterology"*.

INDEX

A

B

L

LaBianca
  Leno ------------------------------ 309
  Rosemary ------------------------ 309
Labrizzetta
  Tony ---------------------------- 277
LaCava
  Louis --------------------------- 263
Lackey
  F. Joseph -------------------- 151, 152
Ladd
  Earl E. ----------------------------30
Lairmore
  L. M. ------------------------------22
Lambert
  Jean ---------------------------- 141
Langan
  John ---------------------------- 275
Langely
  James ------------------------------73
Lansing
  Ed 23
  Edward -----------------------------22
Lauat
  Eva M. (Clark) ----------------------10
Lavender
  Bert (Herman Barker) -------------25
Lawes
  L. A. ---------------------------- 148
Lawrence (or Lorance)
  Mary Jane--------------------------- 6
Lawson
  Jimmy------------------------------22
Lazia
  John ---------------------------- 151
Leavens
  Mona------------------------------ 115
Lee
  Gen. Robert E. ----------------------26

Leek
  Sybil ----------------------------- 341
LeMasters
  Autumn ----------------------256, 325
Lester
  Mark L. --------------------------- 333
Lett
  Milton ---------------------------- 280
Lindbergh
  Ann------------------------------- 137
  Charles, III ----------------------- 137
  Charles, Jr.----------------------- 137
Little
  F. E., Sheriff --------------------- 94
Loftis
  Morris -----------------------289, 312
Lonquist
  Barbara --------------------------- 227
  Patricia -------------------------- 227
Luce
  Frances---------------------------- 131
Luciano
  Lucky ----------------------------- 286
Lyon
  Nathaniel, Brig. Gen. USA ---------3

M

Madala
  John L. --------------------------- 237
Madden
  Owen "Mad Dog"---------------- 286
Magee
  Charles --------------------------- 194
  Walter---- 181, 182, 183, 187, 189,
    192, 194, 197
  Werner---------------------------- 185
Mahoney
  William---------------------------- 139
Makley

CITATIONS AND SOURCES

Chapter 1: BARKER FAMILY HISTORY

1. Battle of Wilson's Creek.
   https://www.nps.gov/wicr/index.htm
2. Bleeding Kansas. http://www.history.com/topics/bleeding-kansas
3. John Brown's Day of Reckoning:
   http://www.smithsonianmag.com/history/john-browns-day-of-reckoning-139165084/?no-ist
4. William Quantrill. Renegade Leader of the Missouri Border War:
   http://www.legendsofamerica.com/mo-quantrill.html
5. Quantrill of Missouri, by Paul R. Peterson.
6. Historic Missourians – Jesse Woodson James:
   http://shsmo.org/historicmissourians/name/j/jamesj/
7. Elias Barker: *Year: 1810; Census Place: Estill, Kentucky; Roll: 6; Page: 3; Image: 00014; Family History Library Film: 0181351* Estill County, Kentucky marriages 1808 – 1820.
   Elias Barker: *1820 U S Census; Census Place: Ravenna, Estill, Kentucky; Page: 47; NARA Roll: M33_17; Image: 59*
8. James Barker: Find A Grave data:
   http://www.findagrave.com/cgi-bin/fg.cgi?page=gr&GRid=149301961
9. Estill County, Kentucky marriages 1808-1820
   Elias Barker: *1830; Census Place: Estill, Kentucky; Series: M19; Roll: 35; Page: 242; Family History Library Film: 0007814*
   Elias Barker: *1830; Census Place: Lafayette, Missouri; Series: M19; Roll: 73; Page: 249; Family History Library Film: 0014854*
   Barker Family genealogy:
   http://searches2.rootsweb.com/th/read/BARKER/1998-11/0910663912
   Eleas [Elias] Barker: *Year: 1840; Census Place: Lafayette, Missouri; Roll: 224; Page: 154; Image: 316; Family History Library Film: 0014856*
   Elias Barker: *Year: 1850; Census Place: District 45, Laclede, Missouri; Roll: M432_403; Page: 141A; Image: 286*

10. Elias Barker: https://www.findagrave.com/cgi-bin/fg.cgi?page=gr&GRid=60500364

11. John Barker: *Year: 1860; Census Place: Union, Laclede, Missouri; Roll: M653_627; Page: 306; Image: 309; Family History Library Film: 803627*
John Barker: *Year: 1870; Census Place: Washington, Stone, Missouri; Roll: M593_823; Page: 143A; Image: 142216; Family History Library Film: 552322*
John Barker: *Year: 1880; Census Place: Flat Creek, Stone, Missouri; Roll: 738; Family History Film: 1254738; Page: 30C; Enumeration District: 121; Image: 0172*

12. John Clark in household of Robert and Delia Clark:
Year: 1850; Census Place: Township 1 N R 4 W, Brown, Illinois; Roll: M432_98; Page: 176A; Image: 569
John Clark in household of John Turner:
Year: 1860; Census Place: Boone, Greene, Missouri; Roll: M653_621; Page: 289; Image: 289; Family History Library Film: 803621
John Clark: *Year: 1870; Census Place: Boone, Greene, Missouri; Roll: M593_777; Page: 10A; Image: 327855; Family History Library Film: 552276*

13. Arizona Clark in household of Reuben Reynolds: *Year: 1880; Census Place: Ash Grove, Greene, Missouri; Roll: 688; Family History Film: 1254688; Page: 161A; Enumeration District: 040; Image: 0023*
Reuben Reynolds in Tulsa: *Year: 1900; Census Place: Vineyard, Lawrence, Missouri; Roll: 870; Page: 20A; Enumeration District: 0088; FHL microfilm: 1240870*
Reuben Ross Reynolds Find A Grave Memorial;
https://www.findagrave.com/cgi-bin/fg.cgi?page=gr&GSln=Reynolds&GSfn=Reuben&GSbyrel=all&GSdyrel=all&GSst=50&GScnty=2960&GScntry=4&GSob=n&GRid=39519268&df=all&

14. Jesse Clark: *Year: 1910; Census Place: Stotts Ward 1, Lawrence, Missouri; Roll: T624_795; Page: 2B; Enumeration District: 0105; FHL microfilm: 1374808.*

Jesse Clark: *Year: 1920; Census Place: Lincoln, Lawrence, Missouri; Roll: T625_932; Page: 11A; Enumeration District: 109; Image: 218*

Jess Clark: *Year: 1930; Census Place: Carthage, Jasper, Missouri; Roll: 1206; Page: 11B; Enumeration District: 0043; Image: 126.0; FHL microfilm: 2340941*

15. Eva M. (Clark) Hayes: *Year: 1930; Census Place: Carthage, Jasper, Missouri; Roll: 1206; Page: 11B; Enumeration District: 0043; Image: 126.0; FHL microfilm: 2340941.*

16. George Beecher Perryman, Jr. Find A Grave: https://www.findagrave.com/cgi-bin/fg.cgi?page=gr&GSln=Perryman&GSbyrel=all&GSdyrel=all&GSst=38&GScntry=4&GSob=n&GSsr=121&GRid=26618762&df=all&.

17. Chesley Reynolds in household of Reuben Reynolds: Year: 1900; Census Place: Vineyard, Lawrence, Missouri; Roll: 870; Page: 20A; Enumeration District: 0088; FHL microfilm: 1240870.

    Chesley Reynolds not found in Tulsa in 1910: *Year: 1910; Census Place: Lake Andes, Charles Mix, South Dakota; Roll: T624_1478; Page: 10B; Enumeration District: 0101; FHL microfilm: 1375491*

    Chesley Reynolds: *Year: 1920; Census Place: Dawson, Tulsa, Oklahoma; Roll: T625_1486; Page: 17A; Enumeration District: 181; Image: 613.*

    Chestley Reynolds: *Year: 1930; Census Place: Tulsa, Tulsa, Oklahoma; Roll: 1936; Page: 7B; Enumeration District: 0132; Image: 186.0; FHL microfilm: 2341670*

18. Mary Goldie (Clark) Vosburg-Hanners obituary: Monday, February 14, 1972. Independent from Long Beach, California, page 27: *"Hanners (Vosburg) Goldie Mary, of 2357 Magnolia Avenue. Born September 1, 1888, Ash Grove, Missouri age 83. Mrs. Hanners is the daughter of Judge Reuben Ross Reynolds and Emma Parker Reynolds. Mrs. Hanners is survived by son, Delbert (Dell) Vosburg, grandchildren Mrs. Carol Ann Bell, James Carey and Charles Melvin Vosburg, and five great-grandchildren."*

19. Edmund D. Parker, Lincoln County, TN 1840: Year: 1840; Census Place: Lincoln, Tennessee; Roll: 531; Page: 89; Image: 183; Family History Library Film: 0024548.

    Edmund D. Parker, McNairy County, TN 1850: Year: 1850; Census Place: District 12, McNairy, Tennessee; Roll: M432_888; Page: 100A; Image: 205.

    Frederic Sewel [Frederick Sewell], McNairy County, TN 1850: Year: 1850; Census Place: District 12, McNairy, Tennessee; Roll: M432_888; Page: 100A; Image: 205.

20. German Suel [German Sewell] Year: 1850; Census Place: District 5, Barry, Missouri; Roll: M432_391; Page: 204A; Image: 414.

21. John Parker: Year: 1850; Census Place: District 5, Barry, Missouri; Roll: M432_391; Page: 199B; Image: 405.

22. John Parker: Year: 1860; Census Place: Cass, Greene, Missouri; Roll: M653_621; Page: 256; Image: 256; Family History Library Film: 803621.

    John A. Parker: Year: 1870; Census Place: Boone, Greene, Missouri; Roll: M593_777; Page: 12B; Image: 328061; Family History Library Film: 552276.

    John Parker: Year: 1880; Census Place: Walnut Grove, Greene, Missouri; Roll: 687; Family History Film: 1254687; Page: 4D; Enumeration District: 031; Image: 0513.

    John Parker: Year: 1900; Census Place: Walnut Grove, Greene, Missouri; Roll: 856; Page: 4B; Enumeration District: 0057; FHL microfilm: 1240856

    John Parker: Year: 1910; Census Place: Walnut Grove, Greene, Missouri; Roll: T624_781; Page: 19B; Enumeration District: 0062; FHL microfilm: 1374794.

23. Lot 202, Block 21, Linzee's 2nd Addition, Book 79, Page 178. John Koblas states this property was located at 108 Jasper Street, Aurora, Missouri ("Ma" The Life and Times of Ma Barker and Her Boys – by John Koblas. Forward by Rick Mattix.

24. George E. Barker, Joplin/Webb City Directories 1904 - 1910: Ancestry.com. U.S. City Directories, 1822-1995 [database online]. Provo, UT, USA: Ancestry.com Operations, Inc., 2011.

25. The Reign of Creepy, by Steve Gerkin: http://thislandpress.com/2011/07/06/creepy-karpis-and-the-tulsa-central-park-gang/
26. George E. Barker, Tulsa, OK City Directors 1914 – 1928: Ancestry.com. U.S. City Directories, 1822-1995 [database on-Line]. Provo, Ut, USA: Ancestry.com Operations, Inc., 2011.

Chapter 2: HERMAN BARKER

1. Herman Barker Tulsa, OK 1914: Ancestry.com. U.S. City Directories, 1822-1995 [database on-line]. Provo, UT, USA: Ancestry.com Operations, Inc., 2011.
2. The Complete Public Enemies Almanac; William J. Helmer and Rick Mattix, page 453.
3. Herman Barker [Bert Lavender] Year: 1920; Census Place: Cottonwood, Powell, Montana; Roll: T625_974; Page: 4B; Enumeration District: 174; Image: 772
4. The Complete Public Enemies Almanac; William J. Helmer and Rick Mattix, page 458.
5. https://www.accessgenealogy.com/oklahoma/biography-of-judge-q-p-mcghee.htm
6. Miami Daily News-Record, Miami, OK. Thursday, July 28, 1931, page 1.
7. File Bremer Kidnapping files, Part 200 of 459.
8. Cornelius Darius Antone: http://www.findagrave.com/cgi-bin/fg.cgi?page=gr&GRid=33865061
9. Michael Francis Slayman to Elizabeth Antone, October 3, 1906, Muskogee, Oklahoma. http://familysearch.org/tree/person/LL9J-74C/details.
   1910 census: Not found
   1920; Lizzie Slayman. Census Place: Tulsa, Tulsa, Oklahoma: T-625_1487; Page 7B; Enumeration District 243: Image: 597. Lizzie Slayman 30, Mary Slayman 12, Francs Slayman 10, Dartha Slayman 6, Myrtle Slayman 1 4/12.
10. Tulsa County Marriages: L. J. Richards to Elizabeth Slayman, 11 February 1922, by Rev. J. M. Page.
11. Creek County Marriage Records: Earl E. Ladd to Mary Carol Antone, July 11, 1914.

12. State V Carol Barker [Hamilton]. First Judicial Court Record, held in [Robert] Nelson Museum of the West, Cheyenne; pp 4.10.32.
13. Troy Taylor, American Hauntings Ink: The Last Great Outlaw Gang: http://troytaylorbooks.blogspot.com/2015/01/the-last-great-outlaw-gang.html.
    U.S. National Library of Medicine. Dr. James Allen Nolan: https://ceb.nlm.nih.gov/fdanj/handle/123456789/12471
14. Oklahoma Historical Society http://www.okhistory.org/publications/enc/entry.php?entry=HE005
15. State V Carol Barker [Hamilton]. First Judicial Court Record, held in [Robert] Nelson Museum of the West, Cheyenne; pp 4.10.32.
16. Ibid.
17. Ibid.
18. Ibid.
19. Ibid.
20. Coroner's Inquest, Arthur E. Osborn, Pine Bluffs, Wyo. August 1, 1927.
21. Finds Trunk of Slayer of Arthur E. Osborn. Pine Bluffs Post, August 19, 1927.
22. $1,000 Reward Is Offered for Osborne Slayer. Billings Gazette (Billings, MT).
23. Only Surviving Bandit Pleads Not Guilty of Slaying Kansas Policeman WICHITA, Kas. Sept 3 – (AP) – Miami Daily News-Record, Miami, Oklahoma, Sunday September 4, 1927.
24. Ibid.
25. Oklahoma Reports: Cases Determined in the Supreme Court of Oklahoma. Volumes 55-56, Pages 209-210. Meek v. Tilghman et al – No. 6418 – Opinion filed Feb 1, 1916.
26. The Complete Public Enemies Almanac. William J. Helmer and Rick Mattix. Page 201.
27. Wichita Eagle, Wichita, Kansas. August 29, 1927
28. Ibid.
29. Ibid.
30. Ibid.
31. Wichita Eagle, Wichita, Kansas. August 29, 1927
32. Ibid.

Hall Undertaking Company (Lawrence and Margie Hall), Funeral
Parlors, 32 S. Main, Phone 800 (See backbone and page 53).
Miami, Ottawa County, Oklahoma City Directory page 97.
Hall, Lawrence (Margie) undtker h613 1st av SW Miami,
Oklahoma City Directory, 1929, page 114.

33. Miami Daily News-Record, Miami, Oklahoma. Sunday,
    September 18, 1927, Page 1.
34. Wichita Eagle, September 1, 1927.
35. Ibid.
    SLAY ANOTHER IN KIMES GANG, Spokesman-Review,
    Spokane, Washington. September 1, 1927.
36. Emporia Gazette, Emporia, Kansas. Stalcup sentenced to life.
    Monday, November 14, 1927, Page 7.

Chapter 3 THE RISE OF THE BARKER-KARPIS GANG

1. Clyde's letter to Henry Ford???
   http://texashideout.tripod.com/comparison.html
2. BANDITS GET $14,200 MINE PAY ROLL, Tulsa Daily World,
   Tulsa, Oklahoma Saturday, September 2, 1922, Page 1.
   5 MEN 2 WOMEN ALL FROM TULSA BANDIT SUSPECTS.
   Seven Held in Miami Pending Probe of Picher Pay Roll
   Robbery.
   Tulsa Daily World, Tulsa, Oklahoma, Thursday, September 7,
   1922.
   St. Louis Post Dispatch, St. Louis, MO, Tuesday, January 16,
   1923, Page 3.
3. The Complete Public Enemies Almanac. William J. Helmer
   and Rick Mattix. Page 455
4. Part 200 of 459. Bremer Kidnapping Files.
5. Herman Barker https://vault.fbi.gov/herman-
   barker/herman-barker-part-01-of-01/view . Page 47.
6. The Alvin Karpis Story. By Alvin Karpis, with Bill Trent. 1971.
   Coward, McCann & Geoghegan, Inc. Chapter 2; pages 26 –
   38.
7. Ibid.
8. Ibid.
9. Ibid.

10. DeVol, Hilem family. Year: 1910; Census Place: Tulsa Ward 2, Tulsa, Oklahoma; Roll: T624_1274; Page: 9A; Enumeration District: 0227; FHL microfilm: 1375287.

11. DeVol, Emma family. Year: 1920; Census Place: Black Dog, Osage, Oklahoma; Roll: T625_1479; Page: 3B; Enumeration District: 78; Image: 210.

12. Newton, Michael. The Encyclopedia of Robberies, Heists, and Capers. New York: Facts on File Inc., 2002. (pg. 81) ISBN 0-8160-4488-0

13. The Alvin Karpis Story. By Alvin Karpis, with Bill Trent. 1971. Coward, McCann & Geoghegan, Inc. Chapter 2; pages 26 – 38.

14. Ibid.

15. The Alvin Karpis Story. By Alvin Karpis, with Bill Trent. 1971. Coward, McCann & Geoghegan, Inc. Chapter 6; pages 80 – 91.

16. Ibid.

17. Ibid.

18. Ibid.

19. Ibid.

20. CREIGHTON ESCAPES FROM STATE PRISON Slayer of Coyne Hatten at Webb City in May, 1931, Was Serving- Life Sentence for Crime. Joplin Globe, July 15, 1944, page 8.

21. Tulsa Tribune, May 23, 1931

22. Part 49 of 459, Bremer Kidnapping Files.

23. September 26, 1931. "Alvin Karpis to Dorothy E. Slayman" Marriage License 2029-00139. Sapulpa, Creek County, Oklahoma.

24. Oregon County Plat Map: http://cdm16795.contentdm.oclc.org/cdm/ref/collection/moplatbooks/id/2417

25. The Alvin Karpis Story. By Alvin Karpis, with Bill Trent. 1971. Coward, McCann & Geoghegan, Inc. Chapter 6; page 59. NIGHT PATROLMAN AT MONETT SHOT. The Sedalia Democrat, Sedalia, Missouri. September 22, 1931, page 8.

26. The Alvin Karpis Story. By Alvin Karpis, with Bill Trent. 1971. Coward, McCann & Geoghegan, Inc. Chapter 2; pages 42, 43. The Complete Public Enemy Almanac. William J. Helmer and Rick Mattix. Page 329.

27. The Alvin Karpis Story. By Alvin Karpis, with Bill Trent. 1971. Coward, McCann & Geoghegan, Inc. Chapter 6; page61. The Compete Public Enemy Almanac. William J. Helmer and Rick Mattix. Page 330.

28. West Plains Gazette, May-June 1982, Number Seventeen. The Shooting of Sheriff Kelly, by Ron Pyron. Pages 14 – 22, 59, 60.

29. Bremer kidnapping part 264 of 576, page 30. FBI.gov The Vault.

30. West Plains Gazette, May-June 1982, Number Seventeen. The Shooting of Sheriff Kelly, by Ron Pyron. Pages 14 – 22, 59, 60.

31. Bremer kidnapping part 21 of 576, page26. FBI.gov The Vault.

32. Ibid.

33. Ibid.

34. Ibid.

35. Bremer kidnapping part 49 of 459, page 8. Identifies license tag of Karpis' 1931 DeSoto as Oklahoma tag number 131-020.

36. Ibid.

37. Bremer kidnapping part 49 of 459, page 15. Mentions personal effects of the Barkers left behind, as well as facts pertaining to Dunlop's will.

38. The Alvin Karpis Story. By Alvin Karpis, with Bill Trent, 1971, Coward, McCann & Geoghegan, Inc. Chapter 6, pages 86, 87.

39. Ibid.

40. Bremer kidnapping part 49 of 459, page 9.

41. Ibid.

42. Ibid.

43. Public Enemies, America's Criminal Past, 1919-1940. William Helmer, with Rick Mattix.

Chapter 4 SAINT PAUL: A REAL GANGSTER'S PARADISE

1. History of Ramsey County and the City of St. Paul – George E. Warner, Charles M. Foote, Edward Duffield, John Fletcher Williams. North Star Publishing Company, Minneapolis, 1881.
2. Ibid.
3. Ibid.
4. Ibid.
5. John Dillinger Slept Here: A Crook's Tour of Crime and Corruption in St. Paul, 1920 – 1936. Paul Maccafee
6. Ibid.
7. O'Connor Layover Agreement: MNpedia.com: http://www.mnopedia.org/thing/oconnor-layover-agreement
8. John Dillinger Slept Here: A Crook's Tour of Crime and Corruption in St. Paul, 1920 – 1936. Paul Maccafee
9. 'DAPPER DAN' HOGAN DIES OF BOMB WOUNDS, St. Paul Pioneer Press, St. Paul, Minn., Wednesday, December 6, 1928.
10. John Dillinger Slept Here: A Crook's Tour of Crime and Corruption in St. Paul, 1920 – 1936. Paul Maccafee
11. The Alvin Karpis Story. By Alvin Karpis, with Bill Trent, 1971, Coward, McCann & Geoghegan, Inc. Chapter 8, pages 105 - 117.
12. The Alvin Karpis Story. By Alvin Karpis, with Bill Trent, 1971, Coward, McCann & Geoghegan, Inc. Chapter 6, pages 86, 87.
13. GUN BANDITS RAID TOWN IN MINNESOTA. Macon Chronicle-Herald from Macon, Missouri, Tuesday, December 29, 1931, Page 1
14. The Complete Public Enemy Almanac. William J. Helmer and Rick Mattix. Page 331.
15. The Alvin Karpis Story. By Alvin Karpis, with Bill Trent. 1971. Coward, McCann & Geoghegan, Inc. Chapter 7, pages 102, 103.
16. SLAIN WOMAN BANDIT'S WIFE, ST. PAUL. Lincoln Star, Lincoln, Nebraska, Page 10.
17. The Alvin Karpis Story. By Alvin Karpis, with Bill Trent. 1971.

Coward, McCann & Geoghegan, Inc. Chapter 12, pages 161-163.

Year: 1900; Census Place: Darwin, Meeker, Minnesota; Roll: 775; Page: 5B; Enumeration District: 0103; FHL microfilm: 1240775: Peter Piefer 34 born September 1865 Illinois, Barbara 32 born May 1868 Germany, Matthias 8 born December 1891 Minnesota, John P. 7 born December 1892, Richard 4 born November 1894.

Year: 1910; Census Place: Litchfield Ward 2, Meeker, Minnesota; Roll: T624_694; Page: 9A; Enumeration District: 0095; FHL microfilm: 1374707: Peter Piefer 44 born Illinois, Barbara age 42 born Germany, Matthias J. age 18, John P. age 17, Richard 14, LeRoy M. age 5.

18. The Alvin Karpis Story. By Alvin Karpis, with Bill Trent. 1971.

19. Coward, McCann & Geoghegan, Inc. Chapter 12, pages 161-163.

20. The Complete Public Enemy Almanac. William J. Helmer and Rick Mattix. Page 333.

21. The Alvin Karpis Story. By Alvin Karpis, with Bill Trent. 1971. Coward, McCann & Geoghegan, Inc. Chapter 3, pages 44 -47.

22. Secret Partners: Big Tom Brown and the Barker Gang. Timothy R. Mahoney. Minnesota Historical Society Press. 2013.

23. Ibid.

24. The Alvin Karpis Story. By Alvin Karpis, with Bill Trent. 1971. Coward, McCann & Geoghegan, Inc. Chapter 6, pages 88,89.

25. On The Rock. Twenty-five years in Alcatraz. By Alvin Karpis, as told to Robert Livesey. 1980. Revised special edition, 2008.

26. The Complete Public Enemy Almanac. William J. Helmer and Rick Mattix. Page 334.
The Alvin Karpis Story. By Alvin Karpis, with Bill Trent. 1971. Coward, McCann & Geoghegan, Inc. Chapter 3, pages 46. 47.

27. Chicago Tribune, August 15, 1933. Page 3.
"Faces Murder Inquiry – [Harvey] Bailey also is wanted in Tulsa County, Okla., for questioning on the killing off J. Earl Smith, Tulsa attorney, whose body was found near the Indian Hills country club, fifteen miles from that place, just about a

year ago. It is the theory that Bailey regarded Smith as a double-crosser and had Harry Campbell and Fred Barker, another pal, kill Smith. Campbell and Barker have not been caught "

28. Cloud County bank robbery, Concordia, Kansas, July 25, 1932.
The Complete Public Enemy Almanac. William J. Helmer and Rick Mattix. Page 335.

29. Beloit robbery: August 18, 1932. Freeport Journal-Standard from Freeport, Illinois · Page 1

30. Robbery of First National Bank of Flandreau, South Dakota. September 1, 1932. The Complete Public Enemy Almanac. William J. Helmer and Rick Mattix. Page 337.

31. Flandreau robbery: September 3, 1932 Deadwood Pioneer-Times from Deadwood, South Dakota · Page 1

Chapter 5: DOC COMES HOME

1. ARTHUR BARKER IS HELD, Tulsa Daily World, Monday July 22, 1918.

2. *Arthur R Barker, Student, b 502 S. Trenton av. Tulsa City Directory, 1919, page 86.*

3. *Joel GAzis-SAx, "Doc" on the Rock: Ripples from the Fall of Arthur Barker.1997.*
    http://www.notfrisco.com/colmatales/barker/

4. "Raymond" Barker enumerated in Tulsa County jail, January 28, 1920. Source Citation: Year: 1920; Census Place: Tulsa, Tulsa, Oklahoma; Roll: T625_1486; Page: 4B; Enumeration District: 215; Image: 937

5. Tulsa Daily News, Tulsa, Oklahoma, 1921 – 1922.

6. SHERRILL'S DEATH CHARGED TO BOYS, Tulsa Daily World, October 27, 1921, pages 1, 2.

7. Ibid.

8. GUARD'S SLAYER GETS LIFE TERM, Tulsa Daily World, January 15, 1922. Page 1, 2
    OFFICERS CATCH AID OF BARKER, Tulsa Daily World, March 5, 1922, page 1

9. The Alvin Karpis Story. By Alvin Karpis, with Bill Trent. 1971.

Coward, McCann & Geoghegan, Inc. Chapter 7, pages 92-94.

10. "The Lawbreakers of Redwood County" by WAYNE E. WEBB & J. I. SWEDBERG, pages 26,27.
The Alvin Karpis Story. By Alvin Karpis, with Bill Trent. 1971. Coward, McCann & Geoghegan, Inc.

11. Ibid.

12. Ibid.

13. The Alvin Karpis Story. By Alvin Karpis, with Bill Trent. 1971. Coward, McCann & Geoghegan, Inc. Chapter 3, pages 48-50. Wahpeton bank robbed, September 30, 1932 The Hutchinson News, Hutchinson, Kansas, Page 1

14. Ibid.

15. Ibid.

16. Ibid.

17. Ibid.

18. The Bismarck Tribune, Bismarck, North Dakota. October 18, 1932, Page 1

19. Ibid.

20. Ibid.

21. Ibid.

22. Ibid.

23. The Complete Public Enemy Almanac. William J. Helmer and Rick Mattix. Page 337.
The Alvin Karpis Story. By Alvin Karpis, with Bill Trent. 1971. Coward, McCann & Geoghegan, Inc. Chapter 7, page 93.

24. Year: 1880; Census Place: Noble, Dickinson, Kansas; Roll: 379; Family History Film: 1254379; Page: 447D; Enumeration District: 070; Image: 0458: Charles Stanley, age 21 (born 1859) in Household of Nicholas D. and Mary J. Stanley. Nicholas D. 58 born Indiana, Mary J., 55 born Indiana. Children: Charles, 21, born Kansas, Hannibal 17, born Kansas. Mary Hewitt, granddaughter, age 11.
Year: 1900; Census Place: Diamond Creek, Chase, Kansas; Roll: 473; Page: 3A; Enumeration District: 0027; FHL microfilm: 1240473: Charles N. Stanley, born July 1862, Kansas, parents born Indiana. Louie, wife, born September 1868, Indiana, parents born Indiana. Children: Harry, born

August 1890, Fred, born December 1891, Matt, born May 1896, Edna, born May 1898.

Year: 1910; Census Place: Narcissa, Ottawa, Oklahoma; Roll: T624_1267; Page: 5A; Enumeration District: 0162; FHL microfilm: 1375280: Chas. Stanley, 51, born Kansas, parents born Indiana. Louie, 41, born Indiana, parents born Indiana. Mother of 10, 6 living. Married 24 years (1886). Children: Matt 12, Edna 11, Dora 9, Floyd, 6.

Year: 1920; Census Place: Quapaw, Ottawa, Oklahoma; Roll: T625_1481; Page: 5B; Enumeration District: 124; Image: 205: N D Stanley, 63, born Kansas, parents born Kansas. Lue, 63, born Indiana, parents born Kansas. Harry 30, Matt 23, Floyd 17.

See also: *"Run Rabbit Run: The Life, The Legend, and The Legacy of Edna "Rabbit" Murray "The Kissing Bandit"*, by Pam Paden Tippet, 2013.

25. OFFICERS CATCH AID OF BARKER. Tulsa Daily World, Sunday, March 5, 1922.
26. Barker-Karpis Gang Summary 1 of 1. I.C.#7-576. Pages 10,11. FBI archives. The Vault.
27. Ibid.
28. The Complete Public Enemy Almanac. William J. Helmer and Rick Mattix. Page 347.
    The Alvin Karpis Story. By Alvin Karpis, with Bill Trent. 1971. Coward, McCann & Geoghegan, Inc. Chapter 5, pages 63 - 66.
29. Wayward Soldier. Verne Miller Time Line: http://www.sdpb.sd.gov/vernemiller/timeline.asp
    Aubrey Miller age 8, and 'Varnon" Miller age 4, in household of Rachel Marlin, Concord, Woodbury County, Iowa: Year: 1900; Census Place: Concord, Woodbury, Iowa; Roll: 466; Page: 3A; Enumeration District: 0149; FHL microfilm: 1240466.
30. Wayward Soldier. Verne Miller Time Line: http://www.sdpb.sd.gov/vernemiller/timeline.asp
31. Ibid.
32. Ibid.
33. Ibid.

34. Ibid.

35. Ibid.

36. Ibid.

37. The Alvin Karpis Story. By Alvin Karpis, with Bill Trent. 1971. Coward, McCann & Geoghegan, Inc. Chapter 5, pages 63 - 66.

38. Ibid.

39. Ibid.

40. Officer Ira Leon Evans: http://www.insidempd.com/2015/12/16/officer-ira-leon-evans/

41. Ibid.

42. J. Edgar Hoover. The Man and His Secrets. By Curt Gentry. W. W. Norton & Company, Inc., 2001. Page 182.

43. The Alvin Karpis Story. By Alvin Karpis, with Bill Trent. 1971. Coward, McCann & Geoghegan, Inc. Chapter 5, pages 63 - 66.

44. National Register of Historic Places in Washoe County: http://noehill.com/nv_washoe/nat1983001117.asp

45. Article: Renown criminal rests in Linwood Cemetery, Paragould Daily Press, Paragould, Arkansas. Friday April 27, 2012.

46. Ibid.

47. The Alvin Karpis Story. By Alvin Karpis, with Bill Trent. 1971. Coward, McCann & Geoghegan, Inc. Chapter 5, pages 73 - 74.

48. The Alvin Karpis Story. By Alvin Karpis, with Bill Trent. 1971. Coward, McCann & Geoghegan, Inc. Chapter 5, pages 75 – 79.

49. Ibid.

50. Ibid.

51. Ibid.
    The Complete Public Enemy Almanac. William J. Helmer and Rick Mattix. Page 348, 349. Note; Alvin Karpis claims the doctor who examined Christman said (Page 79) he was *"in pretty good shape, and shipped him off to a place In the country to recuperate."* Most all other accounts state he died at Miller's house and was taken out to a dry creek bed outside Kansas City, Missouri and secretly buried.

52. Barker-Karpis Gang Summary 1 of 1. I.C.#7-576. Page 11.

53. Year: 1880; Census Place: Precinct 1, Henderson, Texas; Roll: 1310; Family History Film: 1255310; Page: 128D; Enumeration District: 031: Stamps Brannan 31, born Tennessee, Mary J 27, English 4, born Texas, D. B. 2, born Texas, D. C. 33 born Tennessee.

Year: 1900; Census Place: Justice Precinct 5, Cooke, Texas; Roll: 1623; Page: 10A; Enumeration District: 0037; FHL microfilm: 1241623: D. Bird Brannan born August 1877 Texas, Annie born Nov 1881 Georgia, Mattie C born June 1900, Stamps (Father) born December 1848 TN. Widowed, David C (uncle) born December 1846 Tennessee.

Year: 1910; Census Place: Justice Precinct 8, Kaufman, Texas; Roll: T624_1570; Page: 12A; Enumeration District: 0042; FHL microfilm: 1375583: D. B. Brannan 31 born Texas, Annie 28 born Georgia, Paula 10, English 7, Bird 2, Wesley 4/12, S. (Father) 60 born Tennessee:

Year: 1920; Census Place: Port Arthur Ward 3, Jefferson, Texas; Roll: T625_1822; Page: 14A; Enumeration District: 109; Image: 976: David B. Brannan 41 born Texas, Annie A 38 born Georgia, Paula M. age 16 born Georgia, English F age 14 born Texas, Byrd D age 11 born Texas, Wesley W. age 10 born Texas, Charles H. Hester age 27 born Georgia, Lodger.

54. Barker-Karpis Gang Summary 1 of 1. I.C.#7-576. Page 11.

Chapter 6: KIDNAPPING BECAME BIG BUSINESS

1. https://www.fbi.gov/history/famous-cases/lindbergh-kidnapping
2. Ibid.
3. Secret Partners: Big Tom Brown and the Barker Gang. Timothy R. Mahoney. Minnesota Historical Society Press. 2013.
4. John Dillinger Slept Here: A Crook's Tour of Crime and Corruption in St. Paul, 1920 – 1936. Paul Maccafee.
5. Alcohol and Public Policy: Beyond the Shadow of Prohibition edited by Mark Harrison Moore, Dean R. Gerstein.

6. The Alvin Karpis Story. By Alvin Karpis, with Bill Trent. 1971. Coward, McCann & Geoghegan, Inc. Chapter 10, pages 127 - 130.
7. Shotgun Ziegler, Part 1: http://chicagotruecrime.com/shotgun-zeigler-part-i-freddie-fritz-and-shotgun.html.
8. Shotgun Ziegler, Part 2: http://chicagotruecrime.com/shotgun-zeigler-part-ii-big-hits-murder-and-massacre.html.
9. St. Valentine's Day Massacre: http://chicagotruecrime.com/the-st-valentines-day-massacre-part-vi.html.
10. Ibid.
11. The Alvin Karpis Story. By Alvin Karpis, with Bill Trent. 1971. Coward, McCann & Geoghegan, Inc. Chapter 10, pages 127 - 146.
12. Ibid.
13. St. Paul's Historic Family Breweries – MBAA: http://www.mbaa.com/districts/stPaulMpls/about/Pages/District-Memories.aspx
14. Ibid.
15. William and Mary Hamm house: http://saintpaulhistorical.com/items/show/34
16. The Alvin Karpis Story. By Alvin Karpis, with Bill Trent. 1971. Coward, McCann & Geoghegan, Inc. Chapter 10, pages 127 - 146
17. The Complete Public Enemy Almanac. William J. Helmer and Rick Mattix. Page 350.
    Warden Of Kansas Prison Kidnaped by Eight Armed Convicts: Guard Shot. Pampas Daily News, Pampas, Texas, Tuesday May 30, 1933.
18. Underhill, Henry Wilbur (1901 – 1934). http://www.okhistory.org/publications/enc/entry.php?entry=UN016
19. The Alvin Karpis Story. By Alvin Karpis, with Bill Trent. 1971. Coward, McCann & Geoghegan, Inc. Chapter 10, pages 127 - 146

20. Ibid.
21. Ibid.
22. The Complete Public Enemy Almanac. William J. Helmer and Rick Mattix. Page 351.
    Kansas City Massacre/"Pretty Boy" Floyd:
    https://www.fbi.gov/history/famous-cases/kansas-city-massacre-pretty-boy-floyd
23. Ibid.
24. Ibid.
25. Ibid.
26. The Complete Public Enemy Almanac. William J. Helmer and Rick Mattix. The Kansas City Massacre, Pages 352 – 354.
27. Kansas City Massacre/" Pretty Boy" Floyd:
    https://www.fbi.gov/history/famous-cases/kansas-city-massacre-pretty-boy-floyd
28. Ibid.
29. The Alvin Karpis Story. By Alvin Karpis, with Bill Trent. 1971. Coward, McCann & Geoghegan, Inc. Chapter 10, pages 127 - 146
30. Ibid.
31. Secret Partners: Big Tom Brown and the Barker Gang. Timothy R. Mahoney. Minnesota Historical Society Press. 2013.
32. Ibid.
33. Ibid.
34. The Alvin Karpis Story. By Alvin Karpis, with Bill Trent. 1971. Coward, McCann & Geoghegan, Inc. Chapter 10, pages 127 - 146
35. Ibid.
36. Ibid.
37. http://rogertouhygangsters.blogspot.com/2014/10/the-arrest-in-elkhorn.html
38. Ibid.
39. A Byte Out of History: Latent Prints in the 1933 Hamm Kidnapping:
    https://archives.fbi.gov/archives/news/stories/2003/september/hamm090803

40. George "Machine Gun" Kelly"
    https://www.fbi.gov/history/famous-cases/machine-gun-kelly
    http://www.alcatrazhistory.com/mgk.htm
41. Ibid.
42. Tigress: The Life and Times of Kathryn Kelly, by Lawrence J.
    Yaden. http://thislandpress.com/2011/10/15/tigress-the-life-and-times-of-kathryn-kelly/
43. Ibid.
44. Read All About 1933: Charles F. Urschel: http://www.major-smolinski.com/KIDNAP/URSCHEL.html
    Baby-Face Nelson Journal; Machine Gun Kelly, Part 4:
    http://www.babyfacenelsonjournal.com/kelly-4.html
45. George "Machine Gun" Kelly"
    https://www.fbi.gov/history/famous-cases/machine-gun-kelly
46. Ibid.
47. The Alvin Karpis Story. By Alvin Karpis, with Bill Trent. 1971.
    Coward, McCann & Geoghegan, Inc. Chapter 10, pages 148 – 150.
48. The Complete Public Enemy Almanac. William J. Helmer and
    Rick Mattix. The Kansas City Massacre, Page 357.
    Officer Leo Pavlack:
    http://www.southstpaul.org/Index.aspx?NID=334
49. Ibid.
50. The Alvin Karpis Story. By Alvin Karpis, with Bill Trent. 1971.
    Coward, McCann & Geoghegan, Inc. Chapter 10, pages 148 – 150.
51. The Complete Public Enemy Almanac. William J. Helmer and
    Rick Mattix. The Kansas City Massacre, Page 358.
    "City of South St. Paul Police Department History."
    http://www.southstpaul.org/DocumentCenter/View/295
    Chicago Tribune, September 22, 1933. Page 1. Photos Page 44.
52. The Alvin Karpis Story. By Alvin Karpis, with Bill Trent. 1971.
    Coward, McCann & Geoghegan, Inc. Chapter 10, pages 153 – 159.

53. Ibid.

54. Ibid.

55. Ibid.

56. Ibid.

57. Ibid.

58. Ibid.

59. Ibid.

60. Ibid.

61. Ibid.

62. Verne Miller Time Line: http://www.sdpb.sd.gov/vernemiller/timeline.asp

63. 'The End of a Gangster', Says Dying Gus Winkler: Albany Evening News, page 1. October 10, 1933. "Was Gus Winkler's Widow Marked for an Underworld Death?" (Chicago – AP). New York Sun, October 22, 1933. Read All About It. 1933. Gus Winkeler: http://major-smolinski.com/OUTLAWS/WINKLER.html

64. The Alvin Karpis Story. By Alvin Karpis, with Bill Trent. 1971. Coward, McCann & Geoghegan, Inc. Chapter 10, pages 152 – 153.

65. Ibid.

66. Ibid.

67. Louis (Lepke) Burkhalter, part 3 of 4, page 13: vault.fbi.gov

68. http://www.sdpb.sd.gov/vernemiller/timeline.asp Louis (Lepke) Burkhalter, part 3 of 4, page 13: vault.fbi.gov

69. Verne Miller Time Line: http://www.sdpb.sd.gov/vernemiller/timeline.asp

70. The Alvin Karpis Story. By Alvin Karpis, with Bill Trent. 1971. Coward, McCann & Geoghegan, Inc. Chapter 12, page 161. Barker-Karpis gang summary, Part 1 of 1, page 16:

Chapter 7: 1934: THE BREMER KIDNAPPING AND THE END OF THE GANGSTER ERA

1. The Alvin Karpis Story. By Alvin Karpis, with Bill Trent. 1971. Coward, McCann & Geoghegan, Inc. Chapter 12, page 162.

2. Home Brewed Mojo. The Bremer Kidnapping:
   http://homebrewedmojo.blogspot.com/2013/01/the-bremer-kidnapping.html
3. Schmidt Brewery – SUBSTREET:
   http://substreet.org/schmidt-brewery/
   The Alvin Karpis Story. By Alvin Karpis, with Bill Trent. 1971.
   Coward, McCann & Geoghegan, Inc. Chapter 12, page 163.
4. Ibid.
5. Ibid.
6. Obituary of Emily Elizabeth "Betty" (Bremer) Johnson.
   February 14, 15 2009, Pioneer Press, Saint Paul, Minnesota.
7. Couple Sought in Bremer Case Sift. U.S. Agents Try to trace
   Man and Woman Who Occupied Flat. St. Paul Dispatch,
   February 12, 1934, page 1.
   Bremer Kidnap Files, Part 381 of 459, pages 14, 15:

8. 1930 model Lightmaster 3 cell flashlight:
   http://www.flashlightmuseum.com
   Bremer Kidnapping files, Part 29 of 459, pages 92, 93:

   Bremer Kidnapping Files, Part 234 of 459, page 1 (Clerk
   identified as Mrs. Florence Humphrey):
9. Bremer Kidnapping Files, Part 76 of 459, pages 14-17:
10. The Alvin Karpis Story. By Alvin Karpis, with Bill Trent. 1971.
    Coward, McCann & Geoghegan, Inc. Chapter 12, page 164-171.
11. Ibid.
12. Bremer Kidnapping Files, Part 1 of 459. Ibid.
13. Bremer Kidnapping Files, Part 423 of 459:
14. Bremer Kidnapping Files, Part 1 of 459, page 16:
15. Bremer Kidnapping Files, Part 1 of 459, pages 30-33:
16. Ibid.
17. The Alvin Karpis Story. By Alvin Karpis, with Bill Trent. 1971.
    Coward, McCann & Geoghegan, Inc. Chapter 12, page 164-171.
18. Bremer Kidnapping Files, Part 423 of 459, pages 15 – 17:

LEAK IN BREMER CASE CHARGED, St. Paul Daily News, September 2, 1936.

PRIVATE PARLEY DATA GIVEN MOB, DAHILL STATES, St. Paul Daily News, September 3, 1936.

19. Ibid.
20. Barker-Karpis gang summary, part 1 of 1:
21. Ibid.
22. Barker-Karpis gang summary, part 1 of 1:
    Bremer Kidnapping Files, Part 381 of 459, Page 7:
23. Barker-Karpis gang summary, part 1 of 1:
24. Ibid.
25. Ibid.
26. The Alvin Karpis Story. By Alvin Karpis, with Bill Trent. 1971. Coward, McCann & Geoghegan, Inc. Chapter 12, page 164-171.
27. Barker-Karpis gang summary, part 1 of 1:
28. Dr. Joseph P. Moran,
    http://www.legendsofamerica.com/20th-gangsters-m.html
29. On the Rock: Twenty-Five Years in Alcatraz. Alvin Karpis, as told to Robert Livesey. New York: Beaufort Books, 1980, p. 126.
30. http://chicagotruecrime.com/shotgun-zeigler-part-iv-the-1000-corpse.html
31. Ibid.
32. Ibid.
33. Bremer Kidnapping Files, Part 272 of 459, page 7
34. Bremer Kidnapping Files, Part 273 of 459, pages 12-14
35. Bremer Kidnapping Files, Part 310 of 459, pages 5-18
36. Bremer Kidnapping Files, Part 177 of 459, pages 4-16
37. The Complete Public Enemies Almanac; William J. Helmer and Rick Mattix, page 380, 385.
    Bremer Kidnapping Files, Part 51 of 459.
38. The Complete Public Enemies Almanac; William J. Helmer and Rick Mattix, page 381.
    Home Brewed Mojo. The Murder of Eddie Green:
    http://homebrewedmojo.blogspot.com/2013/04/the-murder-of-eddie-green.html

39. Lessons at Little Bohemia: https://www.fbi.gov/video-repository/newss-lessons-at-little-bohemia/view
40. DILLINGER, THE HIDDEN TRUTH - RELOADED, by Tony Stewart
41. Ibid.
42. Ibid.
43. Ibid.
44. Ibid.
45. Faded Glory. Dusty Roads of an FBI Era. John "Red" Hamilton. As Elusive As You Desire.
http://historicalgmen.squarespace.com/hamiltons-fate-sac-earl-j-con/
Dillinger gang section-109, FBI, the vault.
The Complete Public Enemies Almanac; William J. Helmer and Rick Mattix. The Body Identified as John Hamilton. Pages 438 – 442.
46. The Alvin Karpis Story. By Alvin Karpis, with Bill Trent. 1971. Coward, McCann & Geoghegan, Inc. Chapter 11, pages 174, 175.
47. The Alvin Karpis Story. By Alvin Karpis, with Bill Trent. 1971. Coward, McCann & Geoghegan, Inc. Chapter 7, page 99.
48. The Alvin Karpis Story. By Alvin Karpis, with Bill Trent. 1971. Coward, McCann & Geoghegan, Inc. Chapter 11, pages 174, 175.
49. Ibid.
50. The Paris News, Paris, Texas. Friday, April 27, 1984, page 4.
51. The Daily Reporter, Greenfield, Indiana, Friday May 27, 1955, Page 5.
52. On the Trail of Bonnie and Clyde, Then and Now. Edited by Winston G. Ramsey, September 2003.
53. Ibid.
54. Dillinger Gang Gunman Slain by Iowa Police. Tommy Carroll Shot Down in Waterloo: Chicago Tribune, June 8, 1934, page 2.
55. DILLINGER, THE HIDDEN TRUTH – RELOADED, by Tony Stewart.

56. Homer Van Meter Slain. THE NEW YORK TIMES, New York, August 25, 1934
57. The Alvin Karpis Story. By Alvin Karpis, with Bill Trent. 1971. Coward, McCann & Geoghegan, Inc. Chapter 13, pages 176-178.
    Barker-Karpis Gang Summary, Part 1 of 1.
58. The Alvin Karpis Story. By Alvin Karpis, with Bill Trent. 1971. Coward, McCann & Geoghegan, Inc. Chapter 13, pages 178-187.
59. Ibid.
60. Ibid.
61. Bremer Kidnapping Files, Part 300 of 459, page 7.
62. Ibid.
63. Leap Into History: John Dillinger In Delaware County, Indiana, by Brock Krebs.
    Allen County Museum & Historical Society, the Sarber/Dillinger Story:
    http://allencountymuseum.org/ACM2/Sarber-Dillinger_story.html
64. Charles Arthur "Pretty Boy" Floyd.
    http://www.biography.com/people/charles-pretty-boy-floyd-9542085
65. The Alvin Karpis Story. By Alvin Karpis, with Bill Trent. 1971. Coward, McCann & Geoghegan, Inc. Chapter 13, pages 178-187.
66. Ibid.
67. Ibid.

Chapter 8: GATOR JOE

1. Bremer Kidnapping Files, Part 427 of 459, Page 107. Witness Ties Adams To Barker Hideout. Miami Tribune, Miami, Florida, June 8, 1937.
2. For Sale: Ma Barker's Last Home:
   http://www.ocala.com/news/20120822/for-sale-ma-barkers-last-home
3. Bremer Kidnapping Files, Part 250 of 459, Pages 15- 21
4. Ibid.

5. Ibid.
6. The Mammoth Book of Women Who Kill. Edited by Richard Glyn Jones, Constable & Robinson, Ltd., London, 2002.
7. "Shotgun Zeigler" The Strange Case of Fred Goetz, Chicago's Dr. Jekyll and Mr. Hyde PART V "WHO SHOTGUNNED SHOTGUN'?": http://chicagotruecrime.com/shotgun-zeigler-part-v-who-shotgunned-shotgun.html
8. Barker-Karpis Gang Summary, Part 1 of 1.
9. Ex-Agent Recalls Role In Gangster Era: https://www.fbi.gov/video-repository/newss-ex-agent-recalls-role-in-gangster-era/view
10. American Hauntings: Ghosts, Gangsters, Murder & Mayhem in American History: http://troytaylorbooks.blogspot.com/2015_01_01_archive.html
11. Ibid.
12. Statement of Earl J. Connelley, Bremer Kidnapping Part 75.
13. Ibid.
14. Ibid.
15. Ibid.
16. Paranormal and Ghost Society. Gator Joe's and Ma Barker's Hideaway. Scroll down to "January 1935 – The End of the Ma Barker Gang, by Rick Mattix http://paranormalghostsociety.org/GatorJoes%20And%20MaBarkers.asp
17. Statement of Earl J. Connelley, Bremer Kidnapping Part 75, via FADED GLORY: DUSTY ROADS OF AN FBI ERA. Bremer Kidnapping Files, Part 233 of 459, Pages 77-79. Note to Fred Barber from Marien Bradford: *"Dear Mr. Barber, Have given the keys to these friends of Mr. Adams so they can look through the house in view of renting it later. Thought I had better let you know as you were watching it for me. Received the check from Munners house. All o.k. We have a little new baby boy at our house, Carson Bradford the Third. Thanks so much, Lovingly, Marien Bradford. [p.s.] Wish you would show them the house if convenient. If no it is alright for them to look through alone. They might have a*

little trouble with the keys, if so Mr. [illegible] can open the door, I am sure. M.B."

18. Statement of Earl J. Connelley, Bremer Kidnapping Part 75, via FADED GLORY: DUSTY ROADS OF AN FBI ERA.
19. Ibid.
20. Ibid.
21. Ibid.
22. Ibid.
23. Ibid.
24. Ibid.
25. Ibid.
26. Joplin Globe, Joplin MO, January 24, 1935.
27. Sikeston Standard, Sikeston, MO, Tuesday Oct 1, 1935, page 3
28. Miami News-Record, Thursday, October 3, 1935. page 6
29. The Dillinger Days. John Toland. Da Capo Press, New York. 1963.
30. List of weapons found in Barker Hideout. Barker Kidnapping Part 65, via FADED GLORY: DUSTY ROADS OF AN FBI ERA.

Chapter 9: MANHUNT: THE SEARCH FOR ALVIN KARPIS

1. The Alvin Karpis Story. By Alvin Karpis, with Bill Trent. 1971. Coward, McCann & Geoghegan, Inc. Chapter 13, page 187.
2. Ibid.
3. The Complete Public Enemies Almanac; William J. Helmer and Rick Mattix, Page 408.
4. The Alvin Karpis Story. By Alvin Karpis, with Bill Trent. 1971. Coward, McCann & Geoghegan, Inc. Chapter 13, pages 189-201.
5. Bremer Kidnapping Files, Part 88 of 459, page 6.
6. Ibid., page 8.
7. Ibid.
8. Ibid.
9. Ibid.
10. Ibid., page 10.
11. Ibid.
12. Ibid., page 11.

The Alvin Karpis Story. By Alvin Karpis, with Bill Trent. 1971. Coward, McCann & Geoghegan, Inc. Chapter 13, pages 189-201

13. Ibid.
    Bremer Kidnapping Files, Part 88 of 459, pages 10 – 13.
14. The Alvin Karpis Story. By Alvin Karpis, with Bill Trent. 1971. Coward, McCann & Geoghegan, Inc. Chapter 13, pages 189-201
15. Ibid.
    Bremer Kidnapping Files, Part 88 of 459, Page 13.
16. Ibid., page 14.
    The Alvin Karpis Story. By Alvin Karpis, with Bill Trent. 1971. Coward, McCann & Geoghegan, Inc. Chapter 13, pages 189-201
17. Bremer Kidnapping Files, Part 88 of 459, page 15.
18. The Alvin Karpis Story. By Alvin Karpis, with Bill Trent. 1971. Coward, McCann & Geoghegan, Inc. Chapter 13, pages 189-201
19. Ibid.
20. Ibid.
    Barker-Karpis gang summary, the vault, FBI.gov.
21. The Complete Public Enemies Almanac; William J. Helmer and Rick Mattix, Page 409.
22. Gangster Volney Davis's Great Illinois Escape; Yorkville to Wheaton in a Ford V-8. By John Emmering. http://clubs.hemmings.com/nirg-earlyfordv-8/Newsletter/2014/Aug/VolneyDavis.htm
23. Ibid.
24. Ibid.
25. The Complete Public Enemies Almanac; William J. Helmer and Rick Mattix, Page 409.
26. Bremer Kidnapping Files, Part 272 of 459, Page 11.
27. Cincinnati Enquirer, Cincinnati, Ohio, April 28, 1935, page 14. Pottstown Mercury, Pottstown, Pennsylvania, April 29, 1935, page 5.

The Alvin Karpis Story. By Alvin Karpis, with Bill Trent. 1971. Coward, McCann & Geoghegan, Inc. Chapter 15, pages 202-219.

28. Ibid.
29. Ibid.
30. Ibid.
31. Bremer Kidnapping Files, Part 130 of 459, Page 18
32. The Complete Public Enemies Almanac; William J. Helmer and Rick Mattix. The Body Identified as John Hamilton. Pages 438 – 442.
33. Barker-Karpis Gang Summary, vault.fbi.gov
34. Bremer Kidnapping Files, Part 272 of 459, Pages 9-15,
35. Bremer Kidnapping Files, Part 210 of 459, Page 49.
    Bremer Kidnapping Files, Part 272 of 459
    Bremer Kidnapping Files, Part 427 of 459
36. The Alvin Karpis Story. By Alvin Karpis, with Bill Trent. 1971. Coward, McCann & Geoghegan, Inc. Chapter 15, pages 202-219.
    Bremer Kidnapping Files, Part 233 of 459, Page 67.
37. Ibid.
38. Ibid.
39. Ibid.
40. Ibid.
41. Ibid.
42. Ibid.
43. Garrettsville native to share her research into great train robbery from 1935. By Paula Schleis, Beacon Journal staff writer: http://www.ohio.com/news/local/garrettsville-native-to-share-her-research-into-great-train-robbery-from-1935-1.411960
44. The Alvin Karpis Story. By Alvin Karpis, with Bill Trent. 1971. Coward, McCann & Geoghegan, Inc. Chapter 15, pages 202-219.
    Bremer Kidnapping Files, Part 272 of 459, Page 15
    Bremer Kidnapping Files, Part 210 of 459, Page 78
45. Ibid.
46. Barker-Karpis Gang Summary, I.C. #7-576, page 67

47. Barker-Karpis Gang Summary, I.C. #7-576, pages 72, 73.

48. Ibid., page 73

49. Ibid., pages 73, 74

50. The Alvin Karpis Story. By Alvin Karpis, with Bill Trent. 1971. Coward, McCann & Geoghegan, Inc. Chapter 15, pages 220-233.

51. Ibid. Also, Barker-Karpis gang summary, I.C. #7-576.

52. Bremer Kidnapping Files, Part 210 of 459, pages 6-9.

53. Ibid.

54. Ibid.

55. Ibid.

56. The Alvin Karpis Story. By Alvin Karpis, with Bill Trent. 1971. Coward, McCann & Geoghegan, Inc. Chapter 15, pages 220-233.

57. Bremer Kidnapping Files, Part 365 of 459, page 60.

58. The Alvin Karpis Story. By Alvin Karpis, with Bill Trent. 1971. Coward, McCann & Geoghegan, Inc. Chapter 15, pages 220-233.

59. Ibid.

60. Tale of Tennessee and the FBI: Senator K. D. McKellar and J. Edgar Hoover. By Ray Hill August 4, 2013: http://knoxfocus.com/2013/08/a-tale-of-tennessee-and-the-fbi-senator-k-d-mckellar-and-j-edgar-hoover/

61. Ibid.

62. Ibid.

63. Ibid.

64. Ibid.

65. Ibid.

66. The Alvin Karpis Story. By Alvin Karpis, with Bill Trent. 1971. Coward, McCann & Geoghegan, Inc. Chapter 15, pages 220-233.

67. Ibid.

68. Ibid.

69. Ibid.

70. Ibid.

71. The FBI Story. A Byte Out of History. The Alvin Karpis Capture:

file:///C:/Users/Wolf/Documents/Downloads/FBIStory2012%20(2).pdf

72. The Alvin Karpis Story. By Alvin Karpis, with Bill Trent. 1971. Coward, McCann & Geoghegan, Inc. Chapter 15, pages 220-233.
73. Toledo Blade, May 8, 1936
74. Barker-Karpis Gang Summary, I.C. #7-576,

Chapter 10: THE SAD LIFE OF LLOYD WILLIAM BARKER

1. 1916 Tulsa City Directory, Page 68. Barker, Lloyd, Driver 110 E. Cameron, Tulsa.
   1919 Tulsa City Directory, Page 86. Barker, Lloyd W, Driver 702 S Trenton av.
2. Leavenworth files on Lloyd Barker.
   87th Division's WW1 History: https://grahambw.wordpress.com/2011/07/28/87th-divisions-wwi-history/
   The Complete Public Enemy Almanac. William J. Helmer and Rick Mattix. The Rise and Fall of the Last Great Outlaw Gang, page 454.
3. Miami District Daily News, Miami, Oklahoma. Friday, June 17, 1921
4. Joplin Globe, Joplin Missouri, July 6, 1921
5. Roy Hanna, "Tulsa's 'Spawn of Hell' Wiped Out" (Tulsa Tribune, March 22, 1949)
6. Barker, Lloyd: Year: 1930; Census Place: Fort Leavenworth, Leavenworth, Kansas; Roll: 707; Page: 1A; Enumeration District: 0018; Image: 1177.0; FHL microfilm: 2340442
7. Year: 1940; Census Place: Webb City, Jasper, Missouri; Roll: T627_2118; Page: 1B; Enumeration District: 49-35
8. The Crime Times. Doc Barker's Escape from Alcatraz: http://thecrimetimes.blogspot.com/2011/01/jan-13-1939-doc-barkers-escape-from.html
9. Find A Grave. Arthur R. "Doc" Barker: http://www.findagrave.com/cgi-bin/fg.cgi?page=gr&GRid=5856079

10. Find A Grave. George Elias Barker: http://www.findagrave.com/cgi-bin/fg.cgi?page=gr&GRid=10532747
11. William J. Wynne to Jennie V. Farrell, 3 July 1937, Kings County, New York, marriage certificate number 11537
12. 1948 Denver City Directory, Page 88: Barker, Lloyd W (Jean) bartndr h1535 W 46th av apt 1.
13. lloyd-william-barker-part-01-of-012 (Death of) the vault.fbi.gov.
14. The Owosso (Michigan) Argus-Press - Mar 23, 1949 lloyd-william-barker-part-01-of-012 (Death of) the vault.fbi.gov
15. lloyd-william-barker-part-01-of-012 (Death of) the vault.fbi.gov
16. Find A Grave. Jennie Barker: http://www.findagrave.com/cgi-bin/fg.cgi?page=gr&GSln=Barker&GSbyrel=all&GSdyrel=all&GSst=7&GScnty=291&GScntry=4&GSob=n&GRid=100204744&df=all&
17. "The Last of the Barkers" (TIME Magazine, April 4, 1949)
18. Ibid.
19. See also "The Lonesome Death of Lloyd Barker" by Rick Mattix, 2007: https://www.goodreads.com/story/show/7430-the-lonesome-death-of-lloyd-barker

Chapter 11: IN MEMORIUM; END OF WATCH

1. **Thomas J. Sherrill:** Household of Ephraim Sherrill: Year: 1870; Census Place: Linn, Cedar, Missouri; Roll: M593_768; Page: 85A; Image: 43019; Family History Library Film: 552267 Household of Sampson Swingle: Year: 1880; Census Place: Richland, Barton, Missouri; Roll: 673; Family History Film: 1254673; Page: 484D; Enumeration District: 267; Image: 0305 Household of Thomas J. Sherrill: Year: 1900; Census Place: Otter, Kingfisher, Oklahoma; Roll: 1338; Page: 8B; Enumeration District: 0113; FHL microfilm: 1241338

Household of Thomas J. Sherrill: Year: 1910; Census Place: Liberty, Pawnee, Oklahoma; Roll: T624_1268; Page: 2A; Enumeration District: 0179; FHL microfilm: 1375281

Household of Thomas J. Sherrill: Year: 1920; Census Place: Tulsa, Tulsa, Oklahoma; Roll: T625_1487; Page: 1B; Enumeration District: 227; Image: 171

1919 Tulsa City Directory, Page 463: Sherrill, Thomas J. (Lulu B.) helper, Okla Iron Wrks. R 715 Cascade av.

1920 Tulsa City Directory, Page 453: Sherrill, Thomas J. (Lulu) chipper, Okla Iron Wrks r 715 Cascade av.

1931 Tulsa City Directory, Page 482: Sherrill, Thomas J. (Lou) Watchman r 717 N. Owasso av.

2. **Capt. Homer R. Spaulding**
   Officer Down Memorial:
   https://www.odmp.org/officer/16481-captain-homer-r-spaulding

   Household of Homer Spaulding: Year: 1900; Census Place: Cheotah, Creek Nation, Indian Territory; Roll: 1854; Enumeration District: 0063; FHL microfilm: 1241854

   Household of Homer R. Spaulding: Year: 1910; Census Place: Brown, Muskogee, Oklahoma; Roll: T624_1263; Page: 13B; Enumeration District: 0096; FHL microfilm: 1375276

   Household of Homer R. Spaulding: Year: 1920; Census Place: Muskogee Ward 3, Muskogee, Oklahoma; Roll: T625_1477; Page: 7B; Enumeration District: 87; Image: 1078

   1913 Muskogee City Directory Page 366: Spaulding, Homer R. deputy sheriff, res Travelers Hotel.

   1914 Muskogee City Directory Page 240: Spaulding, Homer R. (Edith) deputy sheriff res 1017 Fon du Lac.

   1915 Muskogee City Directory Page 273: Spaulding, Homer R. (Edith) r 919 Columbus

   1916 Muskogee City Directory Page 249: Spaulding, Homer R. (Edith) bailiff r 919 Columbus

   1917 Muskogee City Directory Page 278: Spaulding, Homer R. (Edith) detective 4 919 Columbus av.

1918 Muskogee City Directory Page 300: Spaulding, Homer R. (Edith) (Art Harris Transfer & Storage Co.) r 919 Columbus Phone 1742.
1921 Muskogee City Directory Page 311: Spaulding, Homer R. (Edith) Transfer r 322 S 15th.

3. **Arthur Emil Osborn**
    Officer Down Memorial:
    https://www.odmp.org/officer/10233-deputy-sheriff-arthur-emil-osborn
    Household of William F. Osborn: Year: 1900; Census Place: Edison, Furnas, Nebraska; Roll: 927; Page: 3B; Enumeration District: 0062; FHL microfilm: 1240927
    Household of Earnest F. Osborn: Year: 1910; Census Place: McCook Ward 2, Red Willow, Nebraska; Roll: T624_853; Page: 13A; Enumeration District: 0192; FHL microfilm: 1374866
    Household of Arthur E. Osborn: Year: 1920; Census Place: Pine Bluffs, Laramie, Wyoming; Roll: T625_2027; Page: 3B; Enumeration District: 45; Image: 324

4. **Joseph Earl Marshall**
    Officer Down Memorial:
    https://www.odmp.org/officer/8588-patrolman-joseph-earl-marshall
    Household of Joseph E. Marshall: Year: 1910; Census Place: Bluff, Grant, Oklahoma; Roll: T624_1253; Page: 9A; Enumeration District: 0037; FHL microfilm: 1375266
    Household of Joseph E. Marshall: Year: 1920; Census Place: South Haven, Sumner, Kansas; Roll: T625_553; Page: 14B; Enumeration District: 184; Image: 605

5. **Elisha Lenore Hagler**
    Officer Down Memorial:
    https://www.odmp.org/officer/5903-night-watchman-elisha-lenore-hagler

Household of Jno A. and Dollie Hagler: Year: 1900; Census Place: Kings Prairie, Barry, Missouri; Roll: 838; Page: 10A; Enumeration District: 0007; FHL microfilm: 1240838
Household of Elisha L. Hagler: Year: 1910; Census Place: Monett Ward 3, Barry, Missouri; Roll: T624_767; Page: 12B; Enumeration District: 0005; FHL microfilm: 1374780
Household of Elisha L. Hagler: Year: 1920; Census Place: Monett Ward 1, Barry, Missouri; Roll: T625_904; Page: 2A; Enumeration District: 4; Image: 18
Household of Elisha L. Hagler: Year: 1930; Census Place: Monett, Barry, Missouri; Roll: 1175; Page: 9B; Enumeration District: 0015; Image: 550.0; FHL microfilm: 2340910

6. **Albert Manley Jackson**
   Officer Down Memorial:
   https://www.odmp.org/officer/6995-chief-of-police-manley-jackson
   Household of William A. Jackson: Year: 1910; Census Place: Demun, Randolph, Arkansas; Roll: T624_63; Page: 2B; Enumeration District: 0117; FHL microfilm: 1374076
   Household of William A. Jackson: Year: 1920; Census Place: Demun, Randolph, Arkansas; Roll: T625_77; Page: 7B; Enumeration District: 118; Image: 1090
   Household of Manley Jackson: Year: 1930; Census Place: Demun, Randolph, Arkansas; Roll: 93; Page: 17A; Enumeration District: 0008; Image: 111.0; FHL microfilm: 2339828

7. **Sheriff Calvin Roy Kelly**
   Officer Down Memorial:
   https://www.odmp.org/officer/7421-sheriff-c-roy-kelly
   Household of Calvin Roy Kelly: Year: 1920; Census Place: Saint Francois, St Francois, Missouri; Roll: T625_945; Page: 16B; Enumeration District: 99; Image: 338
   Household of "Bud" Kelly: Year: 1910; Census Place: Calumet, Pike, Missouri; Roll: T624_805; Page: 6A; Enumeration District: 0122; FHL microfilm: 1374818

8. **Ira Leon Evans**
   Officer Down Memorial:
   https://www.odmp.org/officer/4666-patrolman-ira-leon-evans
   Household of Ira L. Evans: Year: 1930; Census Place:
   Minneapolis, Hennepin, Minnesota; Roll: 1096; Page: 38B;
   Enumeration District: 0183; Image: 140.0; FHL microfilm:
   234083
9. **Leo R. Gorski**
   Officer Down Memorial:
   https://www.odmp.org/officer/5595-patrolman-leo-r-gorski
   Household of Leo R. Gorski: Year: 1930; Census Place:
   Minneapolis, Hennepin, Minnesota; Roll: 1095; Page: 6A;
   Enumeration District: 0170; Image: 490.0; FHL microfilm:
   2340830
10. **Leo Pavlak**
    Officer Down Memorial:
    https://www.odmp.org/officer/10452-patrolman-leo-pavlak
    Household of Leo Pavlak: Year: 1930; Census Place: West St
    Paul, Dakota, Minnesota; Roll: 1085; Page: 2A; Enumeration
    District: 0040; Image: 689.0; FHL microfilm: 2340820
11. Side Note: Sinking of the Tuscania:
    http://www.islayinfo.com/lord_robertson_islay_troopships.html
12. **Miles A. Cunningham**
    Officer Down Memorial:
    https://www.odmp.org/officer/3714-patrolman-miles-cunningham
    Household of Miles Cunningham: Year: 1930; Census Place:
    Chicago, Cook, Illinois; Roll: 480; Page: 24A; Enumeration
    District: 1495; Image: 963.0; FHL microfilm: 2340215

Chapter 12: CREATING A MONSTER: J. EDGAR HOOVER AND THE MA BARKER MYTH

1. Outlaw Women: The Wild West's Most Notorious Daughters, Wives, and Mothers. By Col. Robert Barr Smith
2. Roy Hanna, "Tulsa's 'Spawn of Hell' Wiped Out" (Tulsa Tribune, March 22, 1949)
3. Lessons at Little Bohemia: https://www.fbi.gov/video-repository/newss-lessons-at-little-bohemia/view
4. DILLINGER, THE HIDDEN TRUTH - RELOADED, by Tony Stewart
5. Ibid.
6. Ibid.
7. Ibid.
8. Ibid.
9. Ibid.
10. Statement of Earl J. Connelley, Bremer Kidnapping Part 75.
11. Ibid.

About the Author....

W. D. Smith is a graphic artist in Manchester, TN. He is originally from Nineveh, in southern Johnson County, Indiana, the son of the late Willie Robert and Gladys Marie (Rice) Smith. After serving a tour of duty in the United States Air Force, he returned home in 1982. Soon thereafter, he was hired for his very first illustration job. Dr. George W. Simpson, DDS, a dentist in Franklin, Indiana, wrote a new chapter on Occlusion for a dental textbook, and needed an artist. The textbook was _"Johnston's Modern Practice In Fixed Prosthodontics," by Dykema, Goodacre, and Phillips (W.B. Saunders & Company, Philadelphia, PA, 4th Edition, 1985)_. He moved to Manchester, Tennessee in August 1985, where he met Miss Valarie Torano the following year. They were married in 1988, and they are the proud parents of two grown sons; Robert E. Lee Smith, and Thomas J. Jackson Smith.

It was about 2003 when he decided to do a series of self-published Gangster Car art calendars, with the invaluable help of crime authors Rick "Mad Dog" Mattix and Tony E. Stewart. This project eventually led to creating book cover illustration beginning in 2009, for Tony Stewart's book, "The Trash Bag Murderer", about California serial killer Patrick Wayne Kearney. Then in 2010, knowing that to remain competitive in the art field, the author delved into the world of computer graphics, earning his Associate of Science in Graphic Design in 2014 from the Art Institute of Pittsburgh, Online Division. Since then, he has designed several additional book cover illustrations for a wide variety of genres. This book is his first large-scale foray into the world of crime writing, and includes several of his original illustrations.

Made in the USA
Columbia, SC
14 March 2018